Micro Frontends Architecture for Scalable Applications

Master Modular and Efficient Web Development with Micro Frontends, DDD, and CI/CD for Scalable, Distributed Frontend Applications

Vanderlei Alves da Silva

www.orangeava.com

First Published: July 2025

Published By: Orange Education Pvt Ltd, AVA®

Address: 9, Daryaganj, Delhi, 110002, India

275 New North Road Islington Suite 1314 London,
N1 7AA, United Kingdom

ISBN (PBK): 978-93-49888-39-5
ISBN (E-BOOK): 978-93-49888-41-8

Scan the QR code to explore our entire catalogue

www.orangeava.com

Dedicated To

My Beloved Parents:

José Franciso da Silva
Terezinha Alves de Campos Silva

Wife

Eloisa Helena Stephany Picolo

And Daughter

Iris Picolo Silva

Without Whom My Life Would Lose Its Light, and This Creation Could Never Be

About the Author

Vanderlei Alves da Silva is a seasoned Frontend Architect with over 15 years of experience in designing and building distributed systems and cloud-native applications. His career is driven by a deep passion for system architecture and frontend development, helping industry-leading organizations to craft scalable, resilient, and user-focused software.

What drives Vanderlei is the belief that a well-crafted software has the power to solve real human problems – whether it is helping someone's grandmother find what she is looking for on a webpage or solving complex organizational challenges at scale. For him, writing a code is more than just engineering; it is a form of storytelling – every function, every interface, and every design choice contributes to the evolving story of a system.

Throughout his career, Vanderlei has remained deeply committed to innovation and continuous learning. His work spans high-impact client/server applications, and cutting-edge frontend architectures designed to scale with the growing demand. He thrives on the technical and human challenges of building systems that grow gracefully, without compromising usability or performance.

As the author of ***Micro Frontends Architecture for Scalable Applications***, Vanderlei brings together years of practical experience, hard-earned lessons, and forward-looking insights. This book represents not only a consolidation of his knowledge, but also a vision for the future of frontend architecture – especially as artificial intelligence begins to reshape how we build and scale modern applications. His aim is to empower developers and architects alike, to think systemically, build confidently, and architect software that truly serves people!

About the Technical Reviewer

Maksym Hopei is a software engineer, architect, and engineering leader with over a decade of experience designing and building distributed systems at scale. Throughout his career, he has navigated the complexity of modern software architecture–from high-throughput messaging platforms to resilient microservices and AI-integrated systems. His work spans startups and enterprise environments, where he has led cross-functional teams, established engineering best practices, and guided organizations through complex technical transformations.

With deep expertise in backend architecture, observability, cloud infrastructure, and developer experience, Maksym brings a pragmatic, systems-oriented mindset to everything he builds. He is particularly interested in service boundaries, team scaling, system resilience, and the evolving relationship between software systems and intelligent agents. He believes great engineering isn't just about technology–it's about designing systems that are understandable, evolvable, and aligned with the human context in which they operate.

Acknowledgements

There are a few people I would like to thank for their continued support, throughout the writing of this book. First and foremost, I am deeply grateful to my wife for her constant encouragement – I could never have completed this book without her unwavering support.

I am also profoundly thankful to every individual who, throughout the course of my career, has shared their knowledge and experiences with me. Their lessons have helped me grow both personally and professionally, and those learnings have played a vital role in shaping this work.

A special mention goes to Mr. Maksym Hopei, book reviewer, whose friendship I truly cherish. I am proud to have worked alongside him for several years, and now to count him as a companion in the making of this book give me immense pleasure!

My sincere gratitude also goes to the team at Orange Education Pvt Ltd for their trust and support throughout this unforgettable journey of publishing this book.

Preface

The book aims to give a comprehensive understanding, with hands-on examples, and easy to digest reading, about **micro frontends**.

It starts by **defining frontend and backend development**, exploring what is considered a valuable architecture, and introducing various **frontend architecture patterns**.

The core section dives into micro-frontends. It explores the foundational concepts, such as Domain-Driven Design, Decentralized Governance, and Independent Deployments. It explains how these principles enable highly observable (easy-to-monitor) micro-frontends. Readers are then guided through in-depth discussions on integration strategies, their advantages and disadvantages.

Communication and routing are covered next, exploring topics such as Container Applications, State Management, Cross-Application Communication, and Routing. Finally, UI/UX considerations for micro-frontends, and how they interact with different backend patterns are addressed.

The final part focuses on the best practices for testing (unit, integration, and end-to-end), deployment strategies, and security considerations essential for micro-frontend applications. The book concludes with a real-world use case, and a look at the future of micro-frontends, discussing emerging trends, potential directions, and the impact of Artificial Intelligence (AI) will have on it.

Chapter 1: In this chapter, we explore the often perceived dichotomy between frontend and backend development. We have delved into the intricate dance between these two realms and reveal the synergy required to create seamless and dynamic web applications. By the end, readers will understand that true innovation and efficiency in web development come from uniting these fields into a singular, collaborative discipline.

Chapter 2: In this chapter, we investigate the principles of architecture and design, emphasizing their central role in creating resilient and scalable applications. We then turn the focus our lens on the frontend architecture–its definition, main concerns and importance for the whole system.

Chapter 3: In this chapter, we explore the various frontend architectural patterns, providing a comprehensive overview of the design, applicability, advantages and disadvantages of each pattern.

Chapter 4: This chapter introduces the key principles behind the micro frontend architecture. By the the end, readers will have a clear vision that should guide them when adopting it.

Chapter 5: The chapter introduces techniques on how to slice each micro frontend implementation, and how to compose/integrate them accordingly to different needs. It explores the pros and cons of each composition strategy, providing concrete examples to illustrate the different concepts.

Chapter 6: This chapter defines the container/shell application responsibilities in the context of micro frontend architecture. It also touches the state management, cross (micro frontend) application communication, routing requirements, and shared dependencies as well as the related performance concerns, bringing concrete examples to illustrate the concepts.

Chapter 7: This chapter centers attention on user interface and experience requirements from a micro frontend architecture standpoint. It spotlights the advantages and challenges as well as the current available tooling to support it.

Chapter 8: This part covers the available backend integration options, and how they can be used together towards legacy system migrations. The main API standards (REST, GraphQL, gRPC, and WebSockets) as well as SDK client generation.

Chapter 9: This chapter examines the comprehensive landscape of testing strategies essential for modern application development focused in the distinct factors brought by the micro frontend architecture.

Chapter 10: This chapter discusses the importance of a solid automation strategy for deploying the different micro frontends, and the different techniques for managing their releases.

Chapter 11: This chapter introduces techniques for observability in micro frontends using well-known tools such as Datadog and Sentry for application metrics, logging, tracing, real user monitoring, and error tracking.

Chapter 12: In this final chapter, we explore a systematic approach on how to introduce micro frontends incrementally in organizations, using a real use-case to highlight the key actions needed for a successful implementation. Additionally, we have examined other relevant use case to provide a comprehensive overview and offer considerations regarding the future of Micro Frontend architecture, including the present and future usage of artificial intelligence in this space. Thus, readers will have a practical view of the concepts studied so far in a real use-case scenario.

Get a Free eBook

We hope you are enjoying your recently purchased book! Your feedback is incredibly valuable to us, and to all other readers looking for great books.

If you found this book helpful or enjoyable, we would truly appreciate it, if you could take a moment to leave a short review with a 5 star rating on Amazon. It helps us grow, and lets other readers discover our books.

As a thank you, we would love to send you a free digital copy of this book, and a **30%** discount code on your next cart value on our official websites:

www.orangeava.com

www.orangeava.in (For Indian Subcontinent)

☑ **Here's how:**

Leave a review for the book on Amazon.

Take a screenshot of your review, and send an email to **info@orangeava.com** (it can be just the confirmation screen).

Once, we receive your screenshot, we will send you the digital file, within 24 hours.

Thank you so much for your support – it means a lot to us!

Downloading the code bundles and colored images

Please follow the links or scan the QR codes to download the
Code Bundles and Images of the book:

https://github.com/ava-orange-education/-Micro-Frontends-Architecture-for-Scalable-Applications

The code bundles and images of the book are also hosted on
https://rebrand.ly/fae67b

In case there's an update to the code, it will be updated on the existing GitHub repository.

Errata

We take immense pride in our work at **Orange Education Pvt Ltd,** and follow best practices to ensure the accuracy of our content to provide an indulging reading experience to our subscribers. Our readers are our mirrors, and we use their inputs to reflect and improve upon human errors, if any, that may have occurred during the publishing processes involved. To let us maintain the quality and help us reach out to any readers who might be having difficulties due to any unforeseen errors, please write to us at :

errata@orangeava.com

Your support, suggestions, and feedback are highly appreciated.

DID YOU KNOW

Did you know that Orange Education Pvt Ltd offers eBook versions of every book published, with PDF and ePub files available? You can upgrade to the eBook version at **www.orangeava.com** and as a print book customer, you are entitled to a discount on the eBook copy. Get in touch with us at: **info@orangeava.com** for more details.

At **www.orangeava.com**, you can also read a collection of free technical articles, sign up for a range of free newsletters, and receive exclusive discounts and offers on Print Books and eBooks.

PIRACY

If you come across any illegal copies of our works in any form on the internet, we would be grateful if you would provide us with the location address or website name. Please contact us at **info@orangeava.com** with a link to the material.

ARE YOU INTERESTED IN AUTHORING WITH US?

If there is a topic that you have expertise in, and you are interested in either writing or contributing to a book, please write to us at **business@orangeava.com**. We are on a journey to help developers and tech professionals to gain insights on the present technological advancements and innovations happening across the globe and build a community that believes Knowledge is best acquired by sharing and learning with others. Please reach out to us to learn what our audience demands and how you can be part of this educational reform. We also welcome ideas from tech experts and help them build learning and development content for their domains.

REVIEWS

Please leave a review. Once you have read and used this book, why not leave a review on the site that you purchased it from? Potential readers can then see and use your unbiased opinion to make purchase decisions. We at Orange Education would love to know what you think about our products, and our authors can learn from your feedback. Thank you!

For more information about Orange Education, please visit **www.orangeava.com**.

Table of Contents

CHAPTER 1
A Tale of Two Worlds

Introduction

It might seem obvious, but it is a pattern we cannot overlook: trends from the past often find their way back into the spotlight. This phenomenon is evident across various fields such as fashion, politics, and technology. Imagine hiking a familiar trail where certain landmarks, once forgotten, suddenly reappear with newfound significance. Just as styles from the 1970s, 1980s, and 1990s are showcased on billboards as the latest trends, we see political landscapes shifting like the cyclical nature of a well-worn path. The political pendulum swings back and forth, with power and public opinion shifting between different ideologies and parties over time.

In the realm of technology, we witness similar patterns. As we navigate the terrain of full-stack web applications, explored further in the upcoming section, we will see how past innovations re-emerge, reshaping the landscape and guiding us on our journey toward the future.

Structure

This chapter will cover the following topics:

- React Server Components vs Server Side Includes
- Frontend Development
- Backend Development
- Full Stack Web Framework

React Server Components vs Server Side Includes

In order to explore a bit of this *deja vu* feeling and get ourselves warmed up, we will be starting with a small react code snippet:

```
import Header from "../components/Header";
import Main from "../components/Main";
import Footer from "../components/Footer";

const HomePage = () => {
  return (
    <>
      <Header />
      <Main>
        <h2>Welcome to My Website</h2>
        <p>This is the main content area.</p>
      </Main>
      <Footer />
    </>
  );
};

export default HomePage;
```

***Figure 1.1:** React Component*

A basic **HomePage** component that includes (via import statements) three external components: **Header, Main,** and **Footer**, as its first introduction React was an exclusive client (browser) library, just like the other well-known alternatives, such as Angular, Vue.js, and so on. However, with the introduction of Server Components for react, the same component can be executed in the server as well.

To some, that may click memories of Server Side Includes, introduced in the early 1990s:

```
<body>
  <!--#include file="header.html" -->
  <h1>Welcome to My Website</h1>
  <p>This is the main content area.</p>
  <!--#include file="footer.html" -->
</body>
```

***Figure 1.2:** Server Side Includes*

Could that be seen as a similar pattern to fashion cycles and/or political pendulum?

From a positive standpoint, something once seen with clear divergency, seen as two distinct worlds, in great extension reflects from:

- **Single Page Applications (SPAs):** Motivated by the wish to have more interactive pages where actions from users should not require a complete page reload, SPAs led a trend in adding more processing to clients, bringing an ever-growing complexity into the clients and therefore a need for specialized development teams.
- **Backend as data and business logic layer:** Mainly as a consequence of the adoption of SPAs, where they were responsible for all the presentation layers, backend services were seen as solely data and business logic providers.

They have once again fuzzy boundaries. Would one consider the SSI example above a frontend or a backend implementation? Would a server side render react application be a frontend or backend development?

From a negative standpoint, we have all the technological innovations, some of which we shall see during the upcoming chapters, that tell these two implementations apart.

With that in mind, let us explore a bit more about these two worlds, their similarities and differences.

Frontend Development

In a typical setup where backend engineers were responsible for providing some http api based interface (Rest, Graphql, SOAP ...) and frontends were responsible for consuming those and handling all the users' interaction with the system, we have the following scenario.

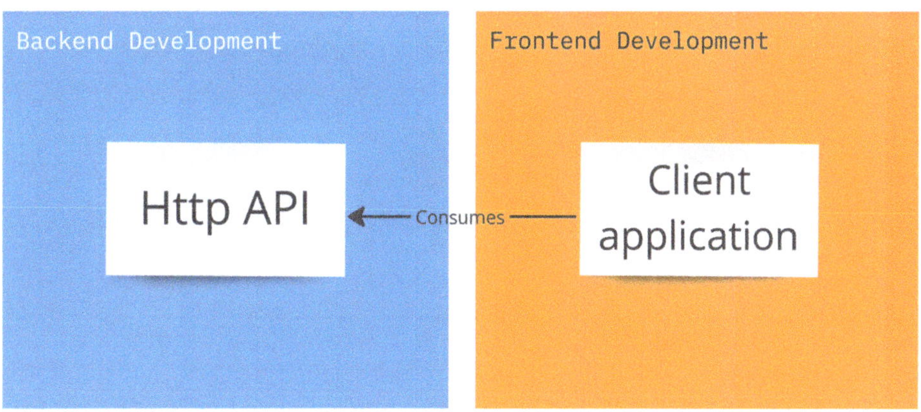

Figure 1.3: *Traditional split between frontend and backend development*

However, the technological pendulum has swung back and a more accurate definition would not be limited to specific clients:

"Frontend development refers to the development part that deals with the user interface (UI) and user experience (UX)."

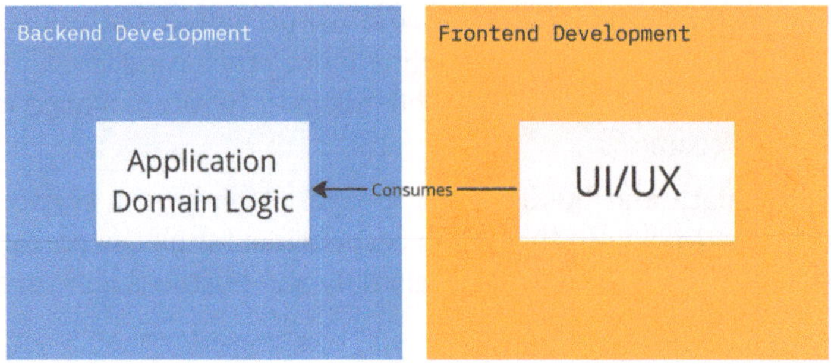

Figure 1.4: *Modern split between frontend and backend development*

It is interesting to note that frontend development has significantly expanded its responsibilities. It is no longer restricted to specific platforms, such as browsers, but now encompasses the entire user interface and experience, regardless of the client/server infrastructure.

Users have in their hands a myriad of devices that can be used to access the application and their expectations are to be able to use it everywhere, from desktop browsers to smartwatches.

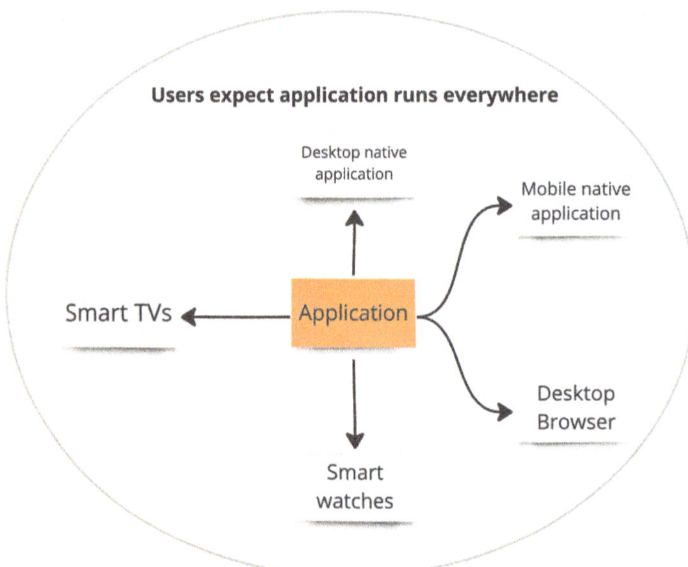

Figure 1.5: *Applications are expected run everywhere*

This evolution brings both great possibilities and new challenges. Concerns related to:

- **Scalability**: The ability of the system to handle increasing loads efficiently, whether by growing in user base, features, or content, online systems are now present everywhere, therefore their loads are reasonable to expect to be way higher than before.
- **Interoperability:** The capability of the frontend to work seamlessly with other systems, platforms, or third-party services, the concerns once limited to different operation systems and/or browser vendors, now it relies on a multitude of different devices with distinct operation systems, browsers, and more importantly, user expectation on how the given interface should behave in that context.
- **Performance:** How quickly and efficiently a frontend application loads and responds to user interactions considering all different kinds of clients it may have.
- **Aesthetics:** The visual appeal and user experience of the application which can be further segmented into:
    - **Design Consistency**: Maintaining a consistent design language across the application and different clients in order to ensure a cohesive look and feel.
    - **Responsive Design**: The application should adapt its layout and design to different screen sizes and orientations, ensuring a good user experience on all devices.
    - **Animation and Interactivity**: Thoughtful use of animations and interactive elements in order to enhance user experience without overwhelming or distracting them.
    - **Accessibility**: Ensuring that the design is accessible to users with disabilities (for example, by providing text alternatives for images, ensuring sufficient color contrast, and making the UI navigable by keyboard);
- **Security:** The ability of the application to protect user data from vulnerabilities and attacks.

They have gained additional layers of complexity. Consequently, the need for new architectural styles has emerged to address these multifaceted demands.

Backend Development

Readers may be at first influenced by expanded responsibilities in the frontend development, inclined to think that the backend development had your responsibilities decreased. This understanding could not be more false—our goals in the software industry today are way bigger and the tasks we have on our hands, way more audacious.

Using a hiking expedition metaphor let us quickly explore from where we came and where we are standing now.

We used to organize ourselves as an entire hiking expedition as one large group where everyone sticks together and does everything collectively. However, as we ventured into more challenging and unpredictable terrain, we realized that this approach was inefficient and limiting. To navigate these adventurous paths more effectively, we had to organize our hiking expedition with various specialized teams, allowing us to distribute responsibilities, enhance decision-making, and ensure better preparedness for obstacles such as steep climbs, river crossings, and rapidly changing weather conditions. Over time, the expedition realized that smaller, more agile sub-groups could improve efficiency and adaptability by enabling faster problem-solving, reducing delays, and allowing each team to focus on their expertise, such as navigation, supplies, or safety. Later, the expedition strategy was further refined by deeply understanding the terrain and tailoring the hiking approach to specific regions, ensuring that each challenge was met with the right skills and preparation.

In this scenario, we depict the following phases:

- **Monolithic Expedition:** In the early days of software development, applications were built as monolithic systems, where all functionalities were tightly integrated into a single, large unit.
- **From Monolithic to Service Oriented Architecture (SOA):** The expedition realizes that moving as one large group is inefficient. SOA emerged as a way to organize these efforts, much like splitting the group into specialized teams, where they are relatively independent, focusing on their tasks while adhering to a shared mission.
- **From SOA to Microservices:** To further enhance flexibility, the expedition breaks down the teams into smaller, self-sufficient groups or individual hikers, each responsible for specific tasks or trail segments, increasing agility and adaptability.
- **DDD Applied to Microservices**: Each small group or hiker now operates with a deep understanding of their specific domain (terrain), using specialized knowledge and language to optimize their part of the journey.

It is relevant to mention that there are still several domains in which monolithic applications are the most appropriate option, notably applications where strong consistency is the main goal or scalability is not a concern.

As for the systems, to mention a few, where scalability, reliability, fault tolerance, performance, and geographical distribution are requisites, the approach proposed by microservices architecture, along with Domain-Driven Design (DDD), has proven consistently to be the most effective one.

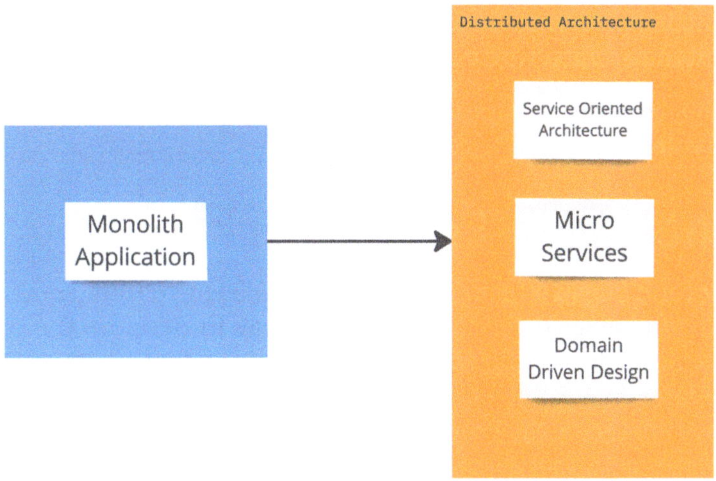

Figure 1.6: *From Monolith to distributed architecture with DDD*

As described in *Figure 1.6*, we have a mindset shift towards distributed architectures where distributed teams are able to focus on their own domains and services, as described in the following schema:

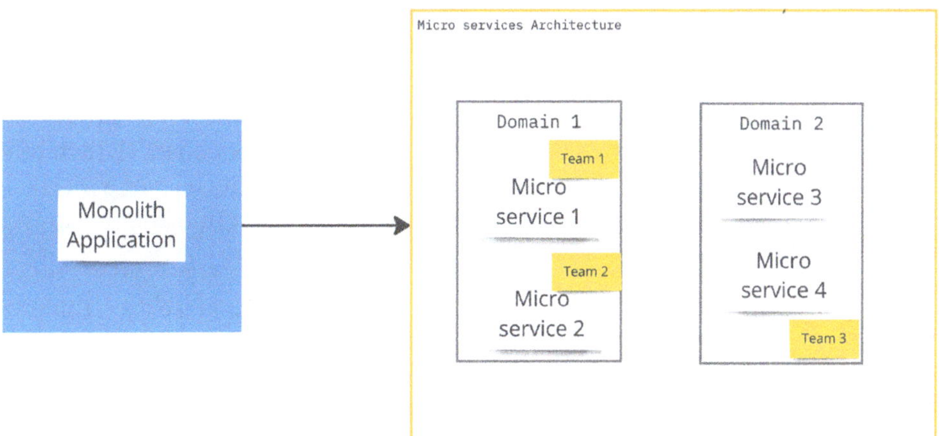

Figure 1.7: *From Monolith to distributed architecture with DDD*

This evolution in backend development illustrates the growing complexity and responsibility in our field. While frontend development has expanded, the backend has not diminished in importance—on the contrary, it has become more strategic and sophisticated. We have moved from monolithic architectures, where everything was tightly coupled, to service-oriented approaches that introduced specialization, and finally to microservices, where agility and scalability take center stage. By applying Domain-Driven Design (DDD), we ensure that each service is deeply aligned with its domain, optimizing performance and maintainability. And as a counterpart evolution, the micro frontend architecture came, to the frontend realm, as:

A natural extension to the successful backend distributed architecture into the frontend development realm.

Full Stack Web Framework

The *Full Stack* term began to gain prominence in the early 2010s, somewhat together with frontend and backend terms, mainly as a way to describe the "old fashioned" developer that was still working with the templating engines, such as SSI, Perls, PHP, and so on, but later come as a counterbalance, a pendulum swinging back, against the specialization proposed by the Frontend and Backend mindsets, arguing in favor of the need of generalist professionals.

Note: *A template engine is a software component that processes templates and dynamically generates output, typically in the form of HTML, XML, or other text-based formats. It allows developers to separate presentation (UI) from business logic by embedding placeholders or logic within a template file, which is then populated with data at runtime.*

It reflects a need for people proficient in both areas, capable of handling both client-side and server-side development tasks, but the level of responsibilities and expertise required imposes a great challenge for developers to keep up with all these demands.

The release of Node.JS enabled the appearance of isomorphic applications - web applications where both the client and server use the same codebase - which offered a more viable solution for the generalist/specialist dichotomy. It relieves a bit the level of expertise in programming languages and all the tooling around them required to maintain systems working.

In this context the appearance of the so-called *Full Stack Web Frameworks* - frameworks that provide a comprehensive set of tools and libraries to support both frontend and backend development - was natural and enabled developers to write code in a similar fashion to what depicted in *Figure 1.1 React Component*, where components execution were not restricted to client anymore, but universally available (running on server and client).

An isomorphic application might look like the following:

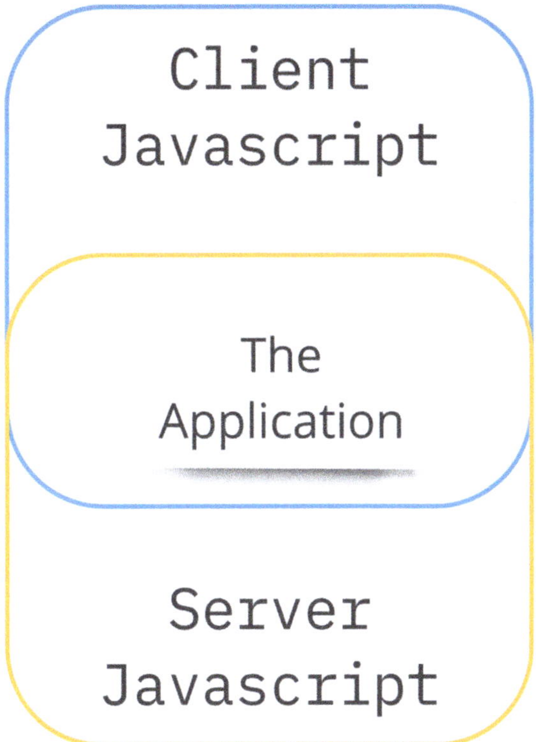

Figure 1.8: *Javascript Isomorphic applications*

The application code sits in between the client and server, containing components that its context executions can be client only, server only, or have both client and server.

The following table shows the major javascript frameworks and their Full Stack Web Framework also referred to server side rendering capability.

Framework	**server side rendering capability**
Angular	*@angular/ssr* package
React	Remix and Next.JS frameworks
Qwik	Already built with server side rendering
Svelte	Sveltekit framework
Vue	*vue/server-renderer* package and Nuxt framework

Table 1.1: *Frameworks and server side rendering capabilities*

Isomorphic applications are not restricted to the JavaScript language. The `<script>` tag was not designed exclusively for JavaScript; its **type** and legacy **language** attributes allowed early browsers to support multiple scripting languages. However, JavaScript became the most convenient and widely adopted option, leading to its monopoly in frontend development.

The WebAssembly open standard specification expands the Full Stack landscape by enabling code written in multiple languages to run in web browsers. This introduces a significant paradigm shift, challenging JavaScript's historical dominance and opening the door to a broader selection of tools and technologies. In this evolving ecosystem, some notable frameworks worth mentioning include:

Full Stack framework	**Language**
Leptos	Rust
Blazor	C#
Dioxus Labs	Rust

Table 1.2: *Full Stack frameworks written on top of WebAssembly*

It is worth noting that these frameworks and the WebAssembly technology as a whole are still in a relatively beginning phase used in niched contexts, but all bring the same idea–of a technology enabling components, written in the same codebase, normally with some decorators, tags and alike to state where should it be executed (client, server or both) and in some cases supported devices (browsers, mobile and so on).

Conclusion

Just as trends from the past resurface to shape the present, developers, just like hikers navigating a well-worn trail, must recognize familiar markers–the recurring dynamics between frontend and backend. Mastering both contexts is paramount for engineers aiming to create valuable applications. This holistic knowledge equips developers with the ability to make knowledgeable decisions, optimize performance, and enhance user experience. It enables them to anticipate how frontend changes can impact backend operations and vice versa, ensuring a seamless and efficient integration. Moreover, it fosters better communication and collaboration within development teams, bridging gaps between different roles and facilitating a more cohesive development process.

Ultimately, a comprehensive grasp of both domains empowers one to select the most appropriate Frontend Architecture and understand the Micro Frontend applicability in this scenario.

In the next chapter, we will dive deeper into the principles of architecture and design, exploring what makes an architecture valuable and how frontend architecture fits into this broader framework.

References

1. https://react.dev/reference/rsc/server-components
2. https://webassembly.org/
3. https://nodejs.org/
4. https://nextjs.org/
5. https://nuxt.com/
6. https://remix.run/
7. https://angular.dev/guide/ssr
8. https://kit.svelte.dev/
9. https://vuejs.org/guide/scaling-up/ssr.html
10. https://www.w3.org/TR/2011/WD-html5-author-20110809/the-script-element.html#scriptingLanguages
11. https://webassembly.org/
12. https://dotnet.microsoft.com/en-us/apps/aspnet/web-apps/blazor
13. https://leptos.dev/

CHAPTER 2
Valuable Architecture

Introduction

As the morning sun rose higher over the rugged peaks, casting a warm, golden hue upon the towering cliffs and winding trails, a group of intrepid hikers began their ascent. Much like the careful planning and deliberate steps required to conquer a mountain, so too is the journey of software engineering, where architecture and design serve as the detailed maps and sturdy boots guiding the way.

Yet could one clearly depict the contrasts found in detailed maps and sturdy boots for hiking in the same fashion for architecture and design in the realm of software development? What is exactly meant by Micro Frontend *Architecture*?

Structure

This chapter will cover the following topics:

- Architecture and Design
  - Software Architecture and Design Building Blocks
  - Exploring a Use Case
  - Frontend Architecture vs Frontend Design
- Frontend Architecture
  - Frameworks
  - Frontend Architecture Aim

Architecture and Design

Architecture lays the foundation, much like the blueprint of a grand edifice. It defines the system's structure, its core components, and the interactions among them, ensuring stability and scalability.

Design, on the other hand, delves into the finer details, refining the features and functionalities within the architectural framework.

However, what does architecture and design look like? Is it a collection of diagrams using some well-known standard format? Is it some formal written document? Or something else?

The reality is: **architecture and design do not look like anything**

They are abstract ideas expressed in a variety of ways, via diagrams, plain English, via draws on whiteboards, via talks, and any other communication tools used to expectantly have all the team with a crystal clear understanding.

And where exactly are the boundaries between the two terms? What exactly are the system's structure and the core components? And the finer details?

The reality is: **there is no clearly defined separation line**

One may ask, understanding frontend as a part of a whole, a domain focused on the input and output of data to individuals that interact with a software application or system, could the term *architecture* still be applied? Or would it be a system detail and therefore *design* a better term?

In order to have a good reasoning on this philosophical question, let's explore the basic concepts around architecture and design and therefore comprehend where the frontend architecture and the micro frontend architecture fit in the bigger picture.

Software Architecture and Design Building Blocks

The following picture depicts a high-level system context down to detailed code, from architecture to design concerns, from the most impactful components to the least ones.

We understand, in this context, impactful components as the ones that:

- if done wrong will require the most effort to be corrected;
- if done wrong will decrease the system maintainability over time;
- if done wrong will decrease the system capability to answer business demands;

In that sense, an application code bug in a payment component, for instance, would definitely be an urgent issue that would require immediate action, but would most likely demand a punctual fix; on the other hand, a wrong architectural decision would for sure demand a whole refactoring on the system and in some cases risk the system's existence.

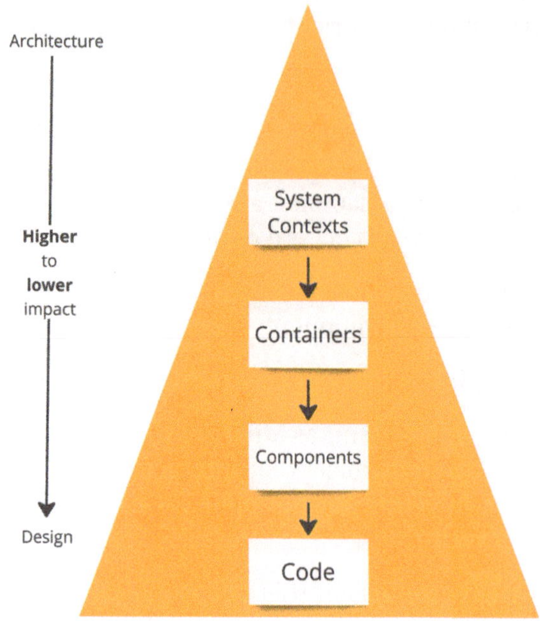

Figure 2.1: *Software Architecture and Design building blocks*

C4 Model

As stated, architecture and design do not look like anything, we could be discussing using plain English or any other desired way, but for our context, we will be using the C4 Model.

The C4 Model proposes an industry standard way to visualize the architecture and design of a software system in a hierarchical manner, from high-level context down to detailed code, as shown in *Figure 2.1*.

For the upcoming examples, we will be using a fictitious booking system where users and operators using the booking system, publish their bookings - their leisure activities, for instance: skydiving, go-karting, laser tags, and so on - to be purchased online from the end customers.

System Contexts

System Contexts refers to the highest level of abstraction. It provides a big-picture view of the software system and its environment, showing how the system interacts with external entities such as users, other systems, and external services.

It aims to understand the scope and boundaries of the system and to identify all external entities that interact with it.

It focuses on **what** the interaction is and not how that would look like.

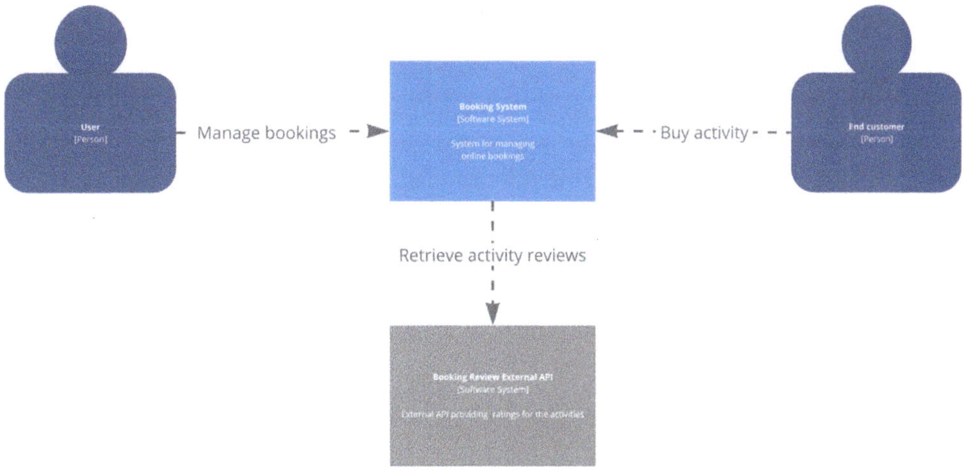

Figure 2.2: *System Context Diagram*

Figure 2.2 shows interactions between the booking system with external users and external systems.

The internals about the system, such as technologies, protocols, and architectures, are not a concern at this stage and consequently, the frontend architecture used is not a concern as well.

Containers

Containers are the second level of abstraction, breaking down the system into high-level technical building blocks. A container represents an application, a service and/or a data store that hosts code or data. It shows the major parts of the system and how they communicate. It bridges the gap between the broader context and the more detailed component and code-level views, making it a crucial tool for architects, developers, and other stakeholders involved in the software development process.

In the following diagram, the Booking System software is decomposed into smaller parts, describing the system in a more fine-grained detail.

Some aspects of this diagram worth exploring:

Micro frontend architecture: The diagram describes one of the ways of implementing the architecture, in which we have a Shell Web Application that adds the individual micro frontends.

Micro frontend alignment with Micro Services architecture: The separation of concerns proposed by the micro service style is reflected in the micro frontend architecture as well. You may notice that for each one of the micro services (Search and Payment APIs), there is a corresponding micro frontend.

Note: *Although not strictly necessary, reflecting the slicing done in the backend architecture—especially when adopting a domain-driven design (for more details, see Chapter 4: Micro Frontend Foundations - Domain-Driven Design)—in the frontend implementation can bring significant advantages, such as strategic alignment, reuse of previously established organizational structure, clear ownership and responsibility, enhanced team autonomy, among others.*

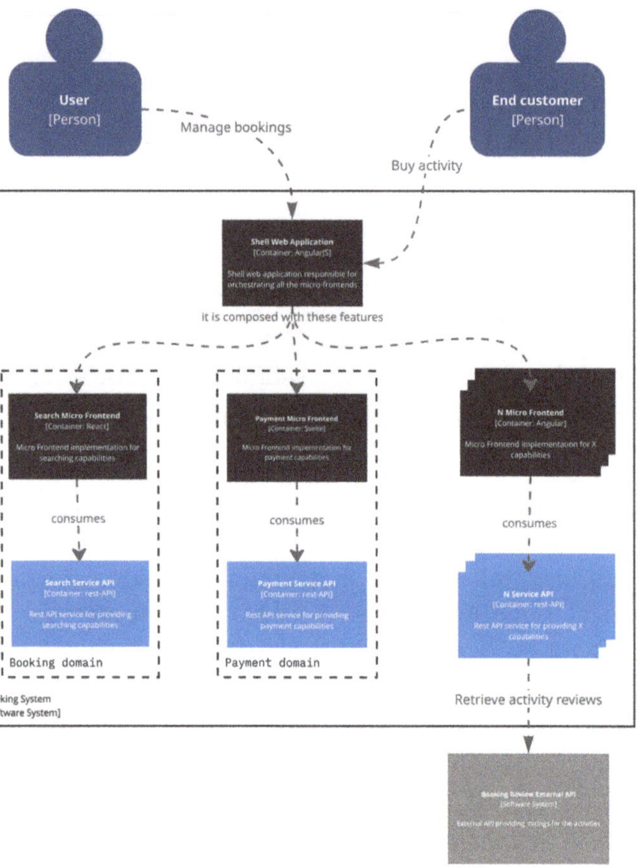

Figure 2.3: *Containers Diagram*

Technology Heterogeneous: each individual micro frontend is not bound to specific technologies, you may notice mentions of Angular, React, and Svelte javascript frameworks.

Domain Driven Design (DDD): We can notice the Booking and Payment domains adding the defining boundaries for both frontend and backend development.

In the upcoming chapters, we will deep dive into the before-mentioned topics; nevertheless, at this stage, it gets clear the relevance in defining the frontend architecture to be used in the system.

Components

Zoom in more, going into the third level of abstraction, components focus on the internal structure of a container. They are individual parts within a container that encapsulate specific functionality.

Its purpose is to understand the structure and organization of code within a container, showing how different parts interact to provide functionality.

At this stage, with a frontend architecture lens, we take each one of the frontend implementations, in our case, each one of the micro frontends, and look at its internals, such as high-level components (mainly molecules and sometimes atoms components from an *Atomic Design* standpoint), routing and state management strategies, API and backend integrations, how the individual UI components interact with each other and so on.

Note: *For details on Atomic Design, please refer to Chapter 7: UI/UX and Design System - Atomic Design*

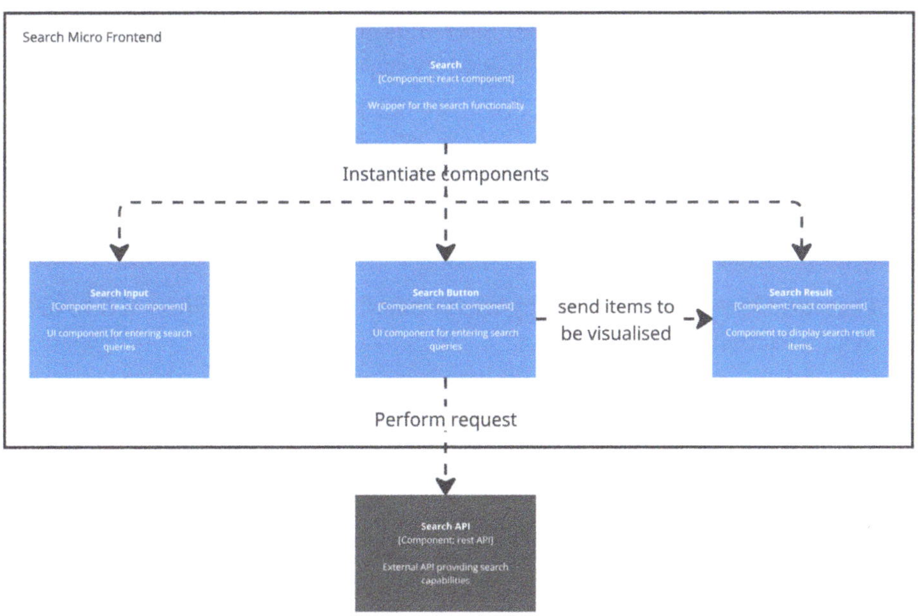

Figure 2.4: *Components Diagram*

Code

And lastly, we naturally have the code and all its structure, modules, classes, functions, methods, unit tests, and so on. Here we aim to understand and map the actual implementation details.

It does come with lots of challenges, and best practices (design patterns, SOLID principles, Clean Code, and so on), which given the rich literature already out there, will not be explored in the context of this book.

Exploring a Use Case

We will be exploring the reasoning taken in order to come up with the aforementioned: *Figure 2.4 Components Diagram*, in which we have a use case for a user searching for activities in a booking system.

Note: *We will not be detailing all required information, in terms of each one of the domain attributes that normally would be demanded for effective implementation; the main goal here is to showcase the reasoning process.*

We first highlight the key business requirements for the feature:

- **Actor:** end-user, person looking for a given activity via a desktop or mobile app
- **Goal:** find the desired activity
- **Main Success Scenario:** the user fills in some filtering criteria (name, availability, price) and finds the activity he/she wants
- **Alternative Flows:** the user does not find the exact match but the system provides similar offers based on the filtering provided and, if available, the user profile
- **Preconditions:** the system users (operators) should have added all the needed activities together with their availabilities
- **Postconditions:** After selecting the activity the user is redirected to select the desired activity availability

With these business requirements, we can safely define:

- The component requirements
    - The activities already being available in the system
    - An optional user profile
- The component domain
    - The activity attributes needed to perform the search
    - The activity attributes to the user visualize them in the search result and be able to select some

- The component boundaries
  - Searching the activity
  - User redirection after an activity selection
- The component goal
  - The user be able to perform searches
  - And select one activity
- The component behavior
  - User should be able to fill in filtering options
  - User should be presented with the results
  - User should be presented with alternative options
  - User should be able to select one

Tip: *The outcomes from this process define a reasonable application programming interface (API) for a Micro Frontend implementation, something that could look like the following code snippet:*

```
interface Activity {
  id: string;
  name: string;
  description: string;
  image: string;
  location: string;
  price: number;
  tags: string[];
  createdAt: Date;
  updatedAt: Date;
}

type ActivitySearch = Partial<Pick<Activity, "name" | "description">>;

type ActivityResult = Pick<
  Activity,
  "name" | "description" | "image" | "location" | "price" | "tags"
>;

interface ActivitySearchUseCase {
  search(search: ActivitySearch): Promise<ActivityResult[]>;
}
```

Figure 2.5: *Searching API Implementation*

In the following *typescript* code snippet, we have a possible API definition for the search micro frontend implementation, where we have the *Activity* interface, representing the micro frontend requirement, so to say the activities stored in the system and the two derived from its types:

- **`ActivitySearch`**: Representing the attributes in which a given activity can be searched for;
- **`ActivitySearch`**: Representing the attributes in which a given search result is presented to users;
- **`ActivitySearchUseCase`**: Lastly the use-case implemented by the micro frontend, the activity search per se.

This reasoning can iteratively be taken for each one of the system use cases.

Frontend Architecture versus Frontend Design

After exploring the four main architecture and design building blocks, we can add an additional piece of information to our *Software Architecture and Design building blocks* figure.

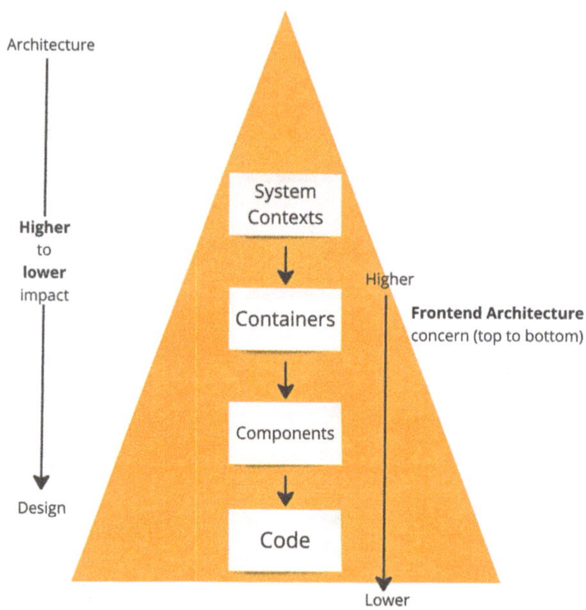

Figure 2.6: *Software Architecture and Design building blocks revisited*

In this revisited version, we have drawn an additional "frontend architecture" line where the frontend architectural concerns are focused on, from top to bottom. Basically excluding the *system context* out of it, understanding the frontend architecture as a container, or as a part of the overall system context.

And though there is no clear separation line between what is architecture and design, readers hopefully have had a clear vision that things done wrong in the system contexts and container diagrams will require the most effort to be corrected and therefore be confidently one of the main architectural points of work.

Back to the philosophical question *frontend architecture vs frontend design*, the answer stands on perspective, the viewpoint taken from a specific system's goal.

From modern and frontend focused systems, where user interface and experience are paramount for business success, the frontend world can not be seen as a technical detail and therefore it is indeed the foundation for systems alike.

In this book, we will dive into the architecture options for scalable applications, understand why Micro Frontend is a natural fit for them, and secondly, comprehend the designs required to achieve these goals.

Frontend Architecture

Frontend architecture definition takes the software architecture definition but focuses on the frontend main container (from a C4 model definition) or containers (depending on the architecture used).

Frontend architecture lays the foundation for the user experience and interface. It defines the frontend system's structure, its core components, and the interactions among them, ensuring stability and scalability.

Consider someone taking a containers diagram, particularly looking into the frontend-related containers, what should this person see? What should he/she understand?

Imagine that you are looking at a house plan; on it, you will see the blueprint for the construction of a building, detailing the layout, structure, and specifications necessary for the entire project. It considers the overall functionality, flow, and integration of different components such as rooms, walls, doors, and utilities. You can easily recognize firstly what it is - a house plan - and, secondly, all the features included, living room, bedrooms, kitchen and so on.

Yet for understanding the whole house architecture, a house plan is not sufficient. Let us say you want to understand how the water will flow in the house, so you start looking into the hydraulic plan. You see a detailed diagram outlining the design and layout of the house's water and fluid-related systems, you notice the water supply and the drainage system, you recognize the Rainwater and Stormwater Management, the pressure systems, and so on.

More importantly, you know what each one of the diagrams is responsible for, they scream at you, and they make clear what they are about.

Just as the hydraulic plan must work in harmony with the house's plan, frontend architecture must integrate seamlessly with the system's overall architecture.

A well-designed frontend architecture enables the postponement of decisions about frameworks, web servers, and other environmental tools. Frameworks should remain flexible options. With a strong architecture, you do not need to commit to Angular, React, Javascript, or Webpack until later in the project. Additionally, it allows for easy changes to these choices if necessary. A good frontend architecture focuses on the use cases and separates them from secondary concerns.

Back to the question: what should someone see when looking into the containers diagram related to the system frontend architecture?

This person should see:

- The business use-cases
- How the different business use-cases will interact with each other
- From which clients (desktop browsers, native mobile apps, smart TVs, and so on) will the users interact with the system
- The same language as the whole system architecture, also known as ubiquitous language, in use

In conclusion, the person should see what the system is about - is it a booking system, a health care system, a customer relationship management system - how the user experience with this system will look like - from which devices will the users interact with the system, which kind of features will each of these devices provide - and how all the different business use-cases will interact with each other and interact with the whole system architecture.

Frameworks

Most of the frontend architectures that we shall explore in the upcoming chapter are, if not completely bound to, very coupled to specific frameworks, and sometimes even created from specific ones. However, for scalable frontend applications, we should aim for framework independence. The ability to change and/or to gradually migrate from one framework to another should guide the frontend architecture definitions.

For that the usage of web standards, such as HTML5, CSS3, ECMAScript specification - standardization for the scripting language that forms the basis for JavaScript - and/or the usage of abstraction layers in order to not expose framework internals when communicating between frontend containers are a valuable approach to improve the overall frontend architecture quality.

Frontend Architecture Aim

If you ask most of the system's stakeholders what the system's goal is, it is very likely you will hear that its goal is to provide the functions that the system is supposed to do. If you have a calculator software, it does need to perform addition, subtraction, division, and multiplication operations.

Nonetheless, for the system architecture and in our context for the frontend architecture, the goal relies on its adaptability, the capability of a given frontend to change as the requirements change.

And that is the main advantage of the Micro Frontend Architecture. Its capability to evolve over time and adjust to the flow of constant changes that successful systems require.

In the end, one of the few certainties in life is the fact that there will be changes.

Conclusion

Throughout our discussion, we have unraveled the foundational principles of architecture and design in software development, emphasizing the delicate balance between the two.

One could have as main takeaways the following:

- Architecture and design do not look like anything
- There is no clearly defined separation line between the two terms
- Architecture focuses on the most impactful components, the ones that if done wrong will require the most effort to be corrected
- Design focuses on the less impactful components

Much like a hiker relying on detailed maps and sturdy boots, a solid architecture and thoughtful design are crucial for navigating the complexities of building software systems. By employing tools such as the C4 model, we have illustrated how these abstract concepts transition from high-level structures to the finer details of code.

We also delved into the unique challenges of frontend architecture, considering its role in defining user experience, scalability, and system integration. By exploring micro frontend architecture and its alignment with microservices, we highlighted how frontend systems should not be viewed as mere technical details but as pivotal elements that ensure a system's adaptability and long-term viability.

With this knowledge in hand, we are now prepared to explore, in the next chapter, the various frontend architectures, examining their strengths and weaknesses, ultimately leading to a deeper understanding of Micro Frontend architecture.

References

1. https://c4model.com/

CHAPTER 3
Frontend Architectural Patterns

Introduction

Architectural patterns are high-level solutions to common problems or challenges in software architecture. They provide a blueprint for structuring software systems by defining fundamental structural organization, components, and their interactions. Next, we will explore the main frontend patterns, their applicability, pros and cons, and ultimately have a clear understanding of when to use and not use the micro frontend architecture.

Structure

This chapter will cover the following topics:

- Static Page Websites
- JAMstack
- Server Side Rendered
- Single Page Applications
- Isomorphic Applications
- Micro Frontends

Static Page Websites

The concept of static page websites dates back to the early days of the World Wide Web in the late 1980s and early 1990s. It is a type of website where each page is delivered to the user exactly as it is stored on the server, without any server-side processing or database interaction. The content of these pages is fixed (or "static") and does not change dynamically based on user input or other factors therefore there is no interactivity between users and the system.

Nowadays, its usage is overall discouraged, (here we meant specifically static page websites without any sort of tooling supporting its content generation, also known as *static site generators*, explored further in the following section), especially due to its hard maintenance, shared features are duplicated, think of a website where all the pages should have a common header and footer for instance, this content would be duplicated in each of the files and following maintenance efforts would increase as the site grows.

Static Page Websites with Static Site Generators

In a modern setup, a static site generator (SSG) - a tool that generates a fully static HTML website from a set of source files, such as templates, content (often written in Markdown or other markup languages), and configuration files - should be considered. With these tools, the maintenance and scalability of the system are improved with slightly increased setup and deployment complexity.

Some known SSG tools:

Tool	Technology
Gatsby	React
Next.js (Static Mode)	React
Scully	Angular
SvelteKit	Svelte
Pelican	Python
Hugo	Golang

Table 3.1: *Known SSG tools*

This setup revamps the Static Page Website usage and shows great applicability to websites where the content does not need to be frequently updated or personalized. In use-cases where simplicity and ease of deployment are the focus, this architecture style could be considered.

Note: *Due to the lack of interactivity, this architecture should not be considered for web applications.*

Websites versus Web Applications

The term *Website* refers to a collection of related web pages that are typically designed to provide information, content, or services to users. They are generally static or semi-dynamic, meaning that their primary purpose is to present content rather than perform complex operations or interactive tasks. It is **content-centric** and focused on delivering content such as text, images, and multimedia. The content is often informational, such as news articles, blogs, or company details.

A web application is a more complex and interactive system designed to perform specific functions or tasks for users. Unlike websites, web apps are often dynamic and can involve complex client-server interactions, data processing, and user-specific functionality. It is **functionality-centric**, they are designed to perform specific tasks or provide interactive functionality. They are often used to manage, process, or analyze data.

Nowadays the distinction between these two terms is less clear than used to. Web applications are way richer in what refers to the degree of interactivity. Anyway, they can be classified considering their focus: websites focus on content, and web applications on functionality.

The difference can be clearly understood with the following diagram:

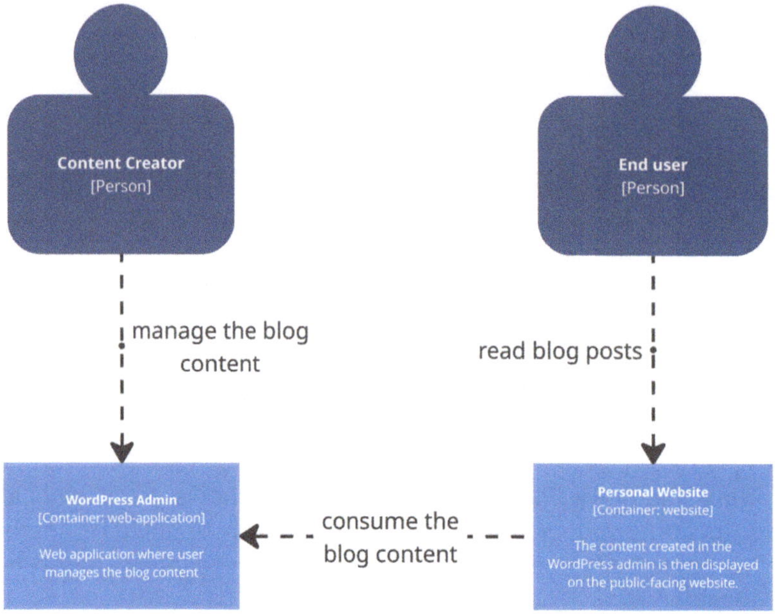

Figure 3.1: *Websites versus Web applications*

In this *WordPress* example, there are two distinct users: the content creator who interacts with the WordPress admin area, a web application focused on the functionality of content management (articles for the user's personal blog), and the end user who interacts with the user's personal website, that is focused on presenting the articles.

JAMstack

JAMstack is a modern web development architecture based on client-side JavaScript, reusable APIs, and prebuilt Markup. The name "JAMstack" comes from these three core elements:

- JavaScript: Handles dynamic functionalities on the client side.
- APIs: Reusable APIs are used to handle server-side operations, such as data fetching, authentication, or processing, often through third-party services.
- Markup: Pre-rendered HTML is generated at build time, usually with a static site generator, which is then served to users.

The architecture makes use of the previously mentioned Static Site Generator (SSG) and adds all the interactivity required through the usage of Javascript and requesting the dynamic data from API services. It enables the traditional split between frontend and backend development where the last focus is on providing the data in some well-known standard such as REST, GraphQL, and so on while the first focus is on the user interface.

It is particularly well suited for use-cases where backend efforts are minor and the focal point is on the frontend, the design integrates well with:

Headless CMS: Backend-only content management system that separates content creation and storage from the presentation layer

Backend as a Service (BaaS): Cloud-based service model that provides developers with a complete backend infrastructure, allowing teams to center attention on the frontend and business logic without worrying about managing servers, databases, authentication, and other backend components.

A Static Page Website architecture can easily be extended to a JAMStack architecture; therefore, it is a viable option for scaling such systems.

The aforementioned WordPress scenario could be seen using JAMStack architecture as the following:

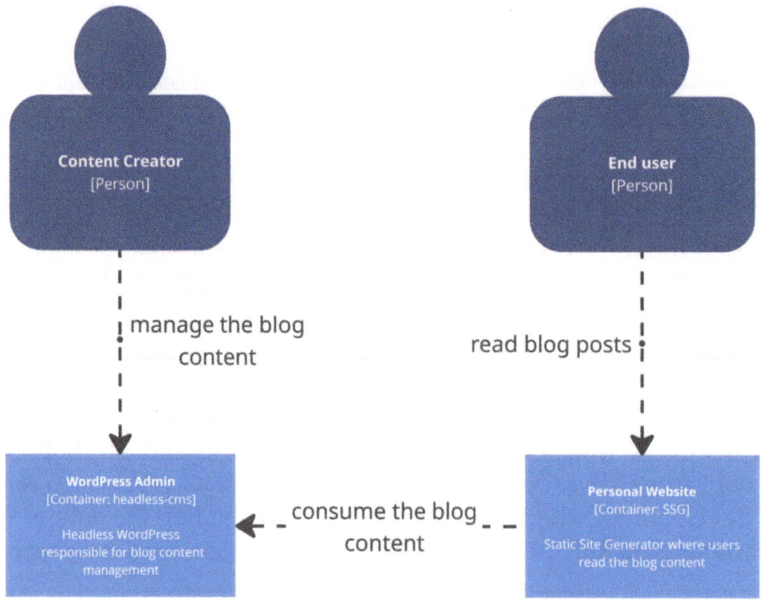

Figure 3.2: *JAMStack*

The headless WordPress CMS usage could be replaced by any other BaaS or a self-made implementation, depending on how much customization the solution requires.

As it assumes a central Static Site Generation the architecture is not recommended for systems where distributed frontend teams are in place as it forces all of them to contribute in a centralized codebase bringing challenges to what concerns the orchestration of these changes. More on this topic will be investigated later.

As it relies heavily on client-side JavaScript for content loading, systems where Search Engine Optimization (SEO) is the main concern should avoid this architecture or should carefully handle SEO matters in order to avoid related issues.

Server Side Rendered

Server-Side Rendered (SSR) applications are web applications or websites where the server generates the complete HTML markup for each page before sending it to the client's browser.

It brings great scalability improvements, especially when compared to Static Page Websites, in what refers to:

Dynamic content: Allows for the generation of dynamic content on the fly based on user requests.

Personalization: Enables the creation of personalized experiences based on user data, such as serving different content to logged-in users or displaying region-specific information. The server can tailor the HTML based on the user's session or cookies.

And great advantages overall:

- **Better Performance on Initial Load:** It offers, assuming that the server is able to handle all the client requests in a reasonable time, faster initial load times compared to architectures that rely heavily on client-side rendering for dynamic content. The server sends fully rendered HTML, reducing the need for the browser to execute large amounts of JavaScript before displaying the content.
- **Reduced application and testing complexity:** The application does not need to be concerned with running on a huge variety of client devices, the dependency on those is only related to the support of HTML, therefore development and testing concerns are restricted to the server.
- **Seamless Integration with Backend Services:** SSR facilitates easier integration with backend services, databases, and APIs. The server can fetch data from multiple sources, process it, and render it into the HTML sent to the client.
- **Security:** The communication between the application and its dependencies (database, backend services, and other external APIs) is known and can easily be monitored. Additionally, in some cases, the traffic over the public internet can be avoided improving the overall system security.
- **Improved SEO:** Search engine crawlers receive fully rendered HTML pages, which is beneficial for indexing dynamic content.

Due to the level of interaction expected for web applications, its sole use in this context is inconceivable, an additional scripting layer in the client would be required to add the needed application interactivity.

Lightweight Javascript Libraries

In this context, to add the interactivity needed in the client, we have the so-called lightweight javascript libraries.

These libraries are a collection of pre-written JavaScript code that is designed to be small in size, easy to use, and focused on a specific set of features or tasks. These libraries are typically minimalistic, offering only the essential functionality needed to accomplish common tasks, without the overhead or complexity of larger frameworks.

Their main focus is on being small so that clients do not need huge requirements in order to run the web application or website.

Some relevant technologies to mention in this category:

HTMX: A modern library that aims to extend HTML capabilities via the usage of HTML attributes. The core idea is about adding dynamic functionality by the usage of HTML attributes such as **hx-get**, **hx-post**, **hx-target**, and others.

A small example taken from the library website:

```
<script src="https://unpkg.com/htmx.org@2.0.2"></script>
<!-- have a button POST a click via AJAX -->
<button hx-post="/clicked" hx-swap="outerHTML">
  Click Me
</button>
```

Figure 3.3: *HTMX code*

The **hx-post** and **hx-swap** attributes on this button tell the library:

When a user clicks this button, issue an AJAX request to /clicked, and replace the entire button with the HTML response

It is worth pointing out that the library does not require most of the setup needed by modern frontend applications, such as:

- Module bundling such as webpack, vite, parcel, and so on.
- Dependency management, the library is dependency-free, requiring only the library script link to work.
- Minification, the library provides a minified version to be used in the product and an unminified one for development purposes
- Any kind of pre-processing in the code, all the code provided is ready for execution in the client

And does not support "advanced" features such as:

- Client routing
- State management

Which should be handled by the server.

jQuery: Still hugely used, despite being outdated, the jQuery library is the precursor of this idea, to know: adding the missing interactivity needed in the clients. In the end, however, we ended up with fat clients leading into the Single Page Application that we shall see in the upcoming sections.

Incremental Server-Side Rendering

Incremental SSR is a hybrid rendering approach for web applications that combines the benefits of Static Site Generation (SSG) and Server-Side Rendering (SSR). It is used in frameworks such as Next.js to optimize performance, load times, and scalability by allowing dynamic content generation while maintaining a high level of caching.

It works by caching the page so that in upcoming requests the app behaves as an SSG application by simply providing the already cached content, until a specific Time-To-Live (TTL) is reached and then a regeneration process happens where the server regenerates the static page, ensuring the data stays fresh while not re-rendering on every request.

It also considers a fallback mode, where pages that have not been rendered yet can either be served as an empty placeholder that fills with data after the SSR process is complete or show the latest cached version while a new version is being generated in the background.

Single Page Applications

On the completely opposite side related to where to render the application content, we have the Single Page Applications (SPAs). The computational load is shifted to the browser which now needs to handle an increased complexity. The application loads a single HTML page and dynamically updates its content as the user interacts with the app.

The architecture revolutionized the level of interactivity in the web platform and brought a real alternative and in most cases a replacement to traditional native applications.

The architecture is particularly suited for the following scenarios:

- **Rich Interactivity:** If your application requires dynamic and highly interactive user interfaces, Single Page Applications (SPAs) are an excellent choice. Examples include dashboards, social media platforms, and messaging apps.
- **Mobile App-Like Experience:** SPAs offer smooth transitions between views, creating a fast, app-like experience with minimal page reloads. They are ideal when you want your application to feel more like a mobile app.
- **Small to Medium-Sized Applications:** SPAs are well-suited for applications where the content is not overly large and the navigation is relatively straightforward. Medium-sized apps with moderate complexity are often a good fit.
- **API-Driven Backends:** If your application relies heavily on APIs for data exchange, SPAs are a natural fit. They handle dynamic data loading and work efficiently with JSON responses.

- **Reduced Page Loads:** SPAs minimize page reloads by loading the application once and dynamically updating content, making them ideal when reducing load times is critical.
- **Enhanced Control over State and Navigation:** SPAs provide better control over user experience, allowing the application to maintain its state during navigation. This is particularly useful for state-dependent applications such as online forms or multi-step processes.

Client Responsibilities

The architecture relies heavily on the browser to handle key functions such as rendering the user interface, managing state, handling URLs, and ensuring security. It plays a pivotal role in ensuring that SPAs are both fast and responsive, while also maintaining critical functionalities such as session management, security, and performance optimization.

Client-Side Rendering (CSR)

The client receives the initial HTML, CSS, and JavaScript files, and renders the entire user interface. Instead of relying on the server for full-page reloads, the browser is responsible for rendering views dynamically.

Client-Side Routing

In SPAs, the client handles navigation between different parts of the application. This means that "page transitions" happen within the browser using JavaScript, without sending a full request to the server.

URL Management: The browser updates the URL to reflect the current view (or "page") using the browser's history API (for example, pushState and replaceState). This ensures that the back/forward buttons work properly in SPAs and that users can bookmark or share URLs for specific states in the app.

History Management: The browser is responsible for managing the history stack, ensuring that navigation works smoothly using the browser's native back/forward buttons.

Data Fetching and State Management

Asynchronous Data Fetching (AJAX/Fetch): Instead of reloading entire pages, the client sends asynchronous HTTP requests to the server for data, often through APIs (such as REST or GraphQL). The browser then handles responses, updates the application state, and rerenders relevant components.

State Management: The client is responsible for maintaining the app's state and ensuring it persists between user interactions.

Session and Authentication Management:

In SPAs, the browser typically handles user session management using cookies, localStorage, sessionStorage, or IndexedDB. This allows users to stay logged in and maintain their session across different interactions.

Note: *Typically in Server Side Rendered applications, the sessions are normally present in the client but not available to scripting, using for instance http-only cookies, reducing therefore the exposure of sensitive information.*

Token Management: When using authentication mechanisms such as JWT (JSON Web Tokens), the browser is responsible for storing the token securely and including it in API requests for user-specific actions or data.

Client-Side Security

- **Cross-Site Scripting (XSS) Prevention**: The browser must ensure that content is sanitized before rendering it to prevent injection attacks.
- **CORS Management**: While fetching resources from APIs or external services, the browser must handle Cross-Origin Resource Sharing (CORS) appropriately.
- **Content Security Policy (CSP)**: Ensuring that only trusted scripts are executed in the browser is a critical responsibility for client-side security, often managed through the browser enforcing the CSP headers.

Caching and Performance Optimization

- **Service Workers:** The browser uses service workers for caching resources and enabling offline access to the application. This can help with faster load times and offline functionality, crucial for improving performance.
- **Resource Caching**: The browser caches static assets such as JavaScript, CSS, and images to improve loading times on subsequent page visits.
- **Lazy Loading**: The browser often uses techniques such as lazy loading (loading resources only when needed) to improve performance by reducing the initial load size.

Handle Client-Side Errors

- **Error Handling and Reporting**: The browser must handle client-side errors such as network failures or exceptions in the JavaScript code. SPAs often rely on the browser to show meaningful error messages or retry failed operations.

- **Fallback Handling**: If the app fails to load or encounters issues, the browser can show fallback error pages or messages, ensuring a graceful user experience.

Modern Frameworks

The appearance of modern JavaScript frameworks such as React, Angular, Vue, and so on, is closely tied to the evolution of Single Page Applications. They were designed to address this increasing complexity.

They bring a component-driven architecture making the code more modular, maintainable, and scalable, and enable reactive data binding, meaning changes to the application state automatically reflect in the user interface without needing to manually manipulate the DOM.

Note: *The* ***Document Object Model (DOM)*** *is a programming interface for web documents, representing the structure of an HTML or XML document as a tree of objects.*

Local-First Architecture

As an ultimate extension of a "fat" client, users could possibly work regardless of being online. Local-first development is an architectural approach where applications store data primarily on users' devices, ensuring functionality regardless of internet connectivity. This paradigm emphasizes user ownership, privacy, and performance by maintaining local data storage and synchronizing with servers or other devices as needed. Web APIs such as *LocalStorage*, *SessionStorage*, *CacheStorage*, and *IndexedDB* were crucial enablers of this model.

The architecture is described in the following diagram:

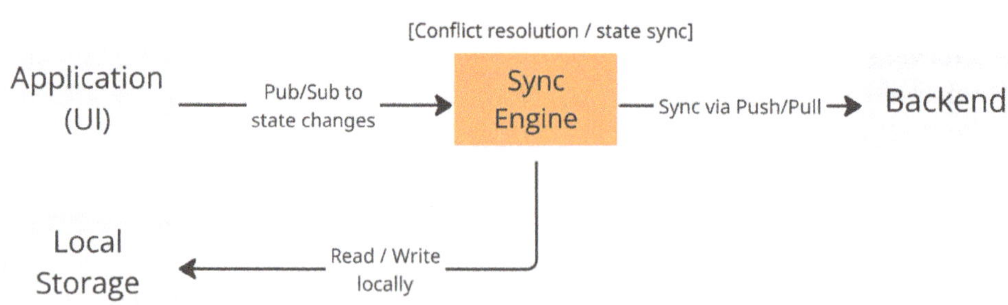

Figure 3.4: *Local First Architecture*

In there, we have:

- **Application UI:** Publishes and subscribes to state changes

- **Local Storage**: It represents any available client storage, most of the time *WebAPIs* previously mentioned, but not restricted to it.
- **Sync Engine**: Listens to changes and ensures sync with local storage and the backend when online.
- **Backend:** It maintains a persistent state so it can be used across different clients.

The main player in the flow is the *Sync Engine*, which abstracts from the client (application UI) the underlying storage, APIS, and backend service infrastructure, allowing the client to interact via a publish and subscribe pattern

The adoption of local-first development is gaining momentum, driven by the success of applications such as *Figma*, *Superhuman*, and *Linear*. These platforms have leveraged local-first principles to offer responsive, collaborative experiences, setting benchmarks in their respective domains.

More details: *https://bricolage.io/some-notes-on-local-first-development/*

Some relevant sync engine library implementations are highlighted as follows:

- **RxDB (Reactive Database):** It is a NoSQL, client-side, JavaScript database designed for real-time applications. It is built on top of RxJS (javascript library for reactive programming using Observables), making it reactive, meaning changes to data trigger automatic updates throughout your application.
- **Zero**: It is an open-source sync engine designed to facilitate local-first development by distributing backend data to the client side, enabling applications to function efficiently with reduced latency and enhanced offline capabilities.
- **Replicache**: It is a client-side sync framework that enables real-time, collaborative, local-first web applications. It integrates with existing backend stacks to provide seamless data synchronization.
- **PouchDB**: An open-source JavaScript database inspired by CouchDB, designed to enable offline storage and synchronization in web applications.
- **Yjs**: A CRDT-based (Conflict-free Replicated Data Type) library focused on enabling real-time collaboration, particularly for text editing, though it can handle other data types as well.
- **ElectricSQL**: A platform that focuses on partial syncing of data from a remote Postgres database to local clients, facilitating local-first application development.

Local-first development is a deliberate architectural choice designed to empower applications with offline functionality, enhanced privacy, and improved performance. By prioritizing local data storage and synchronizing only when necessary, this approach ensures a seamless user experience, even in unstable network conditions.

However, the increased complexity of managing local storage, conflict resolution, and synchronization must not be overlooked. The presence of sophisticated tooling–such as RxDB, Replicache, and ElectricSQL–has significantly lowered the barrier to entry, making local-first applications more feasible than ever. Yet, teams building software must carefully evaluate whether this model aligns with their application's needs, balancing its advantages against the additional overhead it introduces.

Additional Considerations

While SPAs offer seamless user experiences through dynamic content loading, they also introduce challenges in areas such as SEO, performance, and security. And solutions based on server side generated content tend to be more reliable for simpler websites, broader browser compatibility and SEO indexing.

- **SEO Challenges:** SPAs often face difficulties with SEO because their content is loaded dynamically via JavaScript, which can hinder search engine crawlers from properly indexing the website. If SEO is a top priority–especially for public-facing websites such as blogs or e-commerce platforms–SSR architecture might offer better results.
- **Initial Load Time:** SPAs typically load all necessary JavaScript upfront, which can result in longer initial load times. For large or content-heavy applications, this can negatively affect user experience, particularly for users with slower internet connections.
- **Suitability for Simple Websites:** For websites with minimal interactivity or predominantly static content–such as blogs, portfolios, or documentation sites–SPAs may be unnecessary.
- **Browser Compatibility and Performance:** Because SPAs rely heavily on JavaScript, they can encounter performance issues on older browsers or lower-end devices. If your audience includes users with outdated technology, an SSR architecture might provide a more consistent experience.
- **Analytics and Tracking:** Tracking user behavior in SPAs can be more complicated due to the lack of full-page reloads. Analytics tools that depend on page views may require additional configuration to accurately track navigation within an SPA.
- **Security Considerations:** As already highlighted in the *Client-Side Security* section, SPAs, with their heavy use of client-side JavaScript, are more vulnerable to certain security threats. Securing SPAs effectively can demand more effort and vigilance compared to traditional server-rendered applications.
- **Development and Maintenance Complexity:** Developing and maintaining SPAs often involves more advanced tooling and frontend frameworks. If your team is not familiar with these technologies, the associated learning curve can slow down development and increase complexity.

Isomorphic Applications

With an understanding of the SSR and SPAs architecture's pros and cons and the technology advancements that enabled the appearance of the (already explored in *Chapter 1, A Tale of Two Worlds*) isomorphic applications, their appearance feels like a natural step in the frontend development realm.

The architecture aims to bridge the gap between the client/server dichotomy, by allowing both client and server to render the application content:

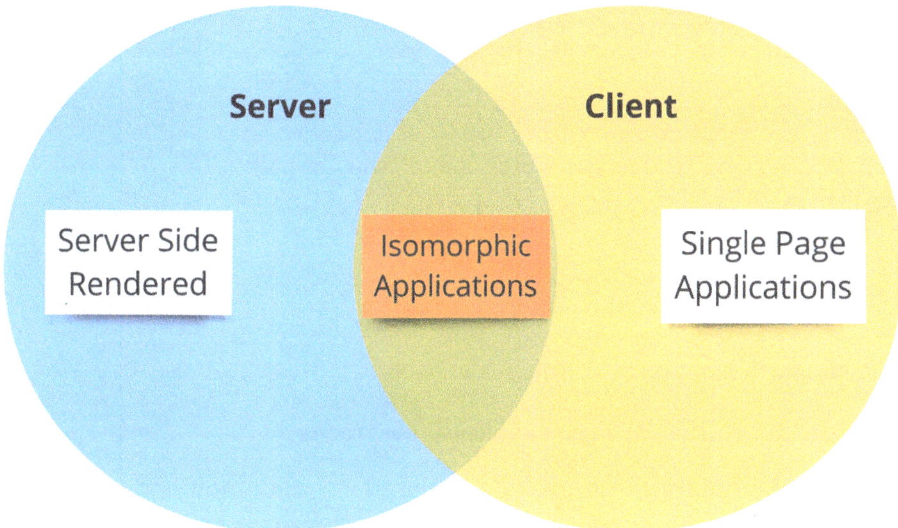

Figure 3.5: *Isomorphic applications*

Rendering Process

The rendering process responsibility is shared between server and client, as described in the following image:

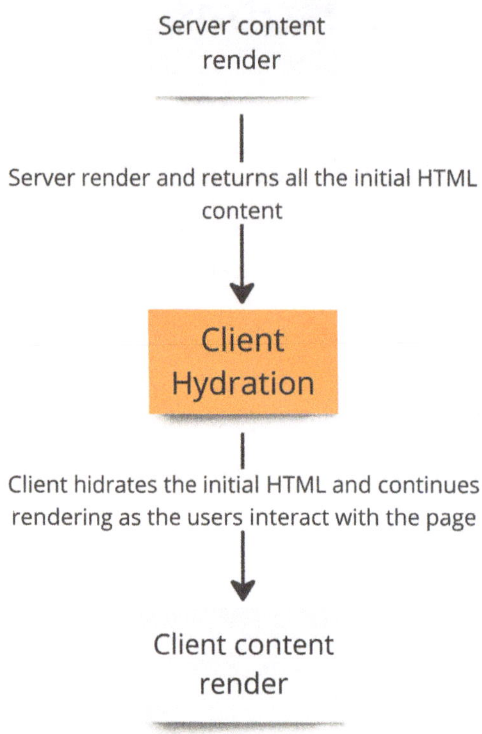

Figure 3.6: *Rendering Process*

At the cost of additional complexity, related to the multi-phased rendering process and the need for client hydration, applications can improve the initial load performance, be SEO friendly, and still have a great level of interactivity with the clients.

Client Hydration

The client hydration is the process of making a server-rendered page interactive by attaching client-side JavaScript functionality to the pre-rendered HTML.

At a high level, it executes the following steps:

1. **Loading the JavaScript Bundle:** Once the HTML is loaded and displayed in the browser, the browser requests and loads the JavaScript bundle containing the framework components and application logic.
2. **Hydrating the Application**: The framework "hydrates" the existing HTML. Meaning, it will attach event listeners and convert the static HTML into a fully interactive application.

3. **Reconciliation**: The framework performs a reconciliation process (the nomenclature may vary depending on the framework, but the idea is the same) to ensure that the virtual DOM matches the actual DOM. It compares the server-rendered HTML (which is the current DOM) with the virtual DOM representation to verify that they are in sync.

4. **Interactive Behavior**: Once hydration is complete, the framework takes over the rendered HTML and enables interactivity. This includes managing state, handling user inputs, and updating the UI dynamically as necessary.

This process does not come for free, and though we get a faster First Contentful Paint (FCP) - a performance key that measures how quickly the first piece of content (text, image, and so on) is painted on the screen - the Time to Interactive (TTI) - a performance key that measures how long it takes for the page to become fully interactive - can drastically be affected.

With this issue in mind, the **Qwik** framework brought the Resumability concept into the scene.

Note: *Qwik is a modern framework that offers instant interactivity, reduced javascript load with improved performance, and efficient Server Side Rendering.*

Resumability

Resumability aims to bring the ability to pause and later resume the state of an application or a component at a particular point in time. With that clients would simply retake the application's state left in the Server Render process, so no hydration would be required for clients.

This can be better understood with the following Qwik example:

```
import { component$ } from "@builder.io/qwik";
import { useSignal, type Signal } from "@builder.io/qwik";

interface CurrentValueProps {⋯
}

const CurrentValue = component$<CurrentValueProps>(({ count }) => {
  console.log("Render: <CurrentValue/>");
  return <div>Current count: {count}</div>;
});

interface IncrementorProps {⋯
}

const Incrementor = component$<IncrementorProps>(({ count }) => {
  console.log("Render: <Incrementor/>");
  return (
    <button
      onClick$={() => {
        console.log("Interaction: +1");
        count.value++;
      }}
    >
      +1
    </button>
  );
});

export default component$(() => {
  console.log("Render: <Counter/>");
  const count = useSignal(0);

  return (
    <div>
      <CurrentValue count={count.value} />
      <Incrementor count={count} />
    </div>
  );
});
```

Figure 3.7: *Qwik Resumability Example*

The example showcases how Qwik handles state and component rendering differently, when running the project, you will notice that all three components are rendered in the server, you can check that by looking at the server terminal, but in the client, each component state is resumed, so not rerendering is performed per any of them (no console logs are shown), only the state increment relatively to the counter increment, when interacting with the counter (clicking +1).

For the full code and instructions on how to execute it, please refer to: *https://github.com/ava-orange-education/-Micro-Frontends-Architecture-for-Scalable-Applications/tree/main/resumability*

Note: *"Traditional" modern frameworks such as Angular, React, and Vue have their initial design focused on SPAs architecture, and though they are constantly bringing innovation toward isomorphic applications, these frameworks' adaptability to new architecture styles imposes a considerable architectural design challenge to the framework/library maintainers. This is a fact that new frameworks such as* ***Svelte*** *and* ***Qwik*** *did not have to deal with, considering that they were built with the isomorphic "mindset" from day one.*

Though a simple concept, its implementation requires a clever implementation.

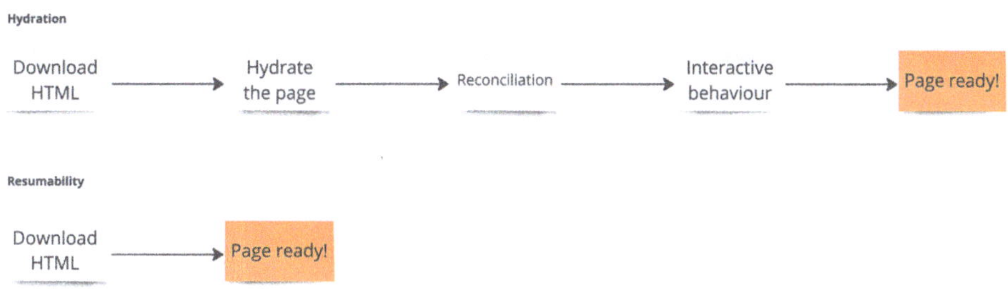

Figure 3.8: *Hydration / resumability*

A closer look to Qwik resumability implementation:

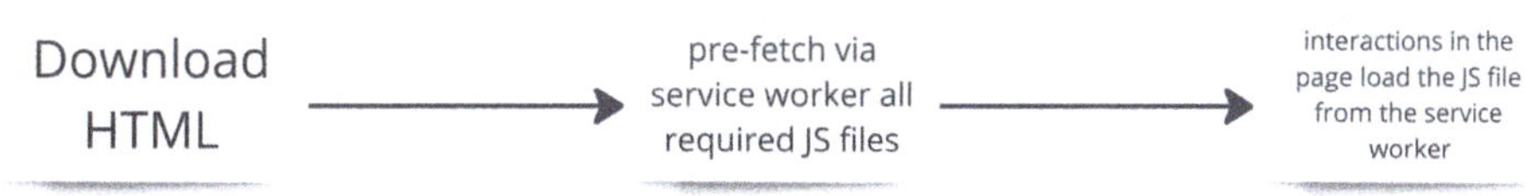

Figure 3.9: *Resumability details*

1. **Download HTML and Prefetch Files:** At this stage, the application downloads all the HTML rendered by the server, along with an additional script to register a service worker. This service worker will prefetch all the necessary JavaScript files for the page.

2. **Page Interaction:** As you interact with the page, the service worker handles requests for the required JavaScript files. Since these files were already downloaded during the prefetch stage, there's no need to rely on network requests during interactions. This not only speeds up performance but also provides offline capability for the application's assets right out of the box.

Note: *A Service Worker is a background task registered for an origin and path that operates in a separate, non-blocking thread, enabling granular control over resource* *requests and caching. It enables features such as offline capabilities, push notifications, background synchronization, and caching.*

For playing around with a Qwik app:

```
pnpm create qwik@latest
/** go through the CLI question, selecting to start a new app with a scaffold basic
project  */

cd <project_directory>

pnpm run preview
```

Figure 3.10: *Qwik initial setup*

After that, investigate the web-page, mainly the html content and the browser network tab to check how the resources are being downloaded as you interact within the page.

Note: *Refer to the chapter references for a link to the framework website and relevant external content that support this chapter.*

While **Qwik** is leading the way with resumability, similar principles are being adopted by other major players, all with the intent to improve the application performance related to the hydration in the client:

- **Partial Hydration**: Frameworks like **Next.js (React)** and **Nuxt.js (Vue)** are experimenting with partial hydration, where only certain parts of the app are hydrated as needed. This is a step toward resumability but still involves more re-initialization than a true resumable framework.
- **Islands Architecture**: Some frameworks, such as **Astro**, are introducing the idea of islands architecture, where specific, isolated components are hydrated on demand, rather than re-hydrating the entire page. This is closer to resumability but does not yet reach the level of fine-grained state restoration as Qwik.

The evolution from traditional Single Page Applications (SPAs) to isomorphic applications reflects the ongoing effort to balance performance, SEO, and interactivity in web development. While SSR-based frameworks have made significant strides in improving initial load times and SEO-friendliness, they introduce complexities such as client-side hydration that can negatively affect Time to Interactive (TTI). The introduction of resumability, pioneered by frameworks such as Qwik, presents an innovative solution to these challenges by eliminating the need for hydration and seamlessly transferring application state from server to client. New frameworks such as Svelte and Qwik, designed with isomorphic capabilities from the outset, are better suited to leverage these advancements, while older, SPA-focused frameworks such as React and Vue face more significant challenges in adapting. As concepts such as resumability, partial hydration, and islands architecture continue to evolve, the web development landscape is steadily moving toward a future where both performance and interactivity are optimized, providing faster and more efficient user experiences.

Micro Frontends

As we have explored the various frontend architectural patterns–each with its own strengths, limitations, and ideal use cases–you might be wondering how to reconcile the benefits of these approaches in large, complex applications?

Imagine having the freedom to combine the flexibility of Single Page Applications, the performance of Server-Side Rendering, and the modularity of Jamstack, all while empowering teams to work independently and deploy their features without stepping on each other's toes.

As we saw in the previous chapter, the great value of an architecture is its adaptability, the capability of a given system to change as the requirements change.

By adopting the Micro Frontend architecture, you are not marrying any specific frontend framework and/or specific frontend architectural pattern, the system remains flexible to adapt itself, within the boundaries of each micro frontend implementation, to any desired frontend architecture and frontend framework.

In this context, the micro frontend architecture is not a replacement for any of the before mentioned architectural styles, but rather a super exceeding architecture which, based on well-defined *public contracts*, will allow the system to use the most applicable frontend architecture and framework to the specific *domain* problem.

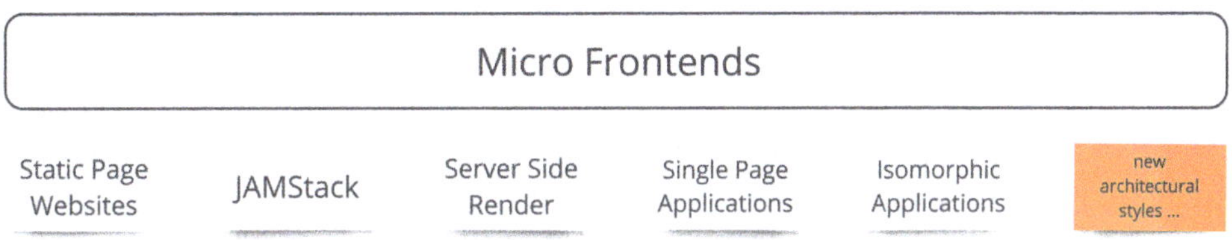

Figure 3.11: *Micro Frontends*

From that, we get some pillars of the frontend architecture:

The domains: Also referenced as slicing, it refers to the boundaries definitions of each micro frontend implementation, what is in and what is out of each implementation. We shall explore that in detail in *Chapter 4, Micro Frontend Foundations* and *Chapter 5, Integration strategies.*

The public contracts: Also referenced by integration strategies, it refers to the language in which all the different micro frontends will talk to each other. Also explored in depth in *Chapter 5, Integration Strategies.*

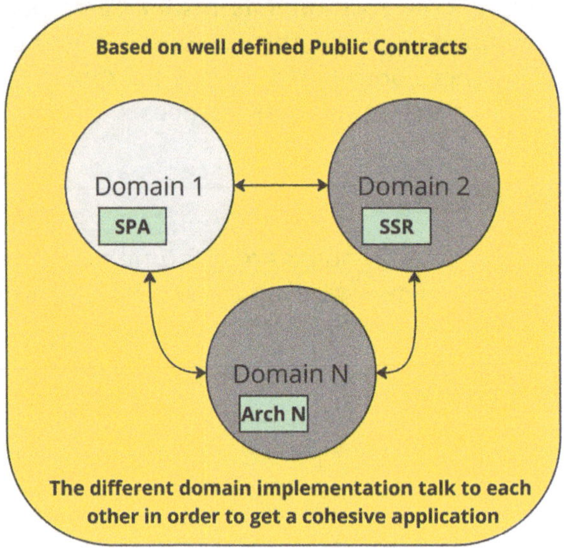

Figure 3.12: *Micro Frontend Domain and Public Contracts*

Origins

The architecture has emerged as a solution to the complexities associated with monolithic frontend applications. It builds on the concept of microservices in the backend and applies similar principles to the frontend by splitting the user interface into small, manageable, and loosely coupled pieces.

Enterprises with large teams and diverse skill sets required solutions where independent teams could work autonomously, without being bottlenecked by dependencies on other teams or central codebases.

Each part, or "micro frontend," can be developed, deployed, and maintained independently by different teams. The architecture, as mentioned, provides a way to bridge the gaps between existing architectures by enabling developers to combine different frontend approaches within a single, cohesive application.

Principle

The Micro frontend architecture is based on the principles of composition and autonomy. The core idea is to divide the frontend into discrete modules, each handling specific features or functionality. These modules are then assembled to create the complete application. The architecture ensures that:

- Each team can choose its own stack and framework (React, Vue, Angular, and so on) for its module, based on the module's requirements.

- The application is rendered as a combination of these modules, with seamless integration despite differences in technology.
- A framework-agnostic approach allows for diverse architecture choices—static, server-side rendered, or Jamstack—within a single application.

Advantages

- **Flexibility in Technology Choice:** Teams can choose the most suitable architecture or framework for their micro frontend, whether it is server-side rendering, Jamstack, or a SPA. This flexibility allows teams to tailor their approach to the specific needs of their module, whether they prioritize performance, maintainability, or user experience.
- **Scalability and Team Autonomy:** The architecture allows for easy scaling of development efforts. Different teams can work on different modules independently without stepping on each other's toes. This significantly reduces dependencies and bottlenecks in the development process.
- **Improved Maintainability:** By breaking down the application into smaller, focused modules, the overall codebase becomes more manageable. Teams can address technical debt, update their modules, or refactor without needing to refactor the entire application.
- **Independent Deployment:** Each micro frontend can be developed, tested, and deployed independently. This leads to faster release cycles and allows teams to push updates to their part of the application without waiting for other teams.
- **Consistent User Experience:** Despite the use of different architectural patterns within the same app, micro frontends allow for a consistent user experience by establishing shared design systems, APIs, and communication protocols. The user seamlessly interacts with different parts of the application, regardless of the underlying architecture.

Challenges

While the micro frontend architecture offers incredible flexibility and autonomy for teams, it is not without its trade-offs. By allowing different teams to develop and deploy independently, micro frontends introduce challenges in coordinating shared resources, managing cross-module communication, and ensuring smooth integration across the entire application. The risk of duplicating dependencies, potential performance overhead from loading multiple micro frontends, and the need for meticulous planning around routing and shared states can complicate development.

Architects need to have these challenges constantly monitored to maintain the whole system architecture in good health during the whole system lifecycle. Follows the list of the most common challenges which will be further discussed as we progress in the book.

Complex Integration and Shared Resources

One of the biggest challenges of the micro frontend architecture is ensuring seamless integration between different modules. Since each micro frontend can be built using different technologies, frameworks, and even design systems, maintaining a cohesive user experience requires careful planning. Teams must align on shared resources such as global stylesheets, fonts, and UI components to prevent visual inconsistencies across the application. More details on that will be explored in *Chapter 7, UI/UX and Design System.*

In addition, communication between micro frontends can be tricky. If different parts of the application need to share state or data (such as user authentication or settings), it requires a carefully designed mechanism to handle cross-module communication. Without this, you risk modules working in silos, leading to inconsistencies or data duplication. More details on that will be explored in *Chapter 6, Communications and Routing.*

Performance Overhead

Micro frontends provide a lot of flexibility, but this can come at the cost of performance. Since each micro frontend is an independently deployable unit, the app may need to load multiple JavaScript bundles, stylesheets, or assets from different sources. This can introduce latency, especially if teams are not diligent about optimizing loading strategies.

Moreover, because each micro frontend could use its own version of libraries or frameworks, users might end up downloading duplicate dependencies, which further increases page load times. To mitigate this, developers must employ strategies such as shared dependencies, lazy loading, and efficient caching, but these optimizations require extra effort and coordination.

Duplication of Dependencies

With micro frontends, each team has the freedom to choose its own tech stack, which can result in dependency duplication. For example, one team might use a different version of React or a CSS library than another, bloating the overall bundle size. This not only impacts performance but also creates difficulties in managing versioning across the app. In traditional monolithic applications, dependencies are usually shared across the entire codebase, but with micro frontends, it is easy to lose track of what's being used where, leading to unnecessary duplication.

Addressing this issue often requires setting up shared libraries or dependency management systems, which can reduce autonomy and reintroduce some of the complexities that micro frontends were meant to solve.

Coordination Overhead

While micro frontends empower teams to work independently, they also introduce the need for increased coordination. Teams must establish protocols for shared concerns such as routing, authentication, and global state management. Without clear guidelines and strong communication between teams, it is easy for inconsistencies to arise.

This coordination is particularly important when it comes to version control and deployment. Teams need to ensure that updates to one micro frontend do not unintentionally break another. While the promise of micro frontends is independent deployment, in practice, some level of synchronization and communication is often necessary, which can slow down development cycles.

Complexity in Routing and State Management

Routing across micro frontends presents another significant challenge. Each micro frontend may have its own routing logic, but they must work together to provide a unified navigation experience for users. Implementing a consistent routing system that allows for smooth transitions between micro frontends requires careful orchestration.

Similarly, state management across micro frontends can become complicated. If the application requires a global state (for example, user authentication, preferences, or shared settings), ensuring that each micro frontend has access to this shared state while maintaining isolation can be difficult. Deciding whether to centralize the state or keep it localized to each micro frontend involves trade-offs that must be carefully weighed. Without proper coordination, inconsistencies or performance issues may arise due to unnecessary state duplication or inefficient data flows.

When Not Use

While the architecture offers exciting opportunities for flexibility and scalability in large, complex applications, it is not always the right choice. In certain cases, the added complexity, overhead, and coordination challenges can outweigh the benefits.

Small or Simple Applications

If your application is small or relatively straightforward and does not aim to scale, micro frontends can introduce unnecessary complexity. A monolithic architecture, where all frontend components are developed together, would likely be easier to manage, test, and deploy. In such cases, the overhead of setting up and maintaining separate micro frontends is overkill and may slow down development rather than speed it up.

Lack of Organizational Scale

Micro frontends are most beneficial for large organizations with multiple teams working on different parts of an application. If you are working with a small team or a single team managing the entire frontend, there is little value in splitting the application into micro frontends. The overhead of managing different codebases, deployments, and coordinating between them is unnecessary when one team can easily handle the full application in a monolithic or modular architecture.

In summary, micro frontend architecture shines in large, complex, and scalable applications where multiple teams need autonomy and independence. However, for simpler projects with smaller teams, the challenges of micro frontends can outweigh their benefits.

Conclusion

In this chapter, we have examined several key frontend architectural patterns, each offering distinct approaches to building modern web applications. By exploring patterns such as Static Page Websites, Server-Side Rendering, Jamstack, Single Page Applications, Isomorphic Applications, and Micro Frontends, we gained a deeper understanding of their design principles, use cases, and trade-offs. Each architecture serves different project needs based on performance, scalability, and complexity.

Equipped with a solid system architectural understanding, in the upcoming chapters, we will delve deeper into the Micro Frontends foundational concepts and practical implementation strategies to know: Domain Driven Design, decentralized governance, independent deployment, and highly observable. This will provide you with the knowledge and tools to build scalable and modular frontend architectures using Micro Frontends, enabling more flexible and maintainable applications.

References

1. https://qwik.dev/docs/concepts/resumable/
2. https://qwik.dev/docs/getting-started/#prerequisites
3. https://developer.chrome.com/docs/devtools/network
4. https://superhuman.com/

5. https://linear.app/
6. https://www.figma.com/
7. https://bricolage.io/some-notes-on-local-first-development/
8. https://rxdb.info/
9. https://pouchdb.com/
10. https://zero.rocicorp.dev/
11. https://replicache.dev/
12. https://pouchdb.com/
13. https://github.com/yjs/yjs
14. https://electric-sql.com/

CHAPTER 4
Micro Frontend Foundations

Introduction

This chapter serves as a primary guide to understanding the core principles that underpin micro frontends, equipping you with the necessary insights for successful adoption.

We will explore the fundamental concepts of domain-driven design, emphasizing the importance of aligning development efforts with business objectives. Decentralized governance will be discussed as a means to empower teams, allowing for greater autonomy and faster decision-making. The notion of independent deployments will highlight the benefits of isolating features and services, facilitating more efficient development cycles. Finally, we will delve into the significance of high observability, ensuring that teams can effectively monitor and manage their applications.

The principles outlined here should guide, but not constrain, the implementation of micro frontends. They represent the core values that the architecture should uphold to maximize its benefits. Any deviations from these values should be carefully monitored to prevent critical shifts that could lead to undesirable side effects.

Structure

In this chapter, we will cover the following topics:

- Domain-Driven Design
- Decentralized Governance
- Independent Deployments
- Highly Observable

Domain-Driven Design

Domain-Driven Design (DDD) is a methodology aimed at creating a shared understanding of the domain within which a system operates. At its core, DDD is not just about coding–it is about creating a shared understanding of the problem domain across the development team and stakeholders, ensuring that the system reflects the business it serves.

This shared understanding creates the environment in which the micro frontend architecture can flourish as a natural extension around the already known *domains*, *subdomains*, and *bounded contexts* communicating via a *ubiquitous language*.

Domain, Subdomains, and Bounded Contexts

The **domain** is the problem space or area of interest that the software aims to address. It represents the business or real-world context in which the system operates.

Within a domain, there can be **subdomains**–smaller, more focused areas of responsibility. DDD categorizes subdomains into three types:

- **Core Subdomains**: The most important and unique parts of the business. This is where you should focus your innovation and development efforts.
- **Supporting Subdomains**: Necessary but not core to the business. These exist to support the core domain, but do not require unique solutions.
- **Generic Subdomains**: Areas that are common across many businesses and can often be implemented with off-the-shelf solutions (for example, authentication, payment gateways).

One of the most critical concepts in DDD is the **bounded context**. A bounded context defines a boundary within which a specific model is applicable. Outside of this boundary, the same terms might have different meanings.

Each bounded context can have its own model, optimized for its specific part of the domain. This reduces complexity by preventing the need for a single, comprehensive model across the entire system.

In the context of micro frontends, bounded contexts translate well. Each micro frontend can operate within its own bounded context, maintaining autonomy and reducing interdependencies between teams.

DDD emphasizes modeling based on the domain rather than technical constraints. In a micro frontend architecture, this principle encourages the design of loosely coupled components that communicate through well-defined interfaces. Each micro frontend can evolve independently, allowing for technologies and frameworks to be chosen based on the specific requirements of the bounded context it represents.

Ubiquitous Language

A key principle of DDD is the use of a ubiquitous language–a common vocabulary shared by both technical and non-technical stakeholders.

The micro frontend implementation should be discussed around this common language, so the understanding is clear for everyone. This shared perception fosters better collaboration, reduces miscommunication, and helps create a user experience that resonates with the end users.

Bringing It All Together

At this point, it should be evident that micro frontend architecture does not introduce entirely new concepts, but rather builds upon established practices. For organizations already embracing these principles, adopting micro frontends should feel like a natural progression. The way micro frontends are divided and aligned with team structures is often already in place, making their implementation straightforward.

The following figure depicts how micro frontends would fit in organizations alike:

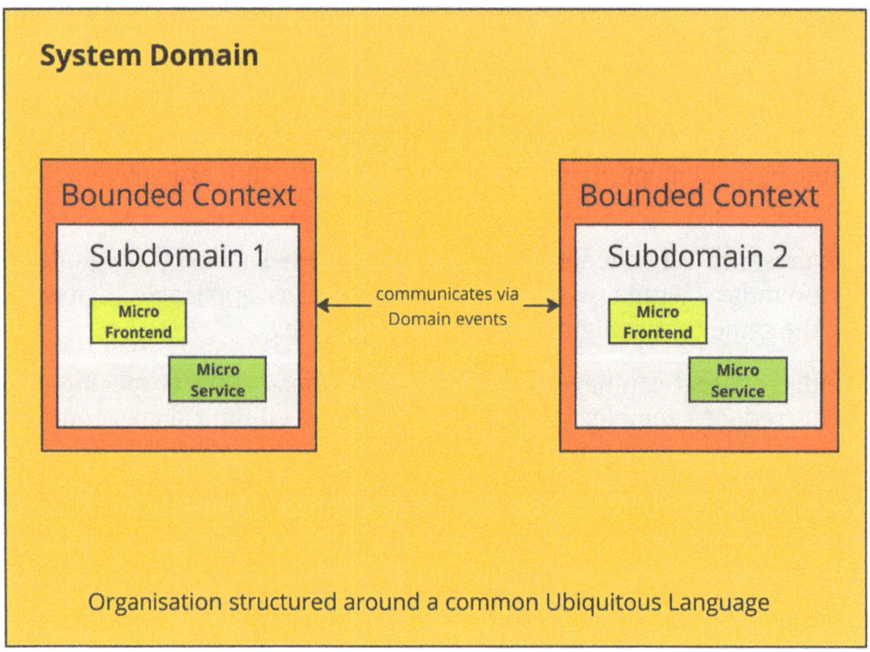

Figure 4.1: *DDD and Micro Frontends*

In a context where the system domain and subdomains are well-defined, each micro frontend would naturally align with the boundaries established by the corresponding subdomain's bounded context. Essentially, each micro frontend serves as the frontend implementation of its specific bounded context. This process can be systematically repeated for each subdomain within the system, ensuring that the micro frontends are not only cohesive but also maintain a clear relationship with the underlying domain architecture.

Strategies for DDD Non-Adherent Organizations

The title may be overly exaggerated, in the sense that DDD adoption in organizations is not a boolean statement, companies do not sign a statement or get some sort of certification that attests that the practice is in place, however, we, as software practitioners, while interacting within a given environment and with a good understanding of the DDD main concepts should be able to gauge the degree of DDD adoption in that given environment.

Some reasonings on how to gauge it could include:

- **Domain concepts understanding**: How deeply the team understands the core concepts of their domain. A company practicing DDD should have clear, well-structured domain models that reflect real business logic.
- **Ubiquitous language:** Do people (developers, domain experts, stakeholders) speak the same language? Listen for consistency and clarity in language when discussing the business domain.
- **Collaboration with Domain Experts:** Are domain experts regularly involved in the development process? Strong DDD practitioners frequently consult subject-matter experts to ensure the software aligns with real-world needs. Look at how the company incorporates feedback from non-technical stakeholders into the development cycle.
- **Handling complexity:** DDD, not surprisingly, involves breaking down large systems into smaller, manageable parts. How is the separation of concerns within the system? Are microservices or modularity applied where needed? How well does the company define boundaries between different parts of their system and ensure clear communication between teams handling different contexts?
- **Adaptability**: How changing requirements are handled? A good DDD practitioner will regularly refine and evolve domain models as the business grows or shifts.

Figure 4.2: *DDD Adherence*

After considering the proposed reasoning, you may feel more confident in assessing your current environment and gaining a clearer understanding of where you stand. From this, you can begin to outline a strategy for gradual adoption.

The further to the left you are on the 'DDD adherence scale,' the more challenging the implementation of micro frontends becomes. However, these challenges should not be viewed as blockers to adopting the architecture.

To mitigate the absence of DDD initiatives in your company, consider the following technical steps:

1. **Define Technical Boundaries:** Each module should handle distinct functionalities, even if the boundaries are not domain-related. For example, one team handles the checkout flow, another handles the user profile.
2. **Contract-First Approach:** Define contracts between different frontend modules. Teams should agree on the APIs and interfaces their implementations expose to other parts of the application.
3. **Loose Coupling through Events and Pub/Sub:** Introduce event-driven communication to manage interactions between modules without tight coupling. Use a Pub/Sub model or message buses (for example, with WebSockets, Server-Sent Events, or even custom event handlers) to allow modules to notify each other of changes without being directly dependent.

Note: *The Pub/Sub model is a messaging pattern where senders (called publishers) do not send messages directly to specific receivers (subscribers). Instead, publishers send messages to a centralized topic or channel, and subscribers subscribe to that topic. The system then ensures that messages are delivered to all subscribers.*

Decentralized Governance

The micro frontend architecture emphasizes the need for alignment between organizational structures and system architecture. It understands, following *Conway's*

Law, that the structure of a system (such as software or hardware) tends to mirror the communication patterns, hierarchies, and organizational structures of the team or company that created it.

Note: *Conway's Law is an observation made by computer programmer Melvin Conway in 1967. It states: "Organizations which design systems are constrained to produce designs which are copies of the communication structures of these organizations."*

The micro frontend architecture fits best with high-performing company structures where authority, decision-making, and control across various entities or levels are decentralized.

Note: *High-performing company structures are mainly described in the book: "Accelerate: Building and Scaling High-Performing Technology Organizations" by Nicole Forsgren.*

The ultimate goal of decentralized governance is to empower teams so that they have the authority to make decisions about their work, including how they build, test, and release software.

Key Points:

- **Autonomy**: Teams have control over their own tools, processes, and workflows, within the guardrails of organizational objectives. They are given the authority to make decisions, leading to faster responses to market changes and customer needs.
- **Local Solutions**: Teams can tailor their approaches based on their specific contexts and challenges, promoting innovation.
- **Decentralized decision-making**: Decisions are made at the team level whenever possible, reducing delays caused by waiting for approvals from higher levels.

This approach contrasts with traditional hierarchical governance models, where decisions are made by a centralized authority, such as a government or a board.

While central initiatives are still valid and, in some cases, needed, they must be carefully implemented and monitored to avoid conflicting with the team's autonomy. The more we have them, the more friction there is in releasing new features.

Independent Deployments

Extending the decentralized governance principle, acting as a supporting tool to enable effective team autonomy, a good and healthy micro frontend architecture should aim to allow independent deployment between the different micro frontend implementations.

We soften the "strong guarantees" but bureaucratic processes proposed by centralized deployment strategies so that teams can deploy to production as frequently as possible in small and incremental changes.

Why it matters: Frequent deployments are a sign of a healthy and fast-paced delivery pipeline. They enable faster feedback from customers, reduce the size of deployments (making them less risky), and provide quicker fixes for any issues.

Deployments should be seen as trivial and mundane work, and processes around it should be automatized, not depending on manual interventions, so that the amount of time it takes to go from code commit to code running in production, also known as *Lead Time for Changes* is decreased.

Still, with the understanding that no system is immune to failure, the same decentralized and straightforward deployment process is a valuable resource for quickly recovering from failures, that goes together with a strong observability setup - discussed in the upcoming sections - which together will lead to a decreased average time that teams take to restore services after an incident that impacts customers.

These actions can be tracked all together so we are able to depict how well the development team goes to what concerns the deployment process.

Key metrics mentioned:

- **Lead Time for Changes:** The amount of time it takes to go from code commit to code running in production.
- **Deployment Frequency:** The frequency with which a team deploys changes to production.
- **Mean Time to Restore:** The average time it takes to restore service after an incident that impacts customers (for example, an outage or a degraded performance issue).
- **Change Failure Rate:** The percentage of changes that result in a failure in production (for example, causing downtime, introducing a bug, or requiring a rollback).

These metrics highlight the key performance traits of teams that have successfully embraced continuous integration (CI) and continuous delivery (CD) practices.

Following is a table based on the *Accelerate State of DevOps Report* 2023, showing these metrics with real numbers based on research done in the year 2023.

Performance level	Deployment frequency	Change lead time	Change failure rate	Failed deployment recovery time	% of respondents
Elite	On demand	Less than one day	5%	Less than one hour	18%
High	Between once per day and once per week	Between one day and one week	10%	Less than one day	31%
Medium	Between once per week and once per month	Between one week and one month	15%	Between one day and one week	33%
Low	Between once per week and once per month	Between one week and one month	64%	Between one month and six months	17%

Figure 4.3: *CI/CD metrics*

The "% of respondents" refers to the percentage of people who participated in the survey and provided specific answers to particular questions. These respondents are typically professionals working in various roles related to software development, IT operations, and engineering.

Note: *The Accelerate State of DevOps Report is an influential annual publication that provides data-driven insights into the practices and capabilities that enable high-performing software development and IT operations. The report is based on rigorous research and surveys, initially stemming from the work described in the book Accelerate: The Science of Lean Software and DevOps, authored by* Nicole Forsgren, *Jez Humble, and Gene Kim.*

The research conducted in the *Accelerate State of DevOps Report* is not restricted to the deployment aspect, but rather encompasses a larger spectrum of the software development lifecycle; yet for the context of micro frontend deployment strategy, it brings solid guidance to what it refers to deployment strategies. Though not explicitly advocating for fully decentralized deployments, its emphasis on flexibility, speed, and efficiency in software delivery and operations, often comes from empowering teams to take ownership of their work, including deployment decisions.

The Fallacy of Control

In a centralized deployment model, decisions regarding releases, architecture, and system changes are typically made by a small group of experts or an overseeing authority, such as a central IT or operations team. This group acts as the gatekeeper for changes, approving or rejecting them based on predetermined rules or frameworks.

One of the most persistent assumptions is that centralizing control results in greater safety and predictability. The logic is simple: by consolidating decision-making power and controlling the flow of information and processes, organizations can prevent risks, ensure compliance, and deliver consistent results.

However, in practice, this approach has significant drawbacks. Centralized control often results in bottlenecks. Each decision must pass through the central authority, creating delays in release cycles. These delays can lead to frustrated teams and a slowdown in innovation, as it takes much longer to test and deploy new features.

One real-world example of centralized bottlenecks can be seen in large enterprises with complex approval chains. Imagine a financial institution that requires every software release to be approved by a central committee. Even the smallest change, like a minor UI tweak or bug fix, must go through multiple levels of review, resulting in weeks or even months of delays. During this time, new vulnerabilities or customer frustrations may arise, all because of the slow, centralized process.

Even worse, centralization tends to assume that a small group can foresee and control all potential issues. However, complex systems do not behave in predictable ways. By the time a central team makes a decision, the environment may have changed. This inability to adapt quickly can introduce new risks, especially in industries where the speed of response is critical.

In contrast, a decentralized approach distributes control across teams. Each team or department has autonomy over their area of the system, making decisions about releases and architecture independently.

This approach is inherently more flexible. Since decisions are made locally, teams can respond quickly to issues or new opportunities without waiting for approvals from a central authority. This agility is critical in today's fast-paced markets, where customer expectations change rapidly, and competitive advantages can disappear overnight.

A good example of decentralization is the microservices architecture used by companies such as Netflix or Amazon. In these systems, different teams manage individual microservices, which can be deployed independently of one another. If the team managing the video player at Netflix discovers a bug, they can fix it and redeploy that service without affecting the rest of the system. This reduces the risk of widespread failures and ensures that customer-facing issues are resolved quickly.

In addition to speed, decentralized systems are often more resilient. When control is distributed, teams are empowered to experiment, innovate, and learn from their mistakes. This fosters a culture of continuous improvement. When failures do occur, they tend to be localized—impacting only a small part of the system. In centralized systems, by contrast, a single point of failure can bring down the entire system.

The Myth of Centralization as a “Safer” Option

One of the key reasons centralization is often viewed as safer is the belief that controlling the flow of changes minimizes risk. But, paradoxically, centralized control can introduce risks by slowing down response times and concentrating power in ways that can obscure potential issues.

Consider an organization that delays a security patch because it needs to go through a lengthy approval process. In today’s threat landscape, where vulnerabilities are exploited within hours of discovery, this kind of delay can be disastrous. By the time the patch is finally deployed, a breach may have already occurred. A decentralized approach, in contrast, allows teams to deploy security patches quickly and independently, reducing the time to fix and minimizing the window of vulnerability.

Moreover, centralized systems often discourage experimentation. Teams that have to navigate a bureaucratic approval process are less likely to innovate or take calculated risks, fearing rejection or delays. Over time, this can lead to stagnation, where the system becomes brittle and resistant to change—making it more vulnerable to external shocks, like a sudden shift in customer demands or a new technological breakthrough by a competitor.

The key takeaway for modern organizations is that distributing control, rather than consolidating it, leads to better outcomes. In embracing decentralization, we not only debunk the myth of centralization’s safety but also unlock the true potential for innovation, growth, and resilience.

Highly Observable

It is paramount for modern distributed systems to be highly observable in order to maintain their reliability and performance over time. It enables teams to gain insights into system behavior, detect issues proactively, and optimize user experiences.

Yet what should exactly be seen as highly observable? What shall one understand by observability?

As stated by R.E. Kálmán, 1960:

“Observability is a measure of how well **internal states of a system** can be inferred from knowledge of its **external outputs**.”

Monitoring / Observability

Though related concepts, Monitoring and Observability serve different purposes and have distinct characteristics.

Monitoring: It refers to the process of collecting, analyzing, and using data to keep track of the health and performance of a system. Monitoring typically involves predefined metrics and alerts to notify teams of potential issues.

It focuses on specific metrics, logs, and events that indicate the performance and health of systems. It is often concerned with detecting known issues and maintaining service levels. Primarily involves quantitative data such as metrics (CPU usage, memory consumption, response times), status codes, and error rates.

Observability: It refers to the capability to infer the internal state of a system based on the data it generates. Observability goes beyond monitoring by providing deeper insights into system behavior and facilitating troubleshooting and diagnostics.

It focuses on understanding the full context of the system's behavior, including unknowns. It emphasizes the ability to explore and analyze data to gain insights into complex interactions and root causes of issues. Encompasses a broader set of data types, including metrics, logs (structured or unstructured), and distributed traces. It emphasizes the importance of context and correlation between these data types to understand the system better.

Note: *Another aspect that is not often discussed in books but is always present in the real world is the intuition software engineers develop over time. This intuition is the ability to instinctively understand or know something without conscious reasoning. It stems from years of experience, expertise, and a gut feeling about how a system is likely to behave or respond under certain conditions.*

We could gauge the level of system awareness as follows:

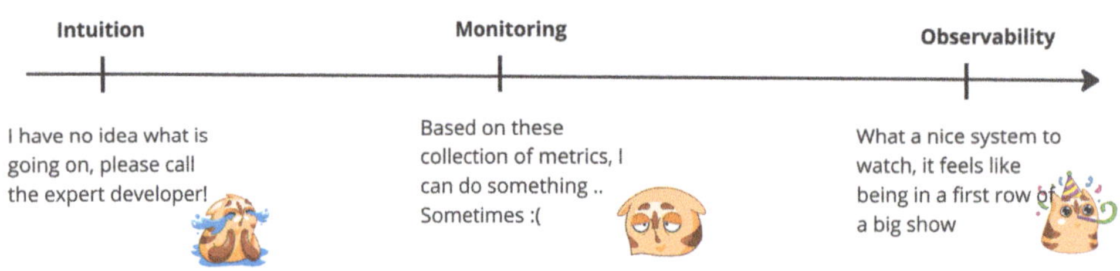

Figure 4.4: *Highly Observable*

With this understanding, we can recognize the importance of highly observable setups in the context of distributed systems and micro frontend architecture. High observability is crucial for navigating the complexity, scale, and challenges inherent in managing multiple interconnected components. While even the best software engineering teams may develop strong intuition for addressing various problems, a system's high observability democratizes the ability to reason about its behavior. This enables a broader range of team members to understand and troubleshoot the running system effectively. It is therefore a vital element of a well-structured micro frontend architecture.

Note: *We will take a closer look at the components and their implementations in Chapter 11, Observability.*

Conclusion

In this chapter, we have explored the foundational principles of micro frontends, emphasizing their alignment with modern architectural practices such as Domain-Driven Design, decentralized governance, independent deployments, and high observability. These pillars collectively empower teams to develop, deploy, and manage their applications more efficiently, with greater autonomy and responsiveness.

Together, these principles form a cohesive strategy for building robust, scalable micro frontend architectures. They encourage a balance between autonomy and alignment, flexibility and control, allowing organizations to meet both their technical and business objectives more effectively.

In the next chapter, *Integration Strategies*, we will build upon this foundation, exploring how different micro-frontend implementations can be composed and integrated to create seamless user experiences, while addressing the varying needs of different use cases.

References

1. https://cloud.google.com/blog/products/devops-sre/announcing-the-2023-state-of-devops-report

CHAPTER 5
Integration Strategies

Introduction

This chapter delves into various strategies for composing micro frontends, examining how different approaches can meet diverse technical and business needs. We will explore how to slice micro frontends, whether per feature or per page, and how to integrate them in both server-side and client-side environments.

Each integration strategy presents its own set of trade-offs, and choosing the right one can significantly impact the overall architecture. Through detailed discussions of techniques such as server-side template composition, edge-side integration, build-time and run-time strategies, and the evolving use of WebComponents and Module Federation, this chapter provides a comprehensive guide to designing an integration plan that aligns with your goals.

This chapter makes use of Docker, Node.js, and Javascript technologies to showcase the integration strategies. It is not in the scope of this book to cover the technology concepts. For the technology documentations, please refer to the References section.

The code used in this chapter can be found at: *https://github.com/ava-orange-education/-Micro-Frontends-Architecture-for-Scalable-Applications*

Structure

This chapter will cover the following topics:

- Per Feature X Per Page Slicing
- Server-Side Template Composition
- Edge-Side Composition
- Client-Side Composition
    - Run-Time Integration via iFrames
    - Run-Time Integration via Javascript
    - Run-Time Integration via WebComponents
    - Module Federation

- Client-Side Composition - Native Apps
    - Native Modules with JavaScript Bridge
    - React Native Module Federation
- Build-Time Integration

Per Feature X Per Page Slicing

Slicing refers to how we divide a larger application into smaller, manageable, and independently deployable pieces. We have explored the alignment that ideally the micro frontend implementations would have with the DDD principles, so that each micro frontend serves as the frontend implementation of its specific bounded context - *Chapter 4, Micro Frontend Foundations*. Technically in this design, we are implementing a *Per Feature Slicing*. This technique does provide a great alignment with the overall system's architecture, as each single micro frontend reflects one application domain; moreover, we avoid double discussion on how to split.

However, the slicing does come with challenges to what it refers to as the different micro frontend integrations. Understanding that at any given moment in an application there can be lots of different micro frontend implementations interacting with each other, brings challenges related, but not limited to:

Routing and Navigation

Coordinating routing between different micro frontends while preserving deep linking, browser history, and SPA behavior.

- Who controls the global router?
- How to handle navigation between domains?
- Potential for conflicting route definitions (imagine different micro frontends competing to change the application router).

Shared State Management

Micro frontends may need to access shared data such as user authentication, feature flags, cart, locale, and so on.

- Where is the global state stored?
- How to avoid tight coupling or reliance on global variables?

Performance and Bundle Size

Multiple micro frontends running on the same page, may result in duplicated dependencies, more JS to parse, and slower page loads.

- Initial load time can suffer, especially on mobile
- Multiple teams might use the same lib but different versions.

Note: *More on those topics can be found in: Chapter 6, Communication and Routing.*

In order to bring more clarity on the topic, let us consider the following hypothetical application:

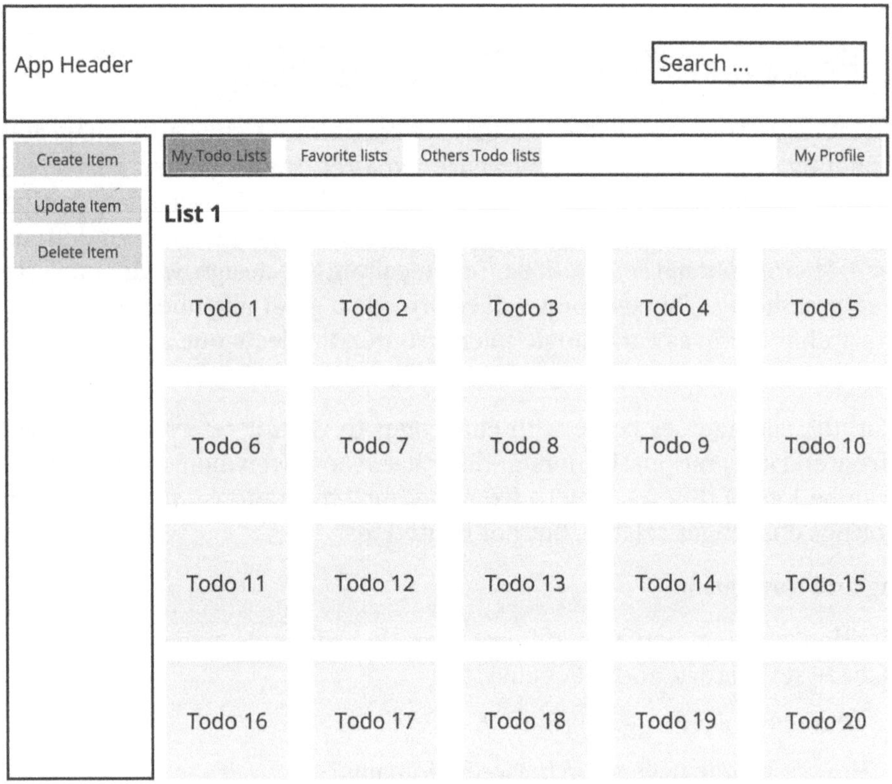

Figure 5.1: *Per Feature Slicing*

The preceding image depicts a hypothetical *ToDo List application*, where users can:

- Create and maintain (add, update, and delete) their own Todo lists;
- Manage favorite Todo lists;
- View and comment on others' Todo lists;
- Manage their own profile;
- Perform a global search among all the system capabilities;

The primary domain of the application revolves around task management, which involves creating, updating, deleting, and organizing tasks (to-dos). And as core, supporting, and generic subdomains, we could have as following:

Core subdomains:

Task Management:

- **Create**: Adding new tasks to the list.
- **Update**: Modifying existing tasks (for example, changing title, due date, status).
- **Delete**: Removing tasks from the list.
- **Prioritization**: Assigning priority levels to tasks.

List Management:

- **Creating Lists**: Users can create multiple lists to organize tasks (for example, Work, Personal) and favorite them.
- **List Organization**: Moving tasks between lists and managing list settings.
- **Interacting with lists**: Commenting on other people lists and receiving comments

Supporting subdomains:

- **User Profile**: Managing user settings such as theme, language, and notification preferences.
- **System searching**: users can search by all the features (lists, users, comments ...) provided in the application

Generic Subdomains

User Management:

- **Authentication**: User registration, login, and logout processes.
- **Authorization**: Role management (for example, user permissions).

Note: *How we are classifying the different domains for the specific use-case does not matter much for our case; it was chosen mainly for educational purposes.*

In the following image, we can see the mapping between the subdomain in the application using per feature slicing.

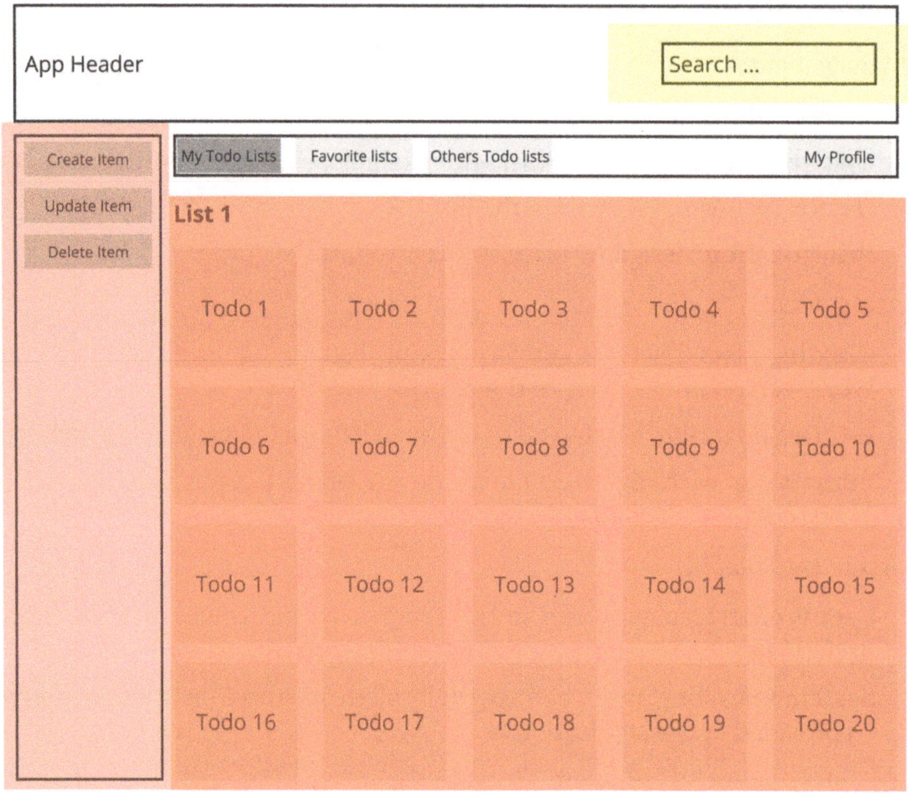

***Figure* 5.2:** *Per Feature Slicing - DDD mapping*

In the mapping, we have:

- The search field, highlighted in yellow would correspond to the *System searching* supporting subdomain;
- And the main red highlighted area would correspond to the *Task management* core domain

In this basic example, we see two distinct micro frontends running on the same page through per feature slicing. As the number of features on a given page increases, so too may the number of micro frontends, leading to the challenges previously mentioned regarding integration and the sharing of common states among the various micro frontend implementations. This topic will be explored further in the following sections.

Note: *The navigation section should be treated as a reusable component so that it can have consistency among the different implementations, but not as a micro frontend implementation on its own. It is just a tool that users use to navigate between the different features (domains) of your app. The same can be said with regard to the header. The main difference is that the last, given the simplicity of the use-case, has pretty* *much no relevant information, it could be managed by the Shell Application, detailed in the upcoming sections. Ultimately and more importantly, navigation and header components have no reference to the sphere of knowledge and activity related to the particular business problem; therefore, they are not seen as a domain and, consequently, not seen as a micro frontend implementation.*

So for this given page, we would have a micro frontend slicing as follows:

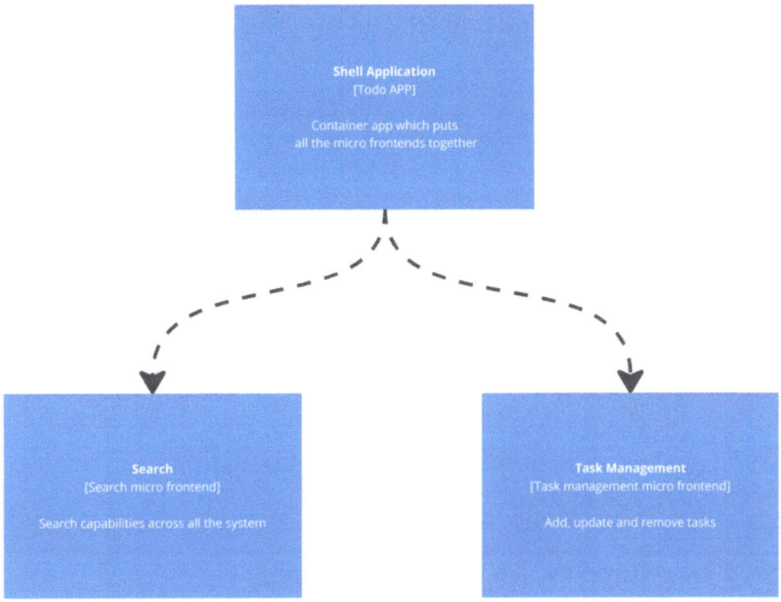

Figure 5.3: *Per Feature Slicing - container diagram*

Per Page Slicing

As for per page slicing, we split the application per page, so each route in the application is treated as an independent micro frontend. From our use-case, we would have the following micro frontends respectively:

- **/list** responsible for managing the to-do lists
- **/list/{id}** responsible for managing tasks within a given list
- **/others-lists** responsible for interacting with other people lists
- **/profile** responsible for managing the user profile

This type of slicing aims primarily to bypass the integration challenges associated with per feature slicing by ensuring that, at any given moment, only a single micro frontend is active on the page. It is a purely technical strategy that helps streamline integration, but it has trade-offs.

A notable drawback is that it can misalign with Domain-Driven Design (DDD) principles and the structure of related microservices. This breaks the ideal of team autonomy around a single business capability and instead creates cross-cutting concerns, tighter coupling, and duplicated logic across pages. As a result, frontend ownership becomes tied to UI routes rather than business domains, reducing cohesion between frontend and backend teams, since the former is UI route-oriented and the latter is domain-oriented, and complicating coordination, scalability, and long-term maintainability (mainly due to the fact that evolving individual parts of the system may involve multiple domains and teams). More on this in *Chapter 4, Micro Frontend Foundations*.

Lastly, it does increase the need for sharing functionalities, as pages normally share common structures, such as in the current use-case, the components *header* and *search* are reused across pages.

Per page slicing can work as an intermediate step in migrating to a micro frontend architecture. Since each new page does not need to integrate with existing ones, this approach is also suitable for implementing isolated features that require minimal or no shared functionality with the rest of the application. However, per feature slicing is generally preferred when possible, as it better supports feature cohesion and reuse.

It is also worth noting that both slicing strategies can coexist within the same architecture–they are not mutually exclusive.

Slicing: Decision Making Flow

Much of the effort involved in implementing a micro frontend architecture relates to how the application is divided (sliced) into the various micro frontends. Although the decisions are inherently context-dependent, a set of questions is presented below, along with subsequent actions to be applied in the decision-making process regarding how to slice the application.

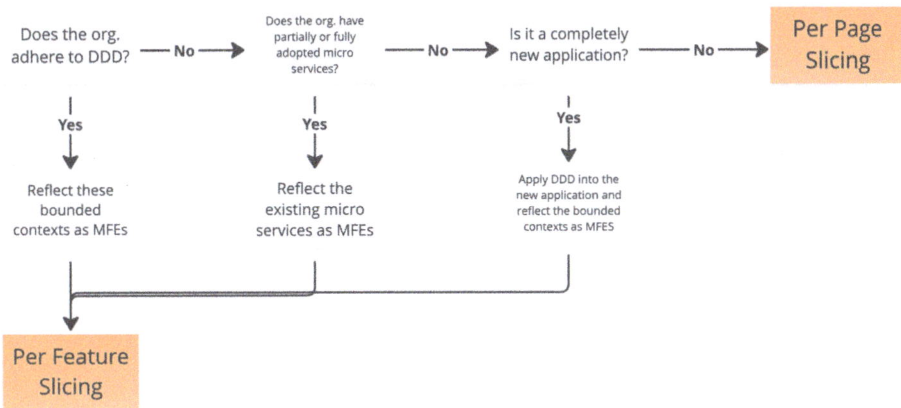

Figure 5.4: *Slicing: Decision Making Flow*

This decision flowchart helps teams decide how to slice an application into Micro Frontends (MFEs) based on the organization's architectural maturity and alignment with Domain-Driven Design (DDD) principles. Here's a breakdown of the logic:

Entry Point: Does the organization adhere to DDD?

If yes, it is likely that the organization already has clear bounded contexts in its backend and domain model. Then we can reflect those bounded contexts as micro frontends. Each MFE aligns with a business domain (for example, Bookings, Payments, UserProfile). Then we can move on and implement a per feature Slicing.

If the answer to this question is a no, then we move on:

Second Decision: Does the organization have partially or fully adopted microservices?

Even if DDD is not fully practiced, if the system has some services, in which the boundaries can be leveraged, this suggests a practical boundary for splitting the micro frontends. And we can again move on to a per feature slicing;

If not, we move on:

Third Decision: Is it a completely new application?

This is a greenfield opportunity, we can apply DDD from the start, define clear bounded contexts, and reflect them in the micro frontends.

Otherwise, we are dealing with a legacy monolith and no DDD or microservices are in place. In this case, the best approach is to go for per page slicing, so we can slice the monolith by pages (/home, /account, /checkout) and easily bootstrap isolated changes.

Shell Application

The Shell Application, also referred to as *Container*, is an important part of the micro frontend implementation, it acts as an aggregator responsible for adding all different micro frontend implementations on a single page. It will compose them in different contexts (server, edge, and/or client), depending on the integration strategy, but the principle is the same. Its responsibility level will vary as well, acting as a simple gateway, for per page slicing integrations to more advanced capabilities in per feature slicing.

A given system is not restricted to a single shell application, you may have different applications with different shells running in different contexts. Imagine for instance an audio streaming service, where users can access the system from different devices, and each one of those could provide its own shell application referencing the same micro-frontend.

For instance, the following audio streaming system where we may have a given micro frontend running in distinct shell applications:

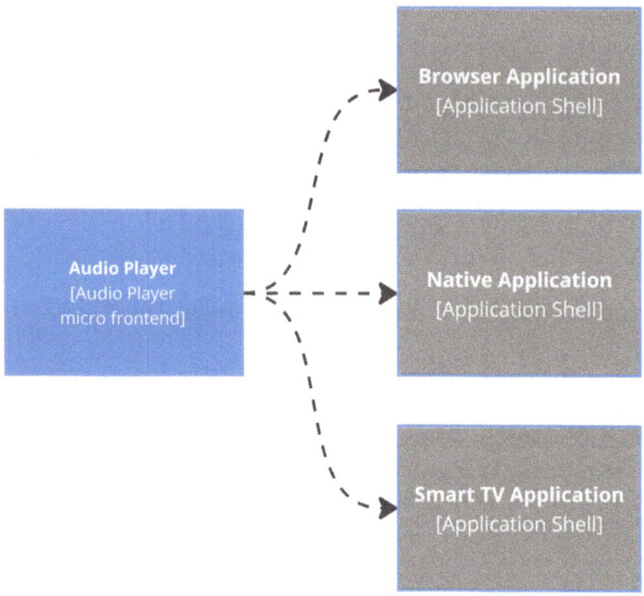

Figure 5.5: *Shell Application*

Server-side Template Composition

The server-side template composition is an integration strategy where different micro frontends (also known in this context as fragments) are assembled on the server before being delivered to the client. This approach allows for assembling and rendering multiple frontend fragments or components into a single HTML document on the server, creating a seamless experience for the end-user.

The server-side template composition generally works as the following:

- **Fragmentation**: Each micro frontend is a separate service responsible for providing a given application feature, such as a list of to-do items, search, user profile, and so on.
- **Server Composition Layer**: A server, *Application Shell*, gathers the rendered fragments or templates from each micro frontend service. This server may use frameworks or template engines (such as Pug, Mustache, Handlebars, and so on) to assemble the HTML fragments into one cohesive page.
- **Delivery**: The server sends the fully assembled HTML to the client.

Note: *A template engine is a software tool or library used in web development to dynamically generate* HTML *(or other text-based formats) by combining static templates with dynamic data. Template engines allow developers to separate the structure of a document* (HTML *layout) from the actual content (data), making code more modular, maintainable, and easier to update.*

Trade offs

While the approach can feel clean and centralized, it brings with it some considerable trade-offs that are often overlooked at the beginning of a project.

Perhaps the most significant issue is that the server has to wait for all the micro frontends to respond before it can return a complete page to the client. This introduces what's commonly known as the "*slowest link*" problem: no matter how fast most services are, the total response time is dictated by the slowest one. If one micro frontend takes 600 milliseconds while the others return in under 100, the user still waits those 600 milliseconds—and possibly longer if retries or timeouts are involved.

Things get even worse when a micro frontend is not just slow but unavailable. If a service fails to respond or times out, and your composition logic does not account for that, the entire page might fail to load. You might return a 500 error, a broken template, or a blank screen. Essentially, your page becomes as reliable as its least reliable dependency.

Another concern is scalability. The composition server becomes a bottleneck, especially under high load. Every page request has to go through it, and it needs to talk to multiple other services in real time, merge their output, and then render the result. This increases infrastructure cost, adds complexity, and can degrade performance quickly if the backend is not carefully optimized.

Caching, too, becomes tricky. Unlike fully static or SSR pages where you can cache the entire HTML output at the CDN, here you are building each page on the fly. Unless cachings are implemented for individual fragments or advanced techniques such as Edge Side Includes (ESI) are explored, the application is stuck with dynamic pages that do not take advantage of global CDNs. This directly impacts performance and scalability, especially when traffic spikes or during global events.

There's also the question of global latency. If your composition server sits in a single region–say, Europe–then users in Asia or South America will not only experience the usual round-trip delay to your origin server, but also inherit the latency of each internal call your server makes to assemble the page. The result: slow Time to First Byte (TTFB), even if the composed HTML is lightweight.

And finally, we run into a more subtle issue: complex error handling. If one of your fragments throws an error or timeout, how does the application degrade gracefully? Does the application render an empty container? Show an error message? Skip the whole section? Building robust fallback behavior for each fragment requires thoughtful composition logic and clear contracts between services.

Designing for Resilience

Thankfully, these challenges are not deal-breakers. With the right strategies, server-side composition can be made significantly more resilient and efficient.

To mitigate these limitations, it is crucial to define timeouts and provide fallback behavior for each micro frontend. When a service exceeds its allotted response time, a default or degraded version can be rendered in its place. This ensures that the page remains usable even if not all components are available. For instance, if the recommendations section responds too slowly, it can be replaced with a placeholder or omitted entirely, preserving access to the core functionality of the page.

Caching also plays a significant role in improving performance and reliability. While full-page caching may not be practical due to dynamic composition, individual fragments can be cached either in memory or at the edge using a CDN. This reduces the load on the composition server and minimizes response times. Fragments with frequent updates can be cached with short expiration windows, while static components benefit from longer caching durations.

Another effective optimization involves shifting the composition process closer to the edge. Services such as Cloudflare Workers or AWS Lambda@Edge can perform template composition at the CDN level, which lowers latency for globally distributed users and reduces the computational burden on origin servers. More details explored in the upcoming section.

A hybrid rendering strategy can provide a balanced solution. Critical content, such as the main page body, may be composed on the server, while non-essential or highly dynamic components—such as footers or personalized widgets—can be loaded client-side after the initial render. This approach enhances perceived performance and reduces the overall complexity of the server-side workload.

Resilience can also be improved through graceful degradation. When certain micro frontends are treated as optional, the system no longer depends on every service to render a complete page. Pages can remain functional with just the essential services, while optional features are included when available, offering a more robust user experience under varying conditions.

Using again our to-do list use-case, we could have something like the following:

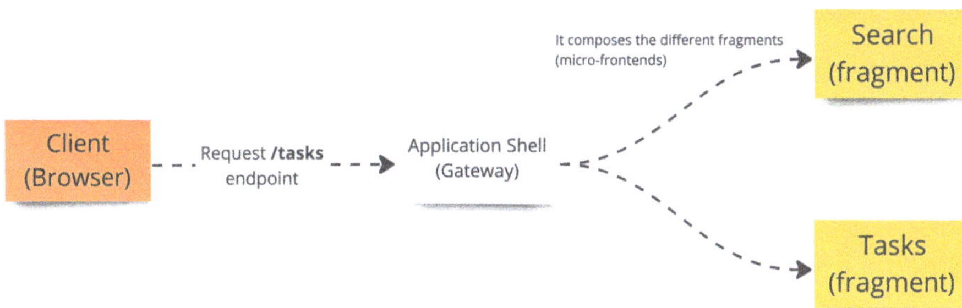

Figure 5.6: *Server-side Template Composition*

Assuming here a use-case where a given user is looking into tasks of a given todo list.

A very basic implementation could look like the following:

A node.JS (based on express framework) acts as a compositional layer (Application Shell) composing the other two (Search and Tasks) fragments also node.JS based on express. The services are independently deployable, and the application shell relies only on their private accessible URLs (*http://tasks:3001 and http://search:3002*). If we needed to have shared features, like in our case, a common header, the Application Shell could simply compose it and all the other micro frontend implementations would not have to care about it.

Note: *Additional requests done from the client are forwarded to the respective fragment implementations, like **/search** and **/view** endpoints.*

As a matter of simplicity, the basic implementation described here does not use any sort of templating engine, framework, timeouts, fallbacks and/or caching strategies, which in a real-world implementation should naturally be considered.

For a complete implementation, refer to: *https://github.com/ava-orange-education/-Micro-Frontends-Architecture-for-Scalable-Applications/tree/main/server-side-template-composition*

Also for a real use case, refer to *Chapter 12, A Micro Frontend Adoption - Other Relevant Use Case*

Basic server-side template composition implementation:

```
const tasksURL = "http://tasks:3001";
const searchURL = "http://search:3002";

// Root endpoint to combine the fragments from the services
app.get("/", async (req, res) => {
  try {
    const [tasksPage, searchField] = await Promise.all([
      axios.get(`${tasksURL}/main`),
      axios.get(`${searchURL}/main`),
    ]);

    res.send(`
      <html>
        <body>
          <header>
            ${searchField.data}
          </header>
          <main>
            ${tasksPage.data}
          </main>
        </body>
      </html>
    `);
  } catch (error) {
    res.status(500).send("Error fetching data from services");
  }
});

// Proxy `/view` requests to Tasks Service
> app.use(…
);

// Proxy `/search` requests to Search Service
> app.use(…
);

app.listen(8008, () => console.log("Gateway Service running on port 8008"));
```

Figure 5.7: *Server-side template composition implementation*

Edge-side Composition

As a slight variation of the server-side template composition, with the goal of reducing the request latency, we have the server-side edge composition which moves the Application Shell or composition layer into the "edge," meaning close to the end user, typically on content delivery networks (CDNs) or edge servers. This approach leverages edge servers' low-latency, distributed nature to deliver parts of the UI swiftly based on user-specific conditions, such as geographical location, device type, or other context.

Note: *An edge server is a server positioned close to the "edge" of a network–meaning near the end users–rather than at a centralized data center.*

Key Elements:

- **Distributed Composition**: Micro frontends are combined at edge servers rather than at the main server or in the client's browser. This reduces the amount of data that needs to travel over long distances and decreases page load times. It is important to note that micro frontend assets must still be fetched from their respective origins. Yet considering efficient caching strategies, we have fewer long-haul trips to compose the pages.
- **Dynamic Personalization**: Edge composition enables a more personalized experience by dynamically selecting the micro frontend components based on contextual information. For example, different content might be served to users based on region or language preferences. The same customization can, naturally, be achieved similarly in traditional server-side rendering, the advantage here lies in the proximity to the user and potentially faster response times.
- **CDN-based Fragment Loading**: By leveraging a CDN to store and load fragments of the UI, it is possible to reduce the load on origin servers. Edge servers can handle much of the routing and assembly, delivering only the necessary micro frontends based on pre-configured rules.
- **Latency Reduction**: Because the UI is composed closer to the user, the Time To First Meaningful Paint (TTFMP) can be faster, improving the user experience. The low latency can be achieved only if most components can be cached at the edge; however, if the edge must request multiple micro frontend parts from central locations, the latency might increase due to compounded long-tail requests.

Edge-side template composition diagram:

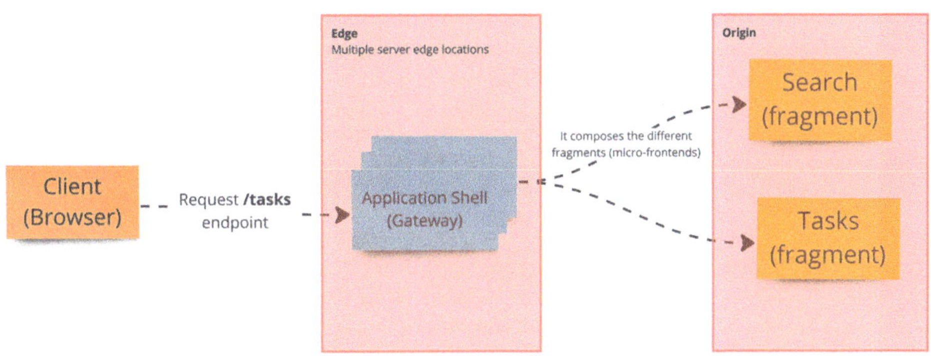

Figure 5.8: *Edge-side template composition implementation*

In this integration strategy, the Application Shell is deployed across multiple edge locations closer to end users, optimizing caching and potentially delivering location-specific content. This design also allows for micro frontend implementations tailored to local requirements, significantly enhancing the scalability of the overall solution.

Back to our to-do list use-case, technically we should move our Application Gateway code so that it runs in an edge location, the implementation can vary considerably based on the system network topology.

A common pattern is about using it together with some Content Delivery Network - CDN in a Serveless manner. In doing so, the network's underlying complexity is delegated to the cloud provider.

Following is a list of known cloud providers, key features, and limitations:

Platform	**Key Features**	**Limitation**
AWS Lambda@Edge	Runs on CloudFront edge locations, customizable caching, security headers, personalized content	Limited memory and execution time; cold starts
Cloudflare Workers	Low-latency with fast startup, KV storage for stateful apps, Durable Objects for persistence	Limited runtime environment (JavaScript/ TypeScript only)
Fastly Compute@Edge	WebAssembly-based execution for very low-latency, caching, and custom routing controls	Requires WebAssembly; limited language support
Google Cloud Functions + CDN	Scales via Cloud Load Balancing and Google CDN, supports HTTP/ HTTPS triggers	Not pure edge; latency may be higher than edge-focused solutions
Akamai EdgeWorkers	Integrated with Akamai CDN, optimized for high-security applications, advanced bot management	Limited to JavaScript; high costs for complex workflows
Azure Functions + Front Door	Global load balancing with Azure Front Door, integration with Microsoft ecosystem	Not fully edge-focused; higher latency for some use cases
Netlify Edge Functions	Built-in with Netlify's CDN, JAMstack-friendly, fast execution with instant deployment	Limited to JavaScript/ TypeScript, requires Netlify platform
Vercel Edge Functions	Edge middleware with Vercel, integrated with Next.js, optimized for frontend frameworks	Primarily for Next.js and Vercel-hosted projects

Table 5.1: *List of edge and serverless technologies*

Edge-side composition offers a promising, scalable model for performance-sensitive and context-aware applications, especially when paired with robust CDN caching and edge compute platforms. However, it shares many of the same challenges as traditional server-side composition (previously explored in the *Server-side Template Composition: Trade Off section*) and introduces new ones around infrastructure complexity and operational consistency across distributed nodes. It's a powerful tool, but one that must be wielded with caution and a deep understanding of the underlying trade-offs.

Client-side Composition

In the client-side composition, each micro frontend is essentially a JavaScript bundle (or a HTML page in an iframe integration), and when a user visits the application, the browser loads and executes these bundles to render the interface. The application shell coordinates this process by fetching the necessary micro frontends and mounting them into predefined locations in the DOM.

In this section, we will be exploring the client integrations assuming the most frequent use-case, the browser as the client. We will be exploring client-site composition in native apps later in this chapter.

Run-time Integration via iFrames

The Run-time integration via iFrames is a technique where individual micro frontends are embedded into a host application using HTML ***<iframe>*** elements.

To showcase the implementation, we will be referring here again to the *ToDo List application* previously described in: ***Per Feature X Per Page Slicing.***

With run time integration via iframe the implementation would look something like the following:

```
<!DOCTYPE html>
<html lang="en">
  <head>
    <meta charset="UTF-8" />
    <meta name="viewport" content="width=device-width, initial-scale=1.0" />
    <title>Main Shell Application</title>
    <style>…
    </style>
  </head>
  <body>
    <header>
      <h1>Shell Application</h1>
      <!-- Search iframe -->
      <iframe src="http://localhost:3001"></iframe>
    </header>
    <main>
      <!-- Tasks iframe -->
      <iframe src="http://localhost:3002"></iframe>
    </main>

    <script>
      // Listen for search results
      window.addEventListener("message", (event) => {
        if (event.data.type === "searchResults") {
          console.log("Search Results Received:", event.data.data);
        }
      });
    </script>
  </body>
</html>
```

Figure 5.9: *Client-side composition via iframes implementation*

On it, we have the application shell composing the micro frontend in the client, which, in this particular case, is also listening to events coming from the **search** micro services via **postMessage,** which were added into the context of the application shell as a matter of simplicity–a fact that in a real case implementation would very likely be delegated to a specific micro frontend. More on this will be explored in *Chapter 6, Communication and Routing*.

For a complete implementation, refer to: *https://github.com/ava-orange-education/-Micro-Frontends-Architecture-for-Scalable-Applications/tree/main/client-side-composition-iframe*

The integration via iFrames brings the highest level of isolation among the client-side composition strategies, it creates a complete sandboxed environment for each embedded application (micro frontend), separating the content, JavaScript, and CSS from the shell application. This makes it very difficult for code in the iFrame to interfere with the shell application, and vice versa.

Because iFrames operate in their own execution contexts, they can enhance security by limiting cross-application access, particularly useful when integrating external applications or third-party content.

However, the same advantages bring considerable drawbacks, to mention a few:

- **Performance Overhead**: iFrames can add to the loading time and increase memory usage, as each frame is effectively a separate browser window. This overhead can impact the application's performance, especially if multiple iFrames are used.
- **Limited Communication**: While it's possible to communicate between iFrames and the host using ***postMessage***, it can be cumbersome and complex to manage. iFrames do not have a shared JavaScript context, requiring additional code for communication and coordination.
- **SEO and Accessibility Issues**: Content within iFrames is often less accessible to search engine crawlers and can present accessibility challenges, particularly for screen readers. This can impact SEO and the user experience for people with disabilities.
- **Layout and Styling Constraints**: iFrames can be difficult to style consistently within the host application. Responsiveness and adaptive layouts may also be challenging to implement, as you do not have direct access to the content within the frame for styling purposes.
- **Cross-Origin Restrictions**: Integrating micro frontends from different domains can lead to cross-origin issues. Configuring Cross-Origin Resource Sharing (CORS) and dealing with restrictions can add to the complexity of using iFrames, especially if the host and micro frontends are served from different origins.
- **Inconsistent User Experience**: Since each iFrame is isolated, achieving a consistent look and feel across the entire application can be challenging. Each micro frontend may render at different times, leading to visual inconsistency during the loading process.

Note: *The* ***`window.postMessage()`*** *method is a powerful browser API for securely sending messages between windows, iframes, or tabs. It enables communication between a main window and an embedded iframe, a popup, or between tabs, even if they are from different origins (namely, domains).*

While iFrames offer good isolation and independence, they come with significant trade-offs, particularly in terms of performance, communication complexity, and user experience. These factors make iFrames suitable for scenarios where strict isolation is required, they prove useful for embedding sensitive elements such as payment forms or authentication screens, where preventing the host application from interfering with or accessing the embedded content is crucial. The same principle applies to integrating third-party tools; embedding partner dashboards, chat widgets, or analytics platforms via an iFrame offers simplicity and containment when dealing with external, uncontrolled systems. However, they are often less ideal for applications that require seamless integration and a cohesive user experience.

Run-time Integration via Javascript

Run-time integration via JavaScript offers a wide range of possibilities, with the core concept being the use of JavaScript to compose various micro frontend applications. Key considerations include the level of flexibility you require and how much you are willing to rely on frameworks.

In its most basic form, integrations can be done via the usage of native JavaScript feature, such as using ***<script />*** tag or via the usage of *import* from ESModules, this strategy gives you full control and flexibility, but it also places responsibility for the entire implementation on your shoulders.

Integration based on the usage ***<script>*** tags

```
<!DOCTYPE html>
<html lang="en">
  <head>
    <meta charset="UTF-8" />
    <meta name="viewport" content="width=device-width, initial-scale=1.0" />
    <title>Shell Application</title>
    <script src="./search/search-component.js"></script>
    <script src="./tasks/tasks-component.js"></script>
  </head>
  <body>
    <h1>Welcome to Feed me!</h1>
    <header>
      <h1>Shell Application</h1>
      <section id="search-component"></section>
    </header>
    <main>
      <section id="tasks-component"></section>
    </main>
  </body>
</html>
```

Figure 5.10: *Client-side composition via Javascript with script tag implementation*

In this simple case, an integration that assumes a certain element in the page containing a specified ID, in this case, the ***search*** micro frontend assumes an html element with a ***search-component*** ID and the ***tasks*** micro frontend assumes a ***tasks-component*** ID.

A slightly more modern variation would make use of the EcmaScript module specification (ES Modules):

```
<script type="module">
  import "./search/search-component.js";
  import "./tasks/tasks-component.js";
</script>
```

Figure 5.11: *Client-side composition via Javascript with ESModules implementation*

Note: *JavaScript ES Modules (ECMAScript Modules) are a standardized way to structure and share JavaScript code across files using import/export syntax. This module system, introduced in ECMAScript 2015 (ES6), allows for more maintainable and reusable code.*

The underlying principle remains the same: not relying on third-party tools, and treating micro frontend integrations and orchestration (discussed further in the following chapters) as the core of the architecture, thus maintaining full control over its implementation details.

A second approach involves using frameworks, which ease the burden of implementing a custom integration strategy.

Let us explore how our ToDo List Application could look like using **Single-SPA**

Single-SPA

Single-SPA (Single Page Application) is a JavaScript framework for building micro-frontends, which provides:

- **Isolation**: Each micro-frontend is isolated from the others in terms of state, logic, and lifecycle.
- **Routing and Navigation:** It enables different applications to be mounted and unmounted depending on the current route. It handles the routing between the applications, ensuring that only the relevant micro-frontends are displayed when a particular URL path is active.
- **Framework Agnostic**: It allows you to mix multiple frameworks on the same page. You can have React, Vue, Angular, and even vanilla JavaScript code running simultaneously without conflicts. It integrates these apps by mounting and unmounting them based on routing or other conditions.

Following is a code snippet where the micro frontends are registered using the API interface provided by Single-SPA:

```
import { start, registerApplication } from "https://cdn.skypack.dev/single-spa";

// Register the search micro frontend
registerApplication(
  "search",
  () => import("./search/search-component.js"),
  (location) => location.pathname === "/" // condition for when to show the search component
);

// Register the tasks micro frontend
registerApplication(
  "tasks",
  () => import("./tasks/tasks-component.js"),
  (location) => location.pathname === "/" // condition for when to show the tasks component
);

// Start the single-spa framework
start();
```

Figure 5.12: *Client-side composition via Javascript with ESModules implementation*

The framework provides a **registerApplication** method which receives the micro frontend application name, the function that should be executed, and the router where the implementation should be active. It can also receive additional parameters, not used in this particular implementation.

The individual micro frontend is expected to implement a **mount** and **unmount** methods:

```
// Search component definition
function SearchComponent() {…
}

// Register the component for single-spa
export const mount = async () => {
  const searchComponent = SearchComponent();
  document.getElementById("search").appendChild(searchComponent);
};

export const unmount = async () => {
  const searchElement = document.getElementById("search");
  if (searchElement) {
    searchElement.innerHTML = ""; // Clear the search component
  }
};
```

Figure 5.13: *Client-side composition via Javascript with Single-SPA implementation*

For a complete implementation, refer to: *https://github.com/ava-orange-education/-Micro-Frontends-Architecture-for-Scalable-Applications/tree/main/client-side-composition-framework*

The framework offers a very lean API integration; yet, decisions at this point need to be very carefully considered. It is important to assess whether it truly adds value or if it introduces unnecessary constraints.

Later changes in how the micro frontend is integrated require considerable team efforts and the odds of being framework-dependent are high.

Following is a list of relevant frameworks with a similar approach, highlighting key features, pros, and cons of each:

Framework	**Key Features**	**Pros**	**Cons**
Piral	- Pluggable architecture - Shared services - Built-in state management	- Offers a plugin system for customization - Manages state and routing effectively	- Higher initial setup and learning curve - Complex configuration for advanced features
Luigi	- Focus on enterprise applications - Routing and navigation management - Secure authentication support	- Built by SAP for enterprise use cases - Strong support for navigation and authentication	- Limited flexibility outside SAP ecosystem - Higher learning curve for non-enterprise cases
Qiankun	- Uses Single-SPA under the hood - Offers easier API for common use cases - Supports lazy loading and prefetching	- Simpler API for Single-SPA features - Provides sandboxing for isolation	- Limited control for advanced scenarios - Tied to Single-SPA's limitations
FrintJS	- Reactive micro frontend framework - Hierarchical composition - Built-in dependency injection	- Built-in dependency injection and hierarchical composition - Focuses on reactivity (React and RxJS)	- Niche usage, smaller community - Limited framework support (React-focused)

Mosaic	- Open-source by Zalando - Server-side and client-side integration - Layout composition with React components	- Powerful layout composition - Tailored for server and client-side integration	- E-commerce focus limits general use cases - Requires React ecosystem for full feature usage

Table 5.2: *List of micro frontend framework*

Additionally, we will explore two more JavaScript integration strategies in detail: integration via Web Components, which leverages the HTML specification to standardize how each micro frontend is exposed; and integration via Module Federation, where micro frontends are expected to utilize a common bundler tool for seamless interoperability.

Run-time Integration via WebComponents

With the integration via the WebComponents, we provide partial isolation compared to the complete isolation of iFrames and the minimal isolation of JavaScript integrations.

It uses the html WebComponent specification as the main contract for integrating different micro frontends; with that understanding, it is expected that each micro frontend register a given custom html tag so it can be integrated by the Shell Application.

Our *ToDo List Application* would look something like:

```
<!DOCTYPE html>
<html lang="en">
  <head>
    <meta charset="UTF-8" />
    <meta name="viewport" content="width=device-width, initial-scale=1.0" />
    <title>Shell Application</title>
    <script type="module" src="./search/search-component.js"></script>
    <script type="module" src="./tasks/tasks-component.js"></script>
    <style>…
    </style>
  </head>
  <body>
    <header>
      <h1>Shell Application</h1>
      <search></search>
    </header>
    <main>
      <tasks></tasks>
    </main>

    <script>
      document.getElementsByTagName("search")[0].onSearch = (results) => {
        console.log("Search Results Received:", results);
      };
    </script>
  </body>
</html>
```

Figure 5.14: *Client-side composition via WebComponents implementation*

In this example, we have links to each one of the micro frontends (*search-component.js* and *tasks-component.js*) which register respectively a *<search />* and *<tasks />* custom html component which are later used.

Also in here, we are not constrained by the ***postMessage*** API; WebComponents offer way more flexibility in how the data is exchanged. In this example, the *<search />* micro frontend triggers an *onSearch* event. Teams are free to define the best API interface for their implementations.

The debugging is also facilitated. Since the scripts run in the same JavaScript and DOM context as the rest of the application, any issue will immediately be visible on the main page; however, errors in a given implementation possibly can crash the whole application.

Partial Isolation: The Shadow DOM provides encapsulation of CSS and markup within the Web Component, which prevents styles from leaking into or out of the component. However, JavaScript isolation is limited; JavaScript in Web Components shares the same global context as the rest of the page.

For a complete implementation, refer to: *https://github.com/ava-orange-education/-Micro-Frontends-Architecture-for-Scalable-Applications/tree/main/client-side-composition-webcomponent*

WebComponents

WebComponents are a set of standardized technologies that enable developers to create reusable and encapsulated custom HTML elements. They allow for the creation of complex UI components that can be easily shared and reused across different web applications, promoting modular design. Web Components consist of four main specifications:

- **Custom Elements**: This allows developers to define new HTML tags and associate them with specific behavior. Custom elements can extend existing HTML elements or create entirely new ones.
- **Shadow DOM:** This provides encapsulation for the styles and markup of a component. By using Shadow DOM, a component can have its own scoped styles and DOM tree, preventing conflicts with the rest of the document.
- **HTML Templates**: These are used to define HTML markup that can be instantiated at runtime. Templates are defined using the <template> tag and can contain any valid HTML, but they are not rendered in the document until they are instantiated using JavaScript.
- **HTML Slots**: It allows developers to define placeholders within a custom element where external content can be inserted. This capability enhances the flexibility and reusability of components by allowing them to accept and render dynamic content while maintaining encapsulation.

Note: *The specification is great for interoperability, since implementation details are hidden from the consumers, allowing different frameworks to be integrated into any web application that supports HTML and JavaScript.*

For more details please refer to: *https://developer.mozilla.org/en-US/docs/Web/API/Web_components*

Module Federation

Last but not least, we have the Module Federation initiative, which has gained significant traction in recent years within the community. It is at the forefront of efforts toward runtime integrations, driving major advancements in the ecosystem.

Module Federation was officially introduced as part of Webpack 5 in 2020. Its primary goal was to enable runtime code sharing between different Webpack builds, allowing developers to load components from remote applications or modules at runtime. With this, each micro frontend became a separate Webpack build capable of exposing and consuming components from other builds during runtime.

One of its standout features is the powerful API interface for handling shared dependencies (which we will explore in detail in *Chapter 6, Communication and Routing*). This significantly reduces the final bundle size.

However, Module Federation was initially limited to the Webpack bundler and required specific configuration, which created some friction around its adoption–especially considering the growing popularity of other bundlers such as Vite, Parcel, and RsBuild in recent years.

Despite these early challenges, the community has steadily addressed them, culminating in the release of Module Federation 2.0. This version decoupled Module Federation from the build tool, allowing teams to use it with their preferred bundler. More importantly, it introduced greater flexibility into the overall micro frontend architecture.

Teams now need to establish a shared understanding of Module Federation as the standard approach for exposing micro frontends. In this context, Module Federation can be viewed as a public contract, much like how WebComponents serve as an interface in runtime integration scenarios. The key distinction, however, is that Module Federation is specifically tailored for micro frontend architecture, providing a broader set of features designed for this purpose.

Its schematic usage can be seen as the following:

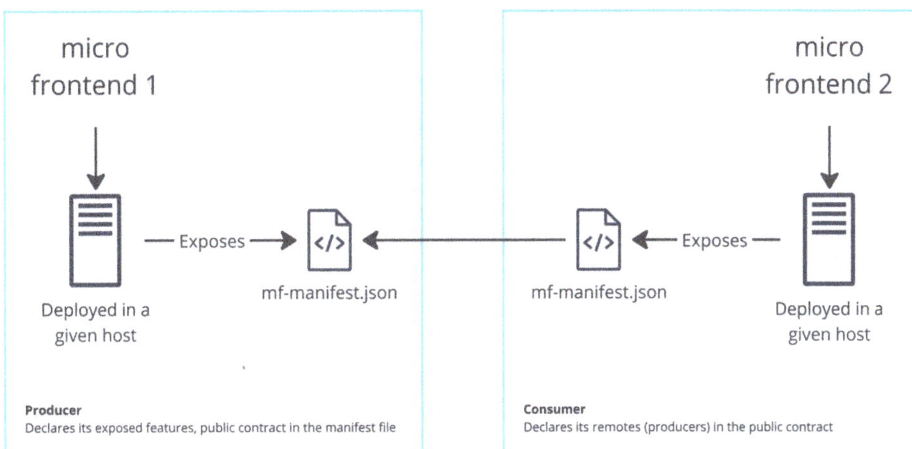

Figure 5.15: *Module Federation Working Flow*

Each micro frontend is independently deployed alongside with its public contract (**`mf-manifest.json`** **file**), declaring its exposed features and/or its remotes, producers which it expects to get certain features from.

Next, we will revisit our *ToDo List Application* with a more compelling use case. This time, we will set up a complete environment consisting of the three already known projects: the Shell Application, and two micro frontends–Tasks and Search–using the following tech stack:

- Rsbuild as bundler;
- React;
- Typescript;
- Module Federation;

The Shell Application main component has the following structure:

```
import './App.css';
import SearchComponent from 'search/search';
import TasksComponent from 'tasks/tasks';
import ActionComponent from 'tasks/actions';
import Menu from './Menu';

const App = () => {
  return (
    <div className="content">
      <header>
        <h1>Shell Application</h1>
        <SearchComponent label="Search for tasks" />
      </header>
      <section className="main">
        <ActionComponent />
        <section className="center">
          <Menu />
          <TasksComponent />
        </section>
      </section>
    </div>
  );
};

export default App;
```

Figure 5.16: *Client-side Composition Module Federation*

On it, the **SearchComponent**, **TasksComponent**, and **ActionComponent** are provided by the *Search* and *Tasks* micro services, which are accessible via http protocol and configured in the module federation as illustrated in the following code snippet:

```
import { defineConfig } from '@rsbuild/core';
import { pluginReact } from '@rsbuild/plugin-react';
import { pluginModuleFederation } from '@module-federation/rsbuild-plugin';

export default defineConfig({
  plugins: [
    pluginReact(),
    pluginModuleFederation({
      name: 'shell_application',
      remotes: {
        search: 'search@http://localhost:3000/mf-manifest.json',
        tasks: 'tasks@http://localhost:3001/mf-manifest.json',
      },
      shared: ['react', 'react-dom'],
    }),
  ],
  server: {
    port: 2000,
  },
});
```

Figure 5.17: *Module Federation Remote consumption*

In this configuration is declared where the remotes (search and tasks micro frontends) are located.

Each one of the providers is expected to expose its public contract via the bundler configuration so that the module federation plugin is able to generate the manifest file (*mf-manifest.json*) to be consumed by the (in the specific case, shell application) consumers, something like the following:

```
import { defineConfig } from '@rsbuild/core';
import { pluginReact } from '@rsbuild/plugin-react';
import { pluginModuleFederation } from '@module-federation/rsbuild-plugin';

export default defineConfig({
  plugins: [
    pluginReact(),
    pluginModuleFederation({
      name: 'tasks',
      exposes: {
        './tasks': './src/tasks/Tasks.tsx',
        './actions': './src/actions/Actions.tsx',
      },
      shared: ['react', 'react-dom'],
    }),
  ],
  server: {
    port: 3001,
  },
});
```

Figure 5.18: *Tasks micro frontend module federation configuration*

The interface is elegantly designed using a plugin-based architecture. In this setup, the **`pluginModuleFederation`** for the *rsbuild* bundler is combined with **`pluginReact`**. It is worth pointing out that the plugins' structure should match the underlying micro frontend application and not the other micro frontends. The manifest file is solely used as public contract. We specify the name of our micro frontend and define the exported features (Tasks and Actions).

Note that the keys from the *exposes* object are the mounting paths, so consumers would import in the case *tasks/tasks* and *tasks/actions*, and list the shared dependencies (react and react-dom).

This approach offers flexibility, allowing us to switch bundlers simply by using a different module federation plugin, or to adopt different JavaScript frameworks while maintaining the same plugin-based architecture.

This configuration generates a manifest file, which consumers can use to discover the micro frontend service:

```
// http://localhost:3001/mf-manifest.json

{
  "id": "tasks",
  "name": "tasks",
  "metaData": {↔},
  "shared": [↔],
  "remotes": [↔],
  "exposes": [
    {
      "id": "tasks:tasks",
      "name": "tasks",
      "assets": {↔},
      "path": "./tasks"
    },
    {
      "id": "tasks:actions",
      "name": "actions",
      "assets": {↔},
      "path": "./actions"
    }
  ]
}
```

Figure 5.19: *Module Federation Manifest file*

Interesting facts to note:

The dependency depth is not limited, producers can act as consumers and vice-versa. In this particular case, for instance, the *Task* micro frontend could consume other micro frontends.

Though not an ideal architecture pattern, cyclical dependencies are allowed. For instance, the Shell Application could consume and provide features for the underlying micro frontends.

The developer ergonomics in this setup offers unique features like:

- **Typing support:** The metadata exported in the manifest file includes typing information, so consumers using some typing feature (most of the time typescript) can get detailed information about your micro frontend API interface.
- **Hot Module Replacement**: The Hot Module Replacement (HMR) is reactive among all the micro frontend projects, changes for instance in a given micro frontend implementation are automatically reflected in the Shell Application.

- **Dev Extensions**: Particularly to react and react-dom as shared dependencies, react chrome extensions work as if it was the same application running.

These benefits are most evident in setups where all micro frontend implementations share a similar tech stack. However, this is not a realistic assumption for many real-world projects. Additionally, the standards surrounding implementations–such as the structure of the manifest file–are still evolving and may undergo significant changes. This instability can introduce considerable friction for projects trying to keep pace with updates.

Despite these challenges, the concepts introduced by Module Federation are worth monitoring and may be particularly useful, currently, in smaller, niche-specific contexts.

For a complete implementation, refer to: *https://github.com/ava-orange-education/-Micro-Frontends-Architecture-for-Scalable-Applications/tree/main/client-side-composition-module-federation*

For more details about the Module Federation 2.0, please refer to: *https://module-federation.io*

Client-Side Composition Digest

The Client-Side Composition Integrations can overall be understood and digested as the following:

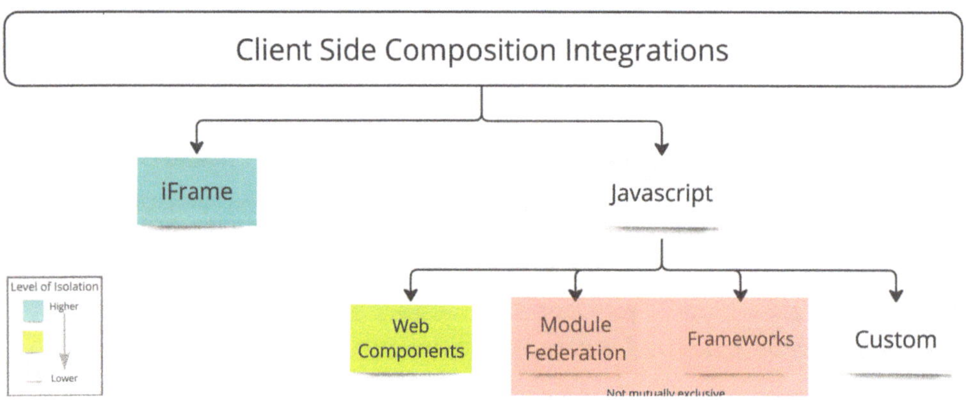

Figure 5.20: *Client-side composition digest*

The chart illustrates the decision-making process for selecting the most suitable client-side composition integration. It starts by evaluating whether the high level of isolation offered by iFrames is necessary. If not, it defaults to JavaScript-based integrations, ranging from the partial isolation provided by Web Components to the complete flexibility of a custom implementation.

A custom implementation typically emerges when the existing patterns do not meet the application needs out of the box. These implementations are tailored to specific requirements, such as tight control over rendering, advanced communication, or legacy constraints. The implementations can vary considerably, ranging from an expected (mounting / unmounting) contract that each micro frontend is expected to implement, a CDN registry where the different micro frontends are registered, custom micro frontend loading functions, and so on.

Note: *Module Federation and micro frontend frameworks are not mutually exclusive, they can be used together, with some frameworks having specific connectors and plugins for that use case. However, this combination should be carefully evaluated to avoid introducing unnecessary complexity into the overall setup.*

The following table highlights the key differences between iFrame, WebComponent, and JavaScript integration (understanding in this category Module Federation and the integration via micro frontend frameworks):

Aspect	iFrame	WebComponent	JavaScript integration
Isolation	Complete, cross-origin restrictions	CSS and structure only; JavaScript shares context	Isolation depends on module scope; shared state can cause issues
Communication	Limited, requires postMessage	Simple, native DOM events	Direct method invocation, but risk of tight coupling
Styling	Completely isolated	Scoped styling	Requires careful namespace handling to avoid conflicts
Performance	Higher resource usage, slower	Low overhead, reactive	Performance depends on the efficiency of the shared modules
SEO & Accessibility	Limited SEO, harder to make accessible	SEO-friendly, better accessibility	
Development Complexity	Separate maintenance, more complex debugging	Unified development, easier debugging	Moderate complexity, but easier to integrate within same framework

Table 5.3: *Key differences between WebComponents and iFrames*

Client-Side Composition: Native Apps

For native mobile applications, the composition principle is the same; however, the technologies available are different. The term micro frontend per se is not frequently connected to the native development, yet the concept of breaking down a big monolith application into smaller independently deployable applications continues. In the literature you may find references to: *Micro Apps*, *Modular Architecture*, *Federated Modules*, *Remote Components*, *Modular Mobile Apps* and the list continues, for our context, as a matter of consistency and hopefully a conversion into a ubiquitous vocabulary, we will be using the same nomenclature adopted by the micro frontend architecture.

In the most simplistic use-case, the native application could be seen just as a container that instantiates a WebView that loads the "normal" application shell and therefore all the consequent micro frontends. By normal, we understand the application shell based on browser technologies.

Note: A *WebView is a native component that allows you to render html content within a native app.*

This integration is great given its "ready-to-go" implementation when comparing to an already existing html-based setup, however for certain use cases, especially when requiring integrations with the device capabilities it may be limited and/or in some cases the user experience may not "feel" like native.

Super Apps

The rise of super apps–platforms that bundle multiple distinct services into a single, seamless mobile experience–has created new momentum for applying micro frontend principles in native mobile development. Super apps such as WeChat, Grab, and Gojek allow users to chat, order food, book rides, and more, all within a unified interface. Technically, they represent a compelling match for micro frontends: independently developed, deployed, and maintained modules that contribute to a cohesive whole. While the idea of micro frontends has already proven effective in the web ecosystem–through techniques such as build-time integration, runtime composition, and shadow DOM encapsulation–their application to native environments remains nascent but promising. In super apps, each internal "mini app" often corresponds to a specific business domain and can benefit from being managed by autonomous teams, using different tech stacks, and updated independently. This naturally aligns with the micro frontend philosophy, where boundaries between features reflect organizational and domain boundaries. As the demand for modular, scalable native platforms grows, micro frontends offer a path to reduce coupling, accelerate feature delivery, and improve cross-functional ownership–just as they have on the web.

Native Modules with JavaScript Bridge

A "more" native approach, when compared to integrating via the usage of WebView, while still reusing web technologies is the Native Modules with JavaScript Bridge integration. In it, each micro frontend (or feature) is built as a module, often in JavaScript, and communicates with native device functionalities through a bridge that handles data passing and method invocation. The bridge translates JavaScript calls to native code (written in Objective-C/Swift for iOS, or Java/Kotlin for Android), allowing JavaScript-based components to interact directly with native capabilities.

Typical Workflow:

1. **Module Initialization**: Native modules are registered within the app and exposed to the JavaScript runtime, which allows them to be accessed like any other JavaScript module.
2. **Data Passing and Method Invocation**: When a JavaScript component needs a native function (like camera access or GPS), it calls the corresponding method on the bridge. The bridge then invokes the native module method and returns results asynchronously.
3. **Event Handling and Communication**: The bridge manages event handling between native and JavaScript, so JavaScript-based components can listen for and react to native events (for example, device orientation changes or push notifications).

By using native modules with a JavaScript bridge, you get a balanced setup that allows you to compose and manage micro frontends effectively while harnessing the native capabilities that mobile platforms offer.

React Native Module Federation

React Native is an open-source framework developed by Facebook (now Meta) that allows developers to build mobile applications using JavaScript and React. React Native enables the development of native mobile apps for both iOS and Android platforms, using the same codebase. It bridges the gap between web development and native mobile development by allowing the use of web development concepts (such as React) while maintaining the performance and feel of a native mobile app.

The technology allows via *Re.Pack* the implementation of Module Federation for the native application

Note: *Re.Pack is a powerful toolkit designed to integrate Webpack with React Native applications. It specifically focuses on enhancing bundling capabilities for React Native by providing Module Federation support and improving the overall developer experience. Re.Pack enables modern web bundling features such as dynamic imports, HMR (Hot Module Replacement), and code splitting within React Native environments.*

This is achieved via the usage of a specific Re.Pack plugin: *Repack.plugin.ModuleFederationPlugin.*

So we can define the micro frontends that the Shell application will be using:

```
import * as Repack from '@callstack/repack';

new Repack.plugins.ModuleFederationPlugin({
  name: 'Tasks',
  remotes: {
    tasks: 'tasks@https://example.com/tasks.container.bundle',
  },
});

new Repack.plugins.ModuleFederationPlugin({
  name: 'Search',
  remotes: {
    search: 'search@https://example.com/search.container.bundle',
  },
});
```

Figure 5.21: *Module Federation in React Native*

In the example the **Tasks** and **Search** micro frontends are bundled as remote components so that they can be injected by the shell application via runtime integration.

```
import { ScriptManager, Federated } from '@callstack/repack/client';

// Resolver function
ScriptManager.shared.addResolver(async (scriptId, caller) => {
  const resolveURL = Federated.createURLResolver({
    containers: {
      search: 'https://example.com/search.container.bundle',
      tasks: 'https://example.com/tasks.container.bundle',
    },
  });

  const url = resolveURL(scriptId, caller);
  if (url) {
    return { url };
  }
});

// Somewhere later...
import Search from 'search/App';
import Tasks from 'tasks/App';
```

Figure 5.22: *Module Federation in React Native, Host application*

This approach still limits us to the constraints of the tooling and the specific tech stack, but it allows us to achieve the ultimate goal of code modularization with independent deployments.

For more details, please refer to: *https://re-pack.dev*

Build-time Integration

A final word in regards to build-time integration, which though should be seen overall as an anti-pattern, understanding that goes against one of the main principles of the micro frontend architecture (Independent Deployments - Explored in *Chapter 4, Micro Frontend Foundations*) and the overall distributed architecture, it may be that for certain environments a controlled and centralized release is a must–in such cases, we can always fallback to the package manager. NPM for web projects, Gradle, Swift Package Manager - Android and iOS respectively, or any other applicable one.

It offers a simpler and more predictable approach to composing applications. Since everything is bundled together during the build process, there is no need to manage complex runtime orchestration or worry about cross-origin issues. Performance tends to benefit as well, because shared libraries are bundled once, reducing duplication and improving load times.

On that, a Shell Application team can control each micro frontend version to be released and add any build checks required prior to release.

A **`package.json`** dependency declaration for NPM.

```
{
  "name": "application-shell",
  "version": "1.0.0",
  "description": "An application for managing tasks",
  "dependencies": {
    "@microfrontend/tasks": "^1.0.0",
    "@microfrontend/seach": "^1.0.0"
  }
}
```

Figure 5.23: *Package.json*

Conclusion

In this chapter, we explored various integration strategies for micro frontends, dissecting them through the lenses of per feature and per page slicing. We examined how different slicing techniques can shape the structure of your application, influencing its modularity, scalability, and maintainability.

By delving into server-side template composition and edge-side composition, we highlighted strategies for handling integration closer to the backend. On the client side, we covered run-time methods such as iFrames, JavaScript, WebComponents, and Module Federation integrations, highlighting their flexibility and trade-offs in isolation and interactivity.

As we moved into the realm of native mobile applications, we discussed how client-side composition translates into native apps through native modules with JavaScript bridges and module federation with react native. Finally, we covered build-time integration, which, while offering simplicity and control, often sacrifices the ability to update components independently post-deployment.

Having established how to integrate micro frontends, the next chapter will dive into the critical aspects of communication and routing within these architectures. We will further explore the concept of a shell application and its pivotal role in orchestrating micro frontends. Additionally, we will address state management, inter-micro frontend communication, routing strategies, and shared dependencies, providing concrete examples to illustrate how these components work together to deliver a cohesive user experience.

References

1. https://docs.docker.com/reference/
2. https://nodejs.org/docs/latest/api/
3. https://developer.mozilla.org/en-US/docs/Web/API/Window/postMessage
4. https://github.com/ava-orange-education/-Micro-Frontends-Architecture-for-Scalable-Applications
5. https://developer.mozilla.org/en-US/docs/Web/API/Web_components
6. https://module-federation.io
7. https://re-pack.dev

Chapter 6
Communication and Routing

Introduction

In micro frontend architecture, the shell application plays a crucial role in orchestrating the different frontend modules. This chapter delves into its responsibilities, focusing on how it manages and coordinates the various micro frontends in a seamless, cohesive experience.

We begin by exploring the shell application, discussing its duties in state management and its role as the backbone for communication across micro frontends. Effective state management is vital to ensure data consistency and prevent duplication of effort, especially when individual micro frontends need to work with shared data or respond to global state changes.

Cross-application communication is another significant aspect of micro frontend systems. In this section, we will examine patterns and mechanisms for enabling micro frontends to exchange information, considering both synchronous and asynchronous approaches. We will also discuss the challenges of isolating individual micro frontends while facilitating necessary interactions between them.

Routing is a critical requirement in any modern web application, and this chapter addresses the challenges of implementing it in a micro frontend environment. We will look at how routing can be coordinated between the shell application and the micro frontends, ensuring consistent navigation and a smooth user experience.

Finally, we will tackle shared dependencies and related performance concerns. When micro frontends share libraries or frameworks, efficient management of these dependencies becomes essential to avoid duplication, reduce bundle size, and improve loading times. By examining real-world examples, we will illustrate best practices for handling shared dependencies while optimizing performance.

By the end of this chapter, you will have a solid understanding of how to effectively manage communication, routing, and shared dependencies within a micro frontend architecture

Structure

In this chapter, the following topics will be covered:

- Shell Application
- State Management
- Cross Application Communication
- Routing
- Shared Dependencies
- The Shell Application Journey

Shell Application

In *Chapter 5, Integration Strategies - Shell Application*, we have defined what a shell application is. Now we need to focus on its responsibilities, especially in the context of horizontal slicing architecture where its duties are more prominent.

It is important to note that the topics explored here are not a fixed list. Instead, they should be adapted to each specific implementation use case to better meet individual needs. In this section, we will focus on the most common responsibilities of a shell application.

Before diving into these topics, it is essential to understand the main goal of the shell application:

"To serve as a stable and predictable platform on which different micro frontends can be built."

The shell application should provide stable, well-defined APIs, events, or interfaces for micro frontends to interact with. These contracts should be versioned and backward-compatible whenever possible to avoid breaking changes that could disrupt individual modules.

Stability can be viewed from two perspectives:

Public Contracts Stability

The frequency of changes made to the public contract over time, together with the number of non-backward-compatible changes required by consumers of these contracts.

Consider a scenario where the shell application specifies React version 18 as a globally shared dependency. This means all micro frontend implementations rely on this version being provided by the shell application. If a critical issue is discovered in React version 18, and a new major, non-backward-compatible update (version 19) is needed, every micro frontend would have to undergo a migration to adopt the new version, in addition to the shell itself.

Such scenarios should be avoided, and this is a key stability goal for the shell application. We will explore this further in the upcoming section on Shared Dependencies.

Another factor affecting public contract stability is the scope of responsibilities assigned to the shell application. The fewer responsibilities it has, the less likely it is to change its public contracts. Therefore, whenever possible, responsibilities should be delegated to individual micro frontend implementations.

Resource Isolation

The other aspect of stability pertains to resource isolation:

A stable platform should ensure that changes, failure, and/or performance issues of one micro frontend do not impact the entire application. For instance, if a micro frontend crashes or fails to load, the shell should handle the error gracefully without compromising the user experience. Similarly, performance issues in one micro frontend should be isolated so they do not negatively affect others.

Predictability in a shell application means consistent behavior across different deployment environments, shared dependencies, global styles, and other shared factors. The shell application must guarantee this consistency to maintain a reliable and seamless user experience.

These two characteristics should be the ultimate goal of the shell application, and the following actions can be seen as ways to achieve these goals.

Note: *Backward-compatible changes are modifications made to a system (for example, an API, component, or application) in such a way that existing clients or consumers can continue to function without requiring any changes. In other words, backward compatibility ensures that new versions of a software system do not break existing integrations or dependent components.*

It is expected that the shell application will handle the following concerns:

- State Management
- Routing
- Cross-Application Communication
- Shared Dependencies
- Bootstrapping and Initialization
- Layout and UI Composition
- Authentication and Authorization
- Error Handling and Resilience
- Lazy Loading and Performance Optimization
- Feature Flags and A/B Testing

In what follows, we are going to explore each one of these concerns.

State Management

State management refers to how an application handles its data, tracks changes, and ensures that the UI is updated to reflect the current state. In a micro frontend architecture, state management can be challenging because the application is split into independent modules (micro frontends), each potentially with its own isolated state. The key challenge is how to manage state in a way that allows these independent modules to coexist and interact without creating inconsistencies or performance bottlenecks.

When designing state management for a micro frontend, it is essential to delineate local state, state that is scoped to a specific micro frontend and not required or relevant outside of its own context, and global state, a state that needs to be shared across multiple micro frontends or has a global impact on the application.

When handling shared state in micro frontends, caution is essential. Once state is exposed, it becomes part of the micro frontend's public contract, requiring any future changes to be managed with backward compatibility in mind. To avoid unnecessary complexity, state should only be exposed when absolutely necessary. It is generally better to keep state private initially, as exposing it later remains an option if the need arises.

Imagine the following use case:

```
// Internal interface:

interface MyComplexInterface {
  // structure of the complex interface
}

interface Task {
  id: string;
  name: string;
  description?: string;
  internalDetails: MyComplexInterface;
}

// ------------------

// Micro frontend interface:
interface TasksComponent {
  onTaskSelected: (task: Task) => void;
}

// Possible usage
// <tasks onTaskSelected={(task) => {}} />
```

Figure 6.1: *Exposing shared state*

A *Tasks* micro frontend exposes a **`onTaskSelected`** event.

In this case, we expose all the internal "complex" state of the **`Task`** interface. Therefore, from this moment, all changes done in this interface need to be carefully managed in order to not introduce breaking changes, thus decreasing the overall application maintainability.

A better variation could look like:

```
// Internal interface:

interface MyComplexInterface {
  // structure of the complex interface
}

interface Task {
  id: string;
  name: string;
  description?: string;
  internalDetails: MyComplexInterface;
}

// --------------

// Micro frontend interface:
type PublicTask = Pick<Task, "id" | "name" | "description">;
interface TasksComponent {
  onTaskSelected: (task: PublicTask) => void;
}

// Possible usage
// <tasks onTaskSelected={(task) => {}} />
```

Figure 6.2: *Exposing shared state*

In this version we are selective in regards to what we expose, the **`PublicTask`** type explicitly selects what information we will expose from the internal **`Task`** interface, in this case, we expose only *id*, *name*, and *description*, not compromising future updates on **`internalDetails`** of the *Tasks* interface.

An understanding of the micro frontend bounded context and its responsibility will also bring valuable insight into what should and should not be a shared state.

A micro frontend should expose state that belongs to its bounded domain and not derived state, state coming from other domains. For more information about bounded context, please refer to: *Chapter 4, Micro Frontend Foundations-Domain-Driven Design.*

With that in mind, we can use the following decision-making-framework:

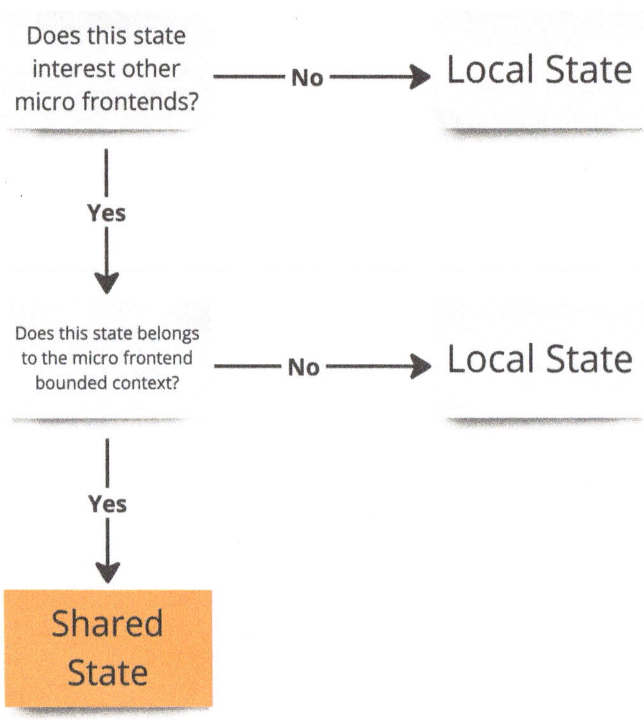

Figure 6.3: *Decision-making-framework*

Once the local and shared state requirements are defined for each micro frontend implementation, the shell application can manage these states using any suitable tools provided by the chosen technology stack.

In the following example, we have a *React* shell application that manages the global state from the two *Search* and *Tasks* web-components with *Signals*.

Note: *Signals is a state management library initially designed for the Preact framework, although it does work with other frameworks. It introduces fine-grained reactivity by using a concept called signals to manage and react to state changes.*

```
import React, { useEffect, useRef } from "react";
import { signal } from "@preact/signals-react";

const tasksSignal = signal([]);

const ShellApplication = () => {
  // it holds references to the web-component elements
  const searchComponentRef = useRef(null);
  const tasksComponentRef = useRef(null);

  useEffect(() => {
    const searchComponent = searchComponentRef.current;

    // Attach the onSearch function
    searchComponent.onSearch = (query) => {
      tasksSignal.value = query;
    };
  }, []);

  useEffect(() => {
    const tasksComponent = tasksComponentRef.current;

    // Update the tasks component whenever tasksSignal changes
    tasksComponent.tasks = tasksSignal.value;
  }, [tasksSignal.value]);

  return (
    <div>
      <h2>Shell Application</h2>
      <search-component ref={searchComponentRef}></search-component>
      <tasks-component ref={tasksComponentRef}></tasks-component>
    </div>
  );
};

export default ShellApplication;
```

Figure 6.4: *Global State Management with React Signals*

The example is simplistic but effectively illustrates global state management in action. In this setup, the global state contains an array of tasks, which will be populated by the **onSearch** event triggered by the Search web component. These tasks will then be consumed by the Tasks web component.

A key aspect of this architecture is the role of the Application Shell, which acts as a message broker. It is responsible for connecting the publisher (the Search web component) with the consumer (the Tasks web component).

Note: *The publish/subscribe (pub/sub) pattern is a messaging pattern in which publishers send messages (events or updates) to a message broker, without knowing which subscribers will receive them. Subscribers express interest in specific topics or types of messages and receive the relevant updates automatically.*

This architecture style can be implemented using native browser capabilities (with the usage of **dispatchEvent** and **addEventListener**) allowing cross application communication without the need for the shell application as we shall see in the next section.

It is important to mention that states are inherently global, such as:

- **window object**: The global object that represents the browser's window, providing access to properties, methods, and global variables.
- **localStorage**: A synchronous key-value storage that persists across sessions. Data is stored in the browser without an expiration time.
- **IndexedDB**: A low-level API for client-side storage of large amounts of structured data.
- **document object**: Represents the DOM (Document Object Model) and provides access to elements, events, and page structure.
- **navigation object:** API interface for controlling and responding to navigation events within a web application

Should be manipulated, ideally, exclusively by the shell application in order to avoid unpredictable side effects and in order to make the implementation environment agnostic (a server-side implementation, component running on the server, would already require that - due to the non-existence of the before mentioned APIs).

We are going to explore in detail the shell interaction with the *navigation* API in the *Routing* section.

Cross Application Communication

While using shared state as a cross-application communication offers a great deal, especially for data that needs to persist longer during the application lifecycle, most of the communication can follow different patterns, so we reduce the degree of dependency in the shell application, thus reducing its complexity.

Conceptually, we could classify them into three main communication models based on the degree of coupling:

Shell-Orchestrated Communication (Frontends Unaware of Each Other)

Micro frontends do not communicate directly. They emit outputs to the shell, and the shell handles state changes, orchestrating inputs and outputs between micro frontends. From the micro frontend's perspective, no cross-application communication exists.

Event-Based Communication (Frontends Suspect Others Exist)

Micro frontends publish and subscribe to events, assuming that other micro frontends might be listening. They do not directly call or query each other. This approach encourages looser coupling.

Common implementations: CustomEvent API, Shared Messaging Services, PostMessage API.

Direct Communication (Frontends Expect Others Exist)

Micro frontends assume the existence of specific other micro frontends. They communicate directly using well-known interfaces (APIs with commands and queries). This brings tighter coupling but can simplify interactions.

Note: *This strategy should be avoided whenever possible in favor of looser coupling mechanisms. It should only be used when the simplicity gain clearly outweighs the maintainability risks.*

Some implementation strategies could look like the following:

Custom Events

With this strategy, we make use of the CustomEvent API, leveraging the native event handling capabilities of the browser so that we achieve event-driven mechanisms that enable communication between the micro frontend applications.

For instance:

```
interface PublicTaskContract {
  id: string;
  name: string;
  description?: string;
}

// A given micro frontend publishes a custom event
const taskEvent = new CustomEvent<PublicTaskContract>("taskSelected", {
  detail: { id: "123", name: "task 1" },
});

window.dispatchEvent(taskEvent);
```

Figure 6.5: *Emitting a custom event*

A given micro frontend implementation defines its public contract, represented by the `PublicTaskContract` interface and then the interested consumers will be subscribed to these events by registering listeners to them:

```
// Another micro frontend consumes the custom event
window.addEventListener("taskSelected", (event: Event) => {
  const customEvent = event as CustomEvent<PublicTaskContract>;
  console.log("Received task item:", customEvent.detail);
});
```

Figure 6.6: *Consuming a custom event*

Note: *The CustomEvent API is a part of the browser's native DOM Events system. It allows developers to create and dispatch their own custom events, complete with optional metadata in the form of a detail object. This API is widely used to enable event-driven interactions, especially for custom components, micro frontends, or any architecture requiring decoupled communication.*

The strategy for a browser-based environment is the most straightforward implementation toward an event-based architecture; however, it does come with some compromises.

The first one is the coupling of the given implementation(s) to a specific environment (the assumption of the *window* object availability therefore the browser environment).

Secondly, there is no grouping mechanism–it all falls into the same global namespace, so depending on the amount of messages triggered, the odds of having naming collisions can be high, and some sort of naming conversion needs to be carefully defined. This also introduces security issues because any active script will be able to listen to these events, imagine a third-party script intercepting and listening to sensitive events like "userLoggedIn".

Lastly, the API is limited to the specific window context, they cannot directly communicate across iframes, Web Workers, or server environments without additional mechanisms.

Shared Messaging Services

The idea of using a shared messaging service comes as an answer to the issues when using native implementations, such as the browser *CustomEvent* API. In this scenario, we add an anti-corruption layer that abstracts from the specific implementations the environment details.

A very basic implementation could look like the following:

```
const EventBus = (() => {
  const events = {};

  return {
    subscribe(namespace, eventName, callback) {
      if (!events[namespace]) {
        events[namespace] = {};
      }
      if (!events[namespace][eventName]) {
        events[namespace][eventName] = [];
      }
      events[namespace][eventName].push(callback);
    },

    publish(namespace, eventName, data) {
      if (!events[namespace] || !events[namespace][eventName]) return;
      events[namespace][eventName].forEach((callback) => callback(data));
    },

    unsubscribe(namespace, eventName, callback) {
      if (!events[namespace] || !events[namespace][eventName]) return;
      events[namespace][eventName] = events[namespace][eventName].filter(
        (cb) => cb !== callback
      );
    },
  };
})();

export default EventBus;
```

Figure 6.7: *Shared Messaging Service*

In this straightforward implementation, we use a Singleton object that provides **`subscribe`** and **`unsubscribe`** methods, allowing consumers to start and stop listening to specific events on a given topic. Additionally, it includes a *publish* method, enabling producers to trigger events for a specified topic.

With that, the micro frontends can produce events, like:

```
import EventBus from "../event-bus/index.js";

// Publish the onSearch event in the tasks topic
EventBus.publish("tasks", "onSearch", results);
```

Figure 6.8: *Shared Messaging Service - Producer*

And consumer can listen to these events, like:

```
import EventBus from "../event-bus/index.js";

// Subscribe to the onSearch event in the tasks topic
EventBus.subscribe("tasks", "onSearch", (tasks) => {
  console.log("Received search results:", tasks);
});
```

Figure 6.9: *Shared Messaging Service - Consumer*

These shared services can be integrated via published packages in a shared registry (for example, npm), or loaded via Module Federation at runtime or any other similar way depending on the specific use-case.

The key advantage here is the flexibility we gain. We can tailor the messaging service to our specific needs, implement robust security checks, restrict its propagation to predefined targets, and adapt it for use in various environments–not just browsers.

This flexibility allows us, to potentially use the CustomEvent API addressing some of the issues previously mentioned, namely, grouping, by the introduction of the namespace concept, and possibly the environment coupling assuming that the implementation would be smart enough to detect whether the *window* object is available, and in case it does not, to fallback to an alternative solution.

Query Parameters

One effective approach to enabling cross-application communication is by encoding the state into the application URL using query parameters. This technique allows the state to be easily shared via the URL, providing a straightforward mechanism for transmitting messages between different applications. Additionally, this technique implements together a routing strategy, further explored in the upcoming section: *Routing: Independent Routing in Each Micro Frontend.*

However, this method comes with limitations. Browsers and servers impose restrictions on URL length, which can limit the amount of information that can be stored. Additionally, security concerns must be addressed: sensitive data should never be included in query parameters. Since URLs are often logged in browser histories and server logs, exposing sensitive information in this way could lead to unintended access or misuse.

In practice, encoding state into URLs is typically used as a supplementary method, complementing other approaches. It is particularly valuable in scenarios where users need (via sharing the application URL) to share the current state of an application with others.

Note: *It is important to mention that in contexts where the micro frontend is unaware of the server routing capabilities, links are created with text fragments, such as* ***#share-value-1=any-value-1&share-value-2=any-value-2****, in order to avoid losing the current route when the user refreshes the page.*

PostMessage API

The PostMessage API is the tool available for cross application communication in a Client-side Composition with run-time integration via iFrames. Architecturally it does behave similar to *Custom Events*, with the difference that the message can target a specific origin, allowing better security guarantees in regards to who is going to receive the message. Also allowing *Shared Messaging Services* using pub/sub or similar patterns to be implemented on top of this technology.

Routing

Routing refers to the way navigation and URL management are handled across the different micro frontends that make up an application. Understanding URL management as the capabilities to reflect the application state at any moment in a potentially shared resource (URL) that can be saved and restarted at any time.

Note: *The URL term is mainly associated with web implementation, yet native apps also need a way to reflect the state of the application in a way that the user can resume their session or continue from a certain state. In mobile apps, this can be achieved through mechanisms such as deep linking (for iOS and Android) or navigation stacks, which manage the state of the UI and can allow the user to navigate between different sections of the app while maintaining context. As a matter of simplicity, we are in this reading simply referring to all of them as URLs.*

The routing strategy involves:

Single Global Router

A single router, at the shell level, controls the entire application's URL structure and exposes a public contract in which individual micro frontends can perform navigation following these restrictions. This central router is responsible for managing the overall navigation, while each micro frontend is responsible for handling its own internal routes.

Global router implementation example:

```
const AppRouter = () => {
  const navigate = useNavigate();

  /** Shell Application Router */
  const onNavigate = (page: AvailableRoutes) => {
    //any possible router validation ..

    navigate(`/${page}`);
  };

  return (
    <Routes>
      <Route path="/" element={<TasksComponent onNavigate={onNavigate} />} />
      <Route path="/profile" element={<ProfileComponent />} />
      <Route path="*" element={<NotFoundComponent />} />
    </Routes>
  );
};

export default AppRouter;
```

Figure 6.10: *Global router implementation example*

In this example, the shell application provides the function in which the individual micro frontend should call in case they are willing to change the application router. On it, we centralize the routing control in the shell which can introduce any checks required in order to make the overall application conform to established criteria.

On the consumer side, in the specific case, the Tasks micro frontend would:

```
import type { MicroFrontendNavigation } from './NavigationPublicContract';

// Micro Frontend implementation which consumes the shell routing public contract
export interface TasksProps extends MicroFrontendNavigation {…
}

export default function Tasks({ onNavigate, ...rest }: TasksProps) {
  return (
    <>
      <div className="tasks">…
      </div>
      <button onClick={() => onNavigate('profile')}>Check your profile</button>
    </>
  );
}
```

Figure 6.11: *Global router implementation consumer example*

The Tasks micro frontend implements the **`MicroFrontendNavigation`** enforces the shell application to provide the navigation function and which at a certain point, in the case on a click of a button, will trigger the application route change.

As for the consumers, in the case, **`ProfileComponent`** which represents a profile micro frontend, that do not want to manipulate the routing, they simply do not implement the public routing interface (**`MicroFrontendNavigation`**).

Independent Routing in Each Micro Frontend

In this approach, each micro frontend manages its own routing, including its own URL structure. The shell application may not know about the internal routing of individual MFEs. This can sometimes lead to URL conflicts, so careful coordination is needed.

This scenario reflects the Query Parameters scenario previously described in: *Cross Application Communication: Query Parameters.*

In a per-feature slicing scenario, where multiple micro frontends coexist on the same page, URL namespaces must be ensured so that different micro frontends do not alter each other's states. For example:

`/page-1/#mf1-value1=any-value&mf1-value2=any-value&mf2-value1=any-value`

In the given scenario, the URL reflects the following structure:

[current page] / [micro frontend identifier] / [param name] = [value]

This allows each micro frontend to implement its routing independently of the others.

Note: *The implementation of this routing strategy is not demonstrated here. However, as a rule, an implementation on top of the browser's routing capability (for example, in the case of a React application, an implementation on top of React Routing) would be necessary.*

In a per-page slicing scenario, the specific route already acts as isolation between different micro frontend implementations, thus simplifying the implementation. The same URL in this context could have the following structure:

`/page-1#value1=any-value&value2=any-value`

[current page] / [param name] = [value]

Routing in Server/Edge-Side Composition

In server-side or edge-side composition, routing responsibilities are handled at the infrastructure or backend level before the user's browser or application loads the page. In this model, the server or edge node acts as the router, interpreting the incoming request URL and dynamically assembling the appropriate combination of micro frontends into a complete response.

Routing strategies for server/edge-side composition typically involve:

- **URL-to-Component Mapping**: The server matches the incoming request path (for example, /dashboard) to a predefined layout that specifies which micro frontends should be included and where.
- **Content Negotiation and Personalization**: Based on request headers, authentication tokens, or geolocation, the server might vary which micro frontends are composed dynamically.
- **Caching and Pre-Composition**: To reduce latency, common compositions can be pre-generated and cached at the edge, with routing still determining which cached response to deliver.
- **Shared or Split Responsibility**: In some architectures, the server decides the overall layout, while each micro frontend still manages its own internal routing once loaded.

This approach reduces the burden on the client to manage complex routing but requires careful coordination between infrastructure, deployment, and micro frontend teams to maintain consistent behavior across entry points.

Example:

A request to /products/electronics could trigger the edge node to compose the `ProductList`, `Recommendations`, and `SearchBar` micro frontends into a unified HTML response even before it reaches the client. Each of these micro frontends could still manage further client-side navigation independently after initial load.

Note: *It is important to highlight that a routing strategy handled exclusively on the server or edge servers is not very realistic, considering that such an approach would require a full page refresh for every navigation. A more likely scenario is the adoption of a hybrid strategy, where server-side routing is used for the initial render of the application, and client-side routing is used for subsequent navigations.*

Shared Dependencies

In a utopian ideal world, the individual pieces (micro frontends) of a given distributed architecture operate completely independently, owning all its dependencies, teams have complete autonomy to choose their tools, libraries, and versions so we achieve maximum independence, resilience, and autonomy as proposed by the *Shared-Nothing* architecture style.

However, there are several challenges that arise when integrating the various parts of the application. One of the first issues is versioning conflicts. Since different micro frontends are often developed independently, each might rely on different versions of the same dependency. When these micro frontends are integrated, the system can break if one part expects a different version of a library than the others. This inconsistency can lead to unexpected behavior or even crashes.

Another significant concern is performance. Multiple micro frontends might bring with them duplicated dependencies, which increases the size of the final bundles. Larger bundles mean slower load times, which negatively impacts the user experience. This problem is not limited to the client-side. Even in server-side integrations, shared dependencies can overload the server, slowing down response times, especially when numerous micro frontends are rendered together.

Compatibility issues also frequently occur. Micro frontends may be built with different frameworks or tools—one might be built in React, another in Angular, and yet another in Vue. Dependencies that work seamlessly in one framework may not be compatible with another, leading to rendering issues or faulty functionality when integrated into the larger system.

The shared dependencies help address many of these problems. By using a common set of dependencies across all micro frontends, teams can ensure, at the cost of less independence, resilience, and autonomy, consistency in the versions of libraries being used, eliminating version conflicts. Shared dependencies also allow for code reuse, which helps reduce the size of each micro frontend's bundle and, in turn, improves performance. By ensuring that the same versions of libraries are used across the application, you also reduce the risk of compatibility issues between different micro frontends built with different frameworks.

It is a critical decision that needs to be made to balance these two conflicting desires. So to say: Independence, resilience, and autonomy versus Efficiency and consistency.

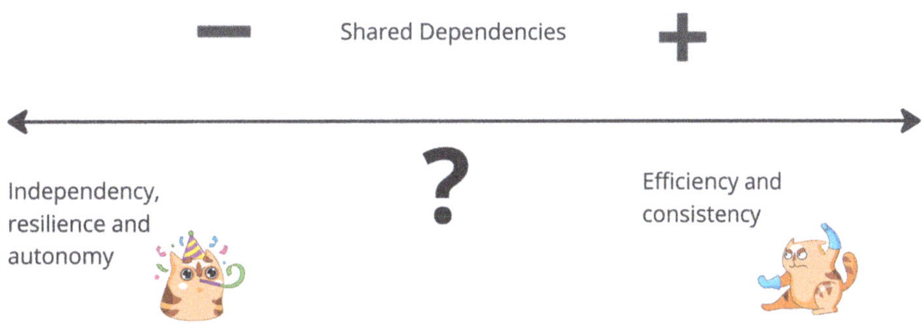

Figure 6.12: *Shared Dependencies*

The exact point where the architecture should stand is bounded to the use case; however, some overall guidelines can be taken:

- There should ideally be no significant compromises, and future changes should always remain possible.
- Performance optimizations should be done based on real issues, not speculative future requirements - YAGNI (You Aren't Gonna Need It). If a specific use case does not exhibit clear signs of poor performance or inconsistency, prioritizing independence, autonomy, and resilience is often the better choice. Shared dependencies, while sometimes necessary, can undermine these qualities and should be used judiciously as a last resort to address the issues mentioned above.

The declarative approach used by Module Federation, supports a great level of flexibility. In this approach, specific implementations declare their shared dependencies and use them when available. If not, they gracefully fall back to loading these dependencies. This design ensures adaptability and robust integration.

```
new ModuleFederationPlugin({
  name: 'microfrontend1',
  shared: {
    react: {
      singleton: true,
      requiredVersion: '^18.0.0',
    },
    'react-dom': {
      singleton: true,
      requiredVersion: '^18.0.0',
    },
  },
});
```

Figure 6.13: *Module Federation: shared dependencies*

The Shell application can at any time decide when to have specific dependencies available as shared ones.

Another common approach is by providing these shared dependencies as CDN links and each specific micro frontend declares it as an external dependency:

The Shell Application:

```html
<!DOCTYPE html>
<html lang="en">
  <head>
    <meta charset="UTF-8" />
    <meta name="viewport" content="width=device-width, initial-scale=1.0" />
    <title>Shell Application</title>
    <script
      type="module"
      src="https://shared.microfrontends.app/react@18.js"
    ></script>
    <script
      type="module"
      src="https://shared.microfrontends.app/react-dom@18.js"
    ></script>

    <!-- the rest of the application -->
  </head>
  <body></body>
</html>
```

Figure 6.14: *CDN Links: shared dependencies*

And in the consumers, for instance, assuming here the Rollup bundler usage, we declare external dependencies:

```js
// rollup.config.js
export default {
  //...,
  external: ["react", "react-dom"],
};
```

Figure 6.15: *CDN Links: shared dependencies bundler config*

A slightly more modern and native implementation would make use of the *importmap* script type:

```html
<script type="importmap">
  {
    "imports": {
      "react": "https://shared.microfrontends.app/react@18.js",
      "react-dom": "https://shared.microfrontends.app/react-dom@18.js"
    }
  }
</script>
```

Figure 6.16: *importmap: shared dependencies*

Note: *The `importmap` script type in the HTML specification allows developers to define how JavaScript modules are resolved when using import statements. It provides a way to map module specifiers (used in import or export statements) to specific URLs, enabling custom resolution logic without needing to rely on a package manager or bundler.*

Shared dependencies provided via CDN links offer fewer guarantees compared to a Module Federation implementation. With CDN links, the shell application must ensure that the shared dependencies are available. However, this approach has the advantage of being independent of any specific bundler and can even be implemented without the use of a bundler at all.

The Shell Application Journey

The shell application in a micro frontend architecture serves as the conductor of a finely tuned orchestra, bringing together disparate components into a harmonious user experience. Its journey begins with **Bootstrapping and Initialization**, where the stage is set for the performance. Here, the shell loads essential configurations, initializes global states, and ensures that every micro frontend follows its own sheet of music, perfectly synchronized under a common tempo and direction. Whether it is connecting to APIs, establishing routing rules, or preparing shared libraries, this foundational phase guarantees that the application starts on solid ground.

With the environment prepared, the shell moves to **Layout and UI Composition**, where it begins crafting the stage for the user experience. Assembling headers, footers, navigation menus, shared styles (in some contexts referred to Design System, which we shall explore in more detail in *Chapter 7, UI/UX and Design System*), and other shared elements, it ensures a consistent design language across the entire application. But this is not a static assembly—each micro frontend dynamically enters and exits the stage based on user interaction or context, seamlessly woven into the larger interface. To make this work smoothly, the shell relies heavily on **Authentication and Authorization** to define who can see what. Only users with the right credentials are granted access to certain parts of the application, ensuring that sensitive data and functionality remain protected.

While orchestrating these elements, the shell also employs **Feature Flags and A/B Testing** as its tools of experimentation and adaptability. New features are cautiously introduced to specific segments of users, and tested in real time for their effectiveness and appeal. These flags act as toggles, giving the shell the flexibility to roll out, modify, or retract features without redeployment, making the system agile and responsive to user feedback.

The last two come as a natural extension of the ability to compose the user interface and handle the application routing.

At the same time, the shell continuously focuses on Lazy Loading and Performance Optimization. Instead of overwhelming the user with an all-at-once approach, it strategically loads components only when they are needed. Critical paths are prioritized, and non-essential elements wait quietly in the wings, ready to appear on demand. This not only improves performance but also ensures that the user's initial interaction with the application is swift and smooth.

But even the best-laid plans encounter turbulence. When something inevitably goes wrong, the shell's commitment to Error Handling and Resilience shines through. Errors are caught and contained, preventing disruptions from spreading through the system. Whether it's a failed API call or a misbehaving micro frontend, the shell gracefully degrades functionality, provides fallback content, and logs incidents for further analysis. This resilience keeps the system afloat, ensuring users remain engaged and confident despite occasional hiccups.

In this ongoing symphony of orchestration, the shell application operates as the unseen maestro, blending initialization, composition, security, experimentation, optimization, and resilience into a seamless performance that serves both users and developers.

Conclusion

In this chapter, we explored the critical responsibilities of the shell application within a micro frontend architecture, emphasizing its role as the backbone of a cohesive and reliable system. By addressing state management, cross-application communication, routing, and shared dependencies, the shell application ensures stability, consistency, and scalability across the ecosystem.

We underscored the importance of clear boundaries between local and shared state, advocating for cautious exposure of data to maintain backward compatibility and reduce complexity. Communication patterns, from native browser events to shared messaging services, were examined to illustrate the trade-offs between simplicity, flexibility, and security.

Routing strategies showcased the balance between centralized control and decentralized independence, ensuring seamless navigation while supporting diverse implementation requirements. Finally, we discussed how shared dependencies, when managed judiciously, can enhance performance and consistency without compromising autonomy.

Together, these elements form the foundation of an effective shell application, capable of orchestrating micro frontends into a unified, high-performing user experience. The principles and practices outlined here provide a roadmap for building resilient systems that adapt to evolving needs, setting the stage for deeper dives into related topics in subsequent chapters.

As we transition to the next chapter, we will shift our focus to UI/UX and Design System, a crucial aspect of micro frontend architecture. This chapter will delve into user interface and experience requirements, emphasizing the importance of consistency across micro frontends. We will examine how a cohesive design system can address these challenges, explore available tooling, and present strategies for implementing and maintaining a unified design across distributed teams. Whether you are aiming for seamless user experiences or striving to maintain a brand identity, this chapter will provide actionable insights to guide your efforts.

References

1. https://github.com/ava-orange-education/-Micro-Frontends-Architecture-for-Scalable-Applications
2. https://developer.mozilla.org/en-US/docs/Web/URI/Fragment/Text_fragments
3. https://developer.mozilla.org/en-US/docs/Web/HTML/Element/script/type/importmap
4. https://preactjs.com/guide/v10/signals/

CHAPTER 7
UI/UX and Design System

Introduction

Delivering a consistent and seamless User Interface (UI) and User Experience (UX) is critical to maintaining user satisfaction and brand identity. However, this becomes especially challenging in distributed architectures such as micro frontends, where applications are composed of independently developed and deployed modules. Without careful coordination, this modularity can lead to fragmented user journeys, inconsistent designs, and a disjointed overall experience.

To address these challenges, the design system approach has emerged as a vital solution. It acts as a centralized framework for ensuring visual and interaction consistency across all modules, regardless of the team or technology stack used to build them. It bridges the gap between independence and cohesion, providing the tools, guidelines, and reusable components necessary to align design and development efforts.

This chapter delves into the concept and importance of design systems in micro frontend architectures, the strategies for achieving design consistency across distributed modules, and practical implementation techniques that enable teams to deliver unified user experiences in this inherently fragmented development paradigm.

Structure

In this chapter, we will cover the following topics:

- Design System
- Micro Frontend Design Consistency
- Implementation Strategy

Design System

A design system should, first of all, not be confused with system design. Though the names are similar, the order makes a great difference. We focus on the design (system) as the collection of elements that will be part of a given user interface and experience by looking into the framework of principles, guidelines, and reusable resources applied to create consistent and scalable user interfaces. It encompasses foundational elements such as design tokens (for example, colors, typography, spacing, motion), semantic color palettes, text styles, spacing scales, responsive grid systems, and animation rules.

These tokens are utilized by reusable components, organized by complexity, ranging from simple elements such as buttons and icons to more complex structures such as navigation bars and forms. This organization follows a hierarchical structure, similar to the Atomic Design methodology.

Additionally, it defines reusable patterns to address common design and interaction challenges, such as deciding whether information should be presented in a dialog or on a new page, and other similar concerns.

All of these elements are guided by principles and standards, including accessibility guidelines, branding rules, and design philosophies, ensuring both inclusivity and brand consistency. The system is supported by a well-documented and centralized resource for educating teams on how to use and extend it, while code libraries provide technical implementations, enabling seamless integration across platforms.

Atomic Design

Atomic Design is a methodology for creating user interfaces by breaking down complex designs into smaller, reusable, and manageable components. Proposed by Brad Frost, it draws inspiration from chemistry, where atoms combine to form molecules, and molecules combine to create organisms. The methodology provides a clear hierarchy for structuring UI components and emphasizes building interfaces from the ground up with a system of interdependent elements.

Components Hierarchy

1. **Atoms:**

The smallest, indivisible building blocks of the UI. They represent basic elements such as buttons, input fields, labels, icons, and colors. These components cannot be broken down further and often serve as the foundation for more complex designs.

2. **Molecules:**

Groups of atoms that work together as a single, functional unit. For example, a search bar molecule might consist of an input field atom, a button atom, and an icon atom. Molecules introduce behavior and interactivity while maintaining simplicity.

3. **Organisms:**

Complex structures that combine molecules and atoms to form distinct sections of a UI. Examples include headers, footers, or product cards. Organisms establish patterns and layouts, creating reusable UI modules.

4. **Templates:**

Page-level structures that arrange organisms into a cohesive layout. They define the overall skeleton of a page without including specific content, serving as a blueprint for how components are organized.

5. **Pages:**

Specific instances of templates, populated with real content. They represent the final user-facing output, allowing designers and developers to test the design's effectiveness with real-world data and content.

Design System / Atomic Design / Frontend Architecture

Once concepts are defined, we can put and work with all of them together - Design System, Atomic Design, and the Frontend Architecture – as depicted in the following figure:

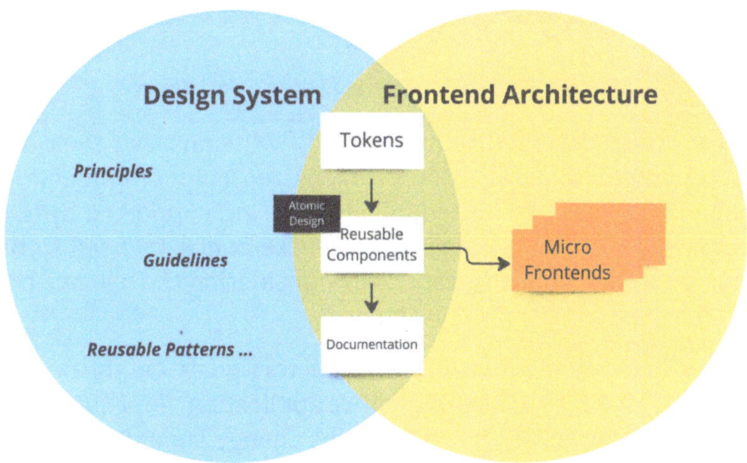

Figure 7.1: *Design System / Atomic Design / Frontend Architecture*

On one side, we have concerns directly related to the implementation of the design system, including its principles, guidelines, reusable patterns, and more.

As a cross-disciplinary topic for the product, UI/UX, and development teams we have tokens and reusable components (following Atomic Design principles), along with their documentation. These components, being the key players in order to achieve UI/UX consistency in the application, will be explored in more detail in the following sections.

Micro Frontend Design Consistency

Similar to the concept of Shared Dependencies discussed in *Chapter 6, Communication and Routing*, the design system serves as another common integration point between different micro frontend applications. However, while shared dependencies focus on code (dependencies) reuse, the design system primarily addresses User Interface (UI) and User Experience (UX) consistency across the application. To achieve this consistency, teams may need to compromise a certain level of independence and autonomy, likely by sharing certain design system implementation patterns, ensuring stronger alignment in UI/UX standards across the system.

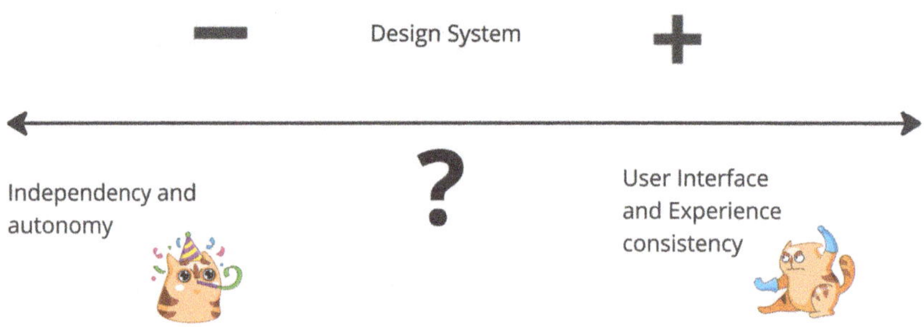

Figure 7.2: *Micro Frontend Design Consistency*

It is of particular interest to the product and UI/UX teams that their design system definitions, incorporated primarily through tokens, reusable components, and patterns (cross-disciplinary concerns illustrated in *Figure* 7.1) are supported by the underlying frontend architecture to ensure consistency. These concerns need to be addressed and understood by all stakeholders, especially considering the balance between team autonomy and the need for UI/UX consistency.

In this context, we face two distinct and contradictory goals. On the one hand, the UI/UX team aims for consistency across the entire application. For example, if there is an update to the system's primary color token, this change should ideally (from the UI/UX perspective) be automatically reflected across all micro frontends. On the other hand, this goal conflicts with the autonomy of individual teams. From a development perspective, each team should have the freedom to manage such updates according to their own preferences and requirements.

While an ideal solution may not exist, it is crucial for all stakeholders to understand the current state of the architecture.

What we are discussing here is two integration strategies, the first one is a runtime integration where each one of the micro frontends would consume it via a CDN link or similar mechanism:

```
<script type="module" src="https://design-system.microfrontends.app"></script>
```

Figure 7.3: *Design System as a CDN Link*

The Design System (DS) can be seen as a standalone application that exports all the DS components (tokens, reusable components, and reusable patterns). In this, every single update in the design system is automatically propagated into the consumers (micro frontend implementation) at the cost of a strong coupling.

The second one is a build time integration where each one of the micro frontends would consume via a given version and update it on a given release:

```
{
  "name": "microfrontend-project",
  "version": "1.0.0",
  "dependencies": {
    "design-system": "^1.0.0"
  }
}
```

Figure 7.4: *Design System as a npm package*

Certainly, a solution considering only one approach would be insufficient to reconcile the two distinct desires. In the following sections, we will explore different implementation strategies for the design system in the context of micro frontend architecture.

Implementation Strategy

The implementation strategy focuses on defining how the design system will be integrated and utilized by the constellation of micro frontends within the system.

The following diagram (*Figure* 7.5) illustrates the cross-disciplinary components arranged on a scale based on their development complexity, accompanied by relevant examples.

Additionally, the diagram highlights components commonly found in UI *frameworks*.

Note: *A design system token is a named, reusable variable that represents a single design decision, such as a color, typography style, spacing value, or animation duration. Tokens are abstract, platform-agnostic representations of UI properties, enabling consistency, scalability, and easier maintenance across design and development processes.*

A UI framework is a pre-built software library or toolkit that provides developers with reusable components, utilities, and patterns for designing and building User Interfaces (UI) efficiently. It serves as a foundation for creating consistent, scalable, and maintainable UIs by offering ready-made solutions to common design and development challenges.

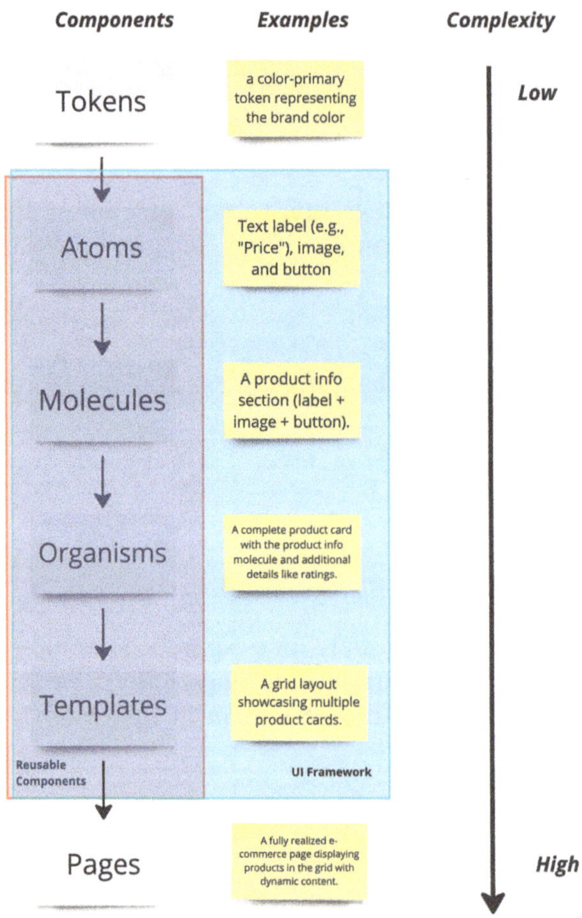

Figure 7.5: *Cross-disciplinary concerns complexity levels*

It is reasonable to assume that the greater the complexity of a component, the stronger the need for versioning. This is due to the increased likelihood of non-backwards-compatible changes, not to mention the inherent component maintenance complexity.

Consider an API interface of a Scheduler or Grid component—these are often highly customizable. Unless we abstract their functionality at the cost of not addressing all system use cases, the chances of requiring future updates to extend their capabilities are significantly higher.

In contrast, for low-complexity components such as a design token—a simple key-value object—the need for breaking changes is minimal. The main requirement is to ensure the keys remain consistent. While issues may still arise from value updates, such as a primary color that lacks sufficient contrast or a spacing token that disrupts layout consistency, these problems are less common and generally easier to manage.

The design system service could export those tokens to be consumed from a CDN link:

```
export default {
  primaryColor: '#1976d2',
  secondaryColor: '#0006ca',
  errorColor: '#d32f2f',
  infoColor: '#0288d1',
  warningColor: '#ed6c02',
  successColor: '#2e7d32',
  fontFamily: '"Roboto", "Helvetica", "Arial", sans-serif',
  fontSize: 14,
  fontWeightLight: 300,
  fontWeightRegular: 400,
  fontWeightMedium: 500,
  fontWeightBold: 700,
  spacing: 8,
  borderRadius: 4,
};
```

Figure 7.6: *Tokens structure*

Later the micro frontend application consumes those values:

```
import { defineConfig } from '@rsbuild/core';
import { pluginReact } from '@rsbuild/plugin-react';
import { pluginModuleFederation } from '@module-federation/rsbuild-plugin';

export default defineConfig({
  plugins: [
    pluginReact(),
    pluginModuleFederation({
      name: 'search',
      remotes: {
        design_system: 'design_system@http://localhost:3002/remoteEntry.js',
      },
      exposes: {
        './search': './src/search/Search.tsx',
      },
      shared: {…
      },
    }),
  ],
  server: {
    port: 3000,
  },
});
```

***Figure 7.7**: Consuming tokens via module federation*

Example using Client-side Composition with Module Federation. In this case, a given micro frontend that acts as a provider, exporting a **`./search`** component additionally acts as a consumer from the tokens exported in the remote `http://localhost:3002/remoteEntry.js`.

Naturally, the CDN link can support any micro frontend integration strategy; for more details, refer to *Chapter 5, Integration Strategies*.

This approach ensures a baseline of consistency for design tokens. However, it provides limited guarantees–for instance, how can we ensure that a Button component correctly applies these token values?

When it comes to reusable components, one might consider *Atom* and *Molecule* components stable enough to be part of a distinct "design system micro frontend." This micro frontend would be responsible for providing all shared components. However, this setup introduces significant coupling: any issue in the design system micro frontend could break the entire application.

A more robust alternative is to use an integration strategy that includes fallback mechanisms. For example, with Module Federation, if there is an issue retrieving the shared resource, the implementation can gracefully handle the failure by providing its own local version.

```
import { defineConfig } from '@rsbuild/core';
import { pluginReact } from '@rsbuild/plugin-react';
import { pluginModuleFederation } from '@module-federation/rsbuild-plugin';

export default defineConfig({
  plugins: [
    pluginReact(),
    pluginModuleFederation({
      name: 'search',
      remotes: {
        design_system: 'design_system@http://localhost:3002/remoteEntry.js',
      },
      exposes: {
        './search': './src/search/Search.tsx',
      },
      shared: {
        '@emotion/react': {
          requiredVersion: '^11',
        },
        '@emotion/styled': {
          requiredVersion: '^11',
        },
        '@mui/material': {
          requiredVersion: '^6',
        },
        react: {
          requiredVersion: '^18',
        },
        'react-dom': {
          requiredVersion: '^18',
        },
      },
    }),
  ],
  server: {
    port: 3000,
  },
});
```

Figure 7.8: *Sharing UI Framework*

In this setup, design system tokens are shared from the design system micro frontend, while reusable components are distributed using Module Federation. This approach leverages Module Federation's fallback capabilities to handle scenarios where the required version is unavailable.

In this particular example, we use the React Material-UI framework, though the same approach can be applied to any other UI framework or a custom-developed solution.

Still, in this context, leveraging Material-UI theming capabilities we can then apply the tokens to the framework theme and therefore have all the reusable components making use of these tokens:

While leveraging a framework-specific solution such as React with Material-UI offers a high degree of component reusability and consistency, it inherently reduces the flexibility to integrate with different technologies. The more tightly the implementation is bound to a specific stack, the easier it becomes to share complex, ready-to-use components, but at the cost of limiting broader adoption across heterogeneous environments. An interesting approach to balance these trade-offs is to allow integration at multiple layers. In the example explored, design system tokens are shared as plain JavaScript objects, enabling a higher degree of flexibility: any micro frontend, regardless of its underlying technology—be it React, Svelte, or another—can still consume and apply the same design definitions. At the same time, for micro frontends that share a similar technology stack, such as React with Material-UI in the example, a more specialized integration can be adopted through the theme creation factory (*Figure* 7.9).

This enables teams to decide based on its specific tech stack the best integration approach to be used, but ultimately still adhering to the same design system definitions, achieving a higher degree of consistency and reducing the integration effort without sacrificing extensibility for other stacks.

```
import { createTheme as createMuiTheme } from '@mui/material/styles';
import tokens from './tokens';

import '@fontsource/roboto/300.css';
import '@fontsource/roboto/400.css';
import '@fontsource/roboto/500.css';
import '@fontsource/roboto/700.css';

export default () => {
  return createMuiTheme({
    palette: {
      primary: { main: tokens.primaryColor },
      secondary: { main: tokens.secondaryColor },
      error: { main: tokens.errorColor },
      warning: { main: tokens.warningColor },
      info: { main: tokens.infoColor },
      success: { main: tokens.successColor },
    },
    typography: {
      fontFamily: tokens.fontFamily,
      fontSize: tokens.fontSize,
      fontWeightLight: tokens.fontWeightLight,
      fontWeightRegular: tokens.fontWeightRegular,
      fontWeightMedium: tokens.fontWeightMedium,
      fontWeightBold: tokens.fontWeightBold,
    },
    spacing: tokens.spacing,
    shape: {
      borderRadius: tokens.borderRadius,
    },
  });
};
```

Figure 7.9: *Applying tokens to the MUI theme*

Note: *React Material-UI (often referred to simply as Material-UI or MUI) is a popular React-based component library that implements Google's Material Design principles. It provides a rich set of pre-designed, customizable UI components that help developers create modern, responsive, and visually appealing user interfaces with minimal effort.*

The full implementation can be found at: *https://github.com/ava-orange-education/-Micro-Frontends-Architecture-for-Scalable-Applications/tree/main/design-system-implementation*

On it we have a solid setup where different micro frontends consume a single design system implementation with consistent styling, all implementations based on a single token structure (*Figure* 7.6). You can update those values and get the different applications automatically updated and all of them sharing the same reusable components (Material UI framework).

While this example is not intended to serve as a definitive guide for implementing design systems in micro frontends, it can certainly be used as a reliable reference.

Conclusion

Design systems play a central part in overcoming the inherent challenges of achieving UI/UX consistency within micro frontend architectures. They serve as a unifying framework that bridges the autonomy of individual teams with the need for a cohesive and seamless user experience.

This chapter has explored the foundational elements of design systems, their alignment with frontend architecture, and the strategies necessary to ensure design consistency. From the simplicity of tokens to the complexity of reusable components, each layer of the design system contributes to building scalable, maintainable, and user-focused applications.

While no single solution perfectly reconciles the tensions between independence and uniformity, understanding and adopting hybrid integration strategies–such as Module Federation with fallback mechanisms–can mitigate risks and enhance resilience. Ultimately, a well-implemented design system is more than a collection of components; it is a shared language that fosters collaboration across disciplines, ensuring that micro frontends deliver not just functionality, but also a unified brand experience.

Next, we will explore how backend integration options–such as Backend For Frontend (BFF), API Gateway, and API Aggregation–can work together to provide the infrastructure needed to support a cohesive micro frontend architecture. Additionally, we will examine key API standards such as REST, GraphQL, gRPC, and WebSockets, as well as strategies for client SDK generation, enabling effective communication between distributed systems and their consumers.

References

1. https://www.figma.com/blog/design-systems-101-what-is-a-design-system/
2. https://atomicdesign.bradfrost.com/chapter-2/
3. https://mui.com/

CHAPTER 8
Backend Patterns

Introduction

As already explored in previous chapters - with more details in *Chapter 1, A Tale of Two Worlds* - there is a strong correlation between the evolution of backend and frontend development patterns. While, at first glance, they may appear to have well-defined boundaries, understanding their structures proves to be an essential factor in establishing solid architectural standards.

In this chapter, we will delve into some of the most commonly used frontend development, backend development patterns, API standards and their implications for the micro frontend architecture, and how these architectures can enable a more efficient adoption of micro frontend patterns.

Structure

In this chapter, we will cover the following topics:

- Backend For Frontend
- API Gateway
- API Aggregation
- API Standards
- Client SDK Generation

Backend For Frontend

Let us imagine the following scenario:

A new development team is formed with the objective of improving a critical part of the system—the checkout process of the company's e-commerce platform—which, over the years, has received criticism regarding its performance and usability. As a side effect, this has led to a significant reduction in online purchases and, consequently, in the company's revenue. Given time and resource constraints, this team does not aim for a profound restructuring of the company's monolithic application but rather focuses on the minimum necessary to address the specific problem.

Note: *Many can relate to this common challenge–the difficulties of scaling monolithic applications.*

The frontend-focused team begins their work by adopting a Run-time Integration approach via WebComponents. They implement an interface following modern UI/UX standards, aligned with the company's current Design System definitions. However, their efforts are strictly limited to the client-side implementation, consuming the existing APIs (backend services) of the monolithic application.

As a result, even though the implementation adheres to modern standards with minimal coupling between presentation layers and application logic, it remains heavily dependent on various APIs exposed by the monolithic application. These APIs often lack consistency in approach, are weakly typed or, in many cases, not typed at all, and exhibit questionable performance.

In such a scenario, the effectiveness of the implementation is diminished and, in many cases, questioned. To end users, it may come across as a mere interface update, ultimately causing confusion rather than delivering value.

In this context, adopting a Backend For Frontend (BFF) approach could significantly enhance the implementation of the micro frontend in question.

This scenario can be represented by the following diagram:

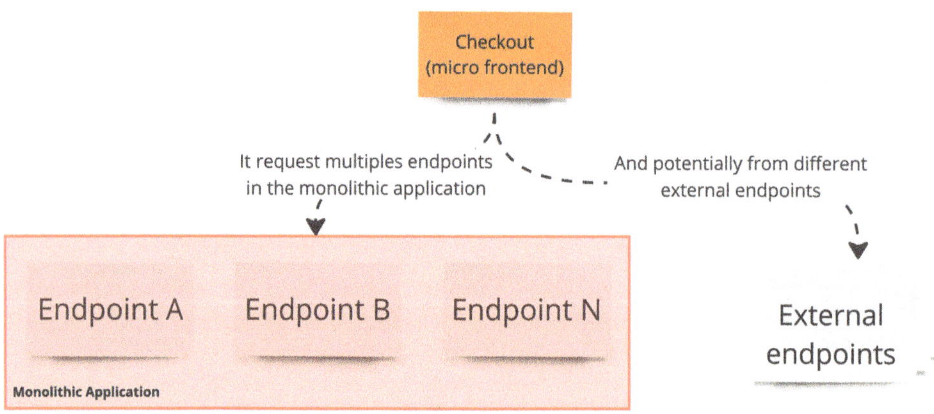

Figure 8.1: *Prior to a BFF adoption*

Once the BFF architectural pattern is adopted, the complexity described above is abstracted away from the frontend implementation. While it is not entirely eliminated, the existence of a backend application dedicated to the micro frontend brings significant advantages:

- **Reduced data transfer between server and client**: The endpoints exposed are exclusively for the micro frontend in question, allowing us to limit the data transfer strictly to what the application needs.

- **API standardization**: Monolithic applications often reflect diverse approaches adopted over the years (who has not worked on a monolithic codebase and felt like an "archaeologist," uncovering various development patterns established over time that, due to the sheer size of the codebase, were not consistently applied throughout?). With the BFF, we can ensure API standardization for the client (micro frontend).
- **Improved typing**: The adoption of standards such as OpenAPI can automate the type generation process for the frontend application through auto-generated SDKs. Tools such as Swagger/OpenAPI Generator, GraphQL Code Generator, and tRPC can generate SDKs directly from the API schema.
- **Performance improvement**: Although performance improvements may be minor and indirect, the BFF can implement caching mechanisms, alleviating high loads on low-performance services.
- **A step towards distributed architecture**: Last but not least, adopting a BFF is an important step in migrating to a distributed architecture.

The same scenario, incorporating the BFF pattern, can be represented with the following diagram:

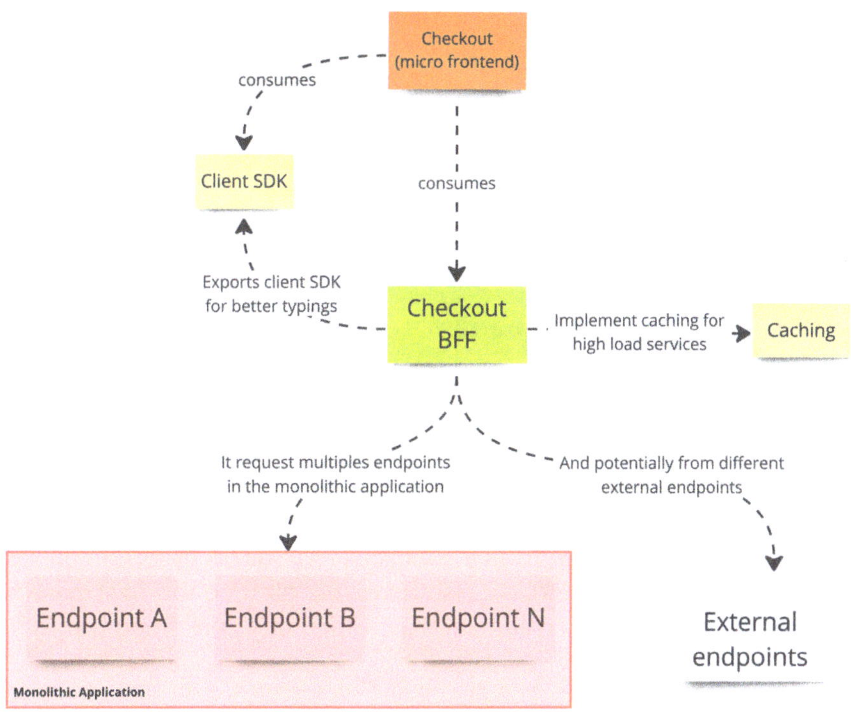

***Figure 8.2:** After BFF adoption*

Note: *The OpenAPI Specification (OAS) is a standard, language-agnostic format for defining and documenting RESTful APIs. Originally known as the Swagger Specification, it has become a widely adopted industry standard for API development and is now maintained by the OpenAPI Initiative, a Linux Foundation project.*

The use of the BFF pattern in Server-Side Template Composition integrations is not applicable—or rather, it is already inherent—since, in this context, each micro frontend is already a "BFF" or simply a backend application.

API Gateway

From a strictly frontend development perspective, the primary differentiating factor between the BFF and API Gateway patterns lies in the factor of exclusivity, or referring to the latter, the lack thereof.

The API Gateway pattern abstracts the complexity of the various microservices existing in distributed systems from its clients (our already well-known and beloved frontend applications).

In architectures based on monolithic frontend systems, a very common configuration follows more or less the following diagram:

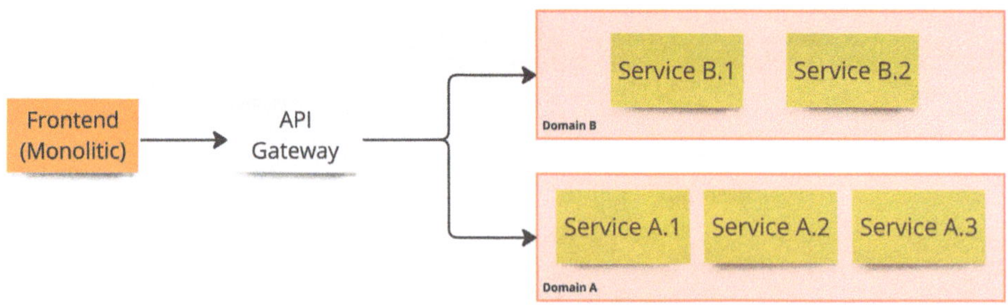

Figure 8.3: *API Gateway*

Without delving into backend-focused improvements (caching, load balancing, centralized control and management, among others), this configuration brings significant benefits to the monolithic frontend, which has simplified consumption of the various APIs. Here, we also set aside the difficulties related to aligning the various services to a minimally consistent interface. Imagine a product discovery API with patterns that are totally different from a checkout API. In this case, complexity would not be entirely hidden from the client. However, we assume the best-case scenario where the various services indeed align and are efficiently consumed through the API gateway.

Considering a migration scenario to a distributed architecture on the client side, we would have something like the following:

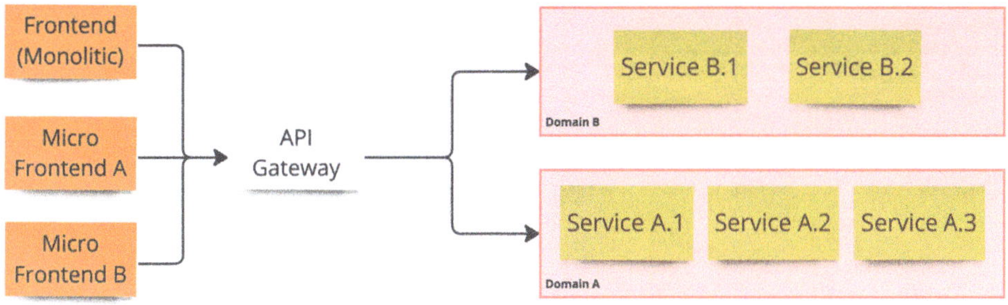

Figure 8.4: *API Gateway + Micro Frontends*

In this scenario, we have a hypothetical transition where a monolithic frontend coexists with two other micro frontends, A and B. This scenario presents some challenges: modifications to the API Gateway tend to become more complex as the number of consumers increases, and it becomes less capable of satisfying the specific demands of certain consumers, since it is not the sole consumer of the functionalities.

It is a choice where we lose adaptability in exchange for easier management of similar functions.

Note: *The two patterns can coexist in a context where the API Gateway acts handling common cross-cutting concerns such as authentication, rate limiting, routing, and so on. Imagine an API Gateway that intercepts requests sent to a specific Kubernetes cluster and forwards the request to the requested service. However, in this case, from the client's (frontend application) perspective, it would be as if it were consuming the required API directly, possibly a BFF.*

API Aggregation

Discussions around microservices and micro frontend architectures–covered earlier in this book, particularly in *Chapter 5, Integration Strategies- Per Feature vs. Per Page Slicing*–often describe an idealized 1-to-1 relationship between a microservice and its corresponding micro frontend. While this model may be conceptually clean, real-world systems often diverge from it. In practice, we encounter 1-to-N relationships in both directions: a single micro frontend consuming multiple microservices, or a single microservice being consumed by multiple micro frontends.

The API Aggregation pattern is especially useful in scenarios where a single micro frontend must consume data from multiple microservices. It consolidates multiple backend requests into a single API call, simplifying data access and reducing client-side complexity.

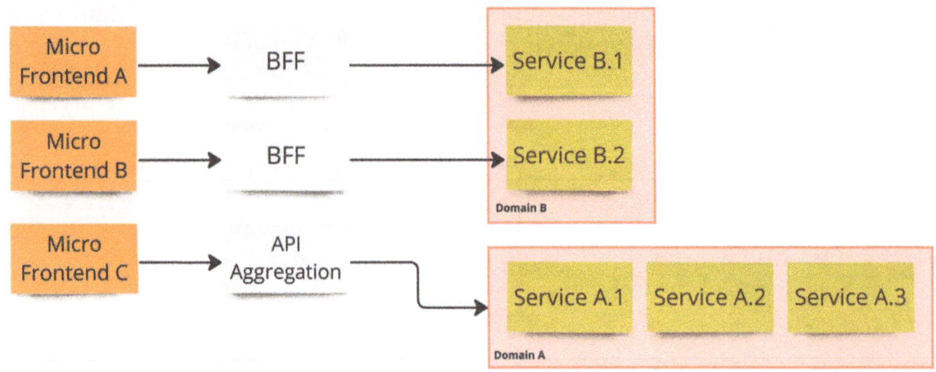

Figure 8.5: API *Aggregation*

This scenario is illustrated in *Figure* 8.5, where Micro Frontend C consumes data from three microservices within Domain A. From the frontend's perspective, this aggregated interface behaves similarly to an API Gateway—but from a broader architectural standpoint, it is functioning as an API Aggregation layer.

====

In this scenario, we have a situation where the three microservices from domain A are consumed by Micro Frontend C. From the narrow perspective of this micro frontend and domain A, the API Aggregation acts as an API Gateway. However, from the system architecture's perspective, it effectively functions as an API Aggregation.

Also keep in mind that, though not described in *Figure* 8.5, unlike BFF which assumes a single client, single frontend application consuming it, a given API Aggregation may have one or multiple clients consuming it.

It is important to note that, unlike the Backend for Frontend (BFF) pattern, which is typically designed for a single frontend, an API Aggregation layer may serve multiple consumers. In this sense, API Aggregation is not a competing pattern, but rather a complementary technique that can be implemented within a BFF or an API Gateway. The most important architectural distinction lies in the number and type of consumers, and in how the aggregation is applied—whether it serves a single client, or multiple frontends or services.

API Standards

Standards are a hot topic in engineering, and we struggle daily to deal with the various standards (or the lack thereof).

The story goes something like this:

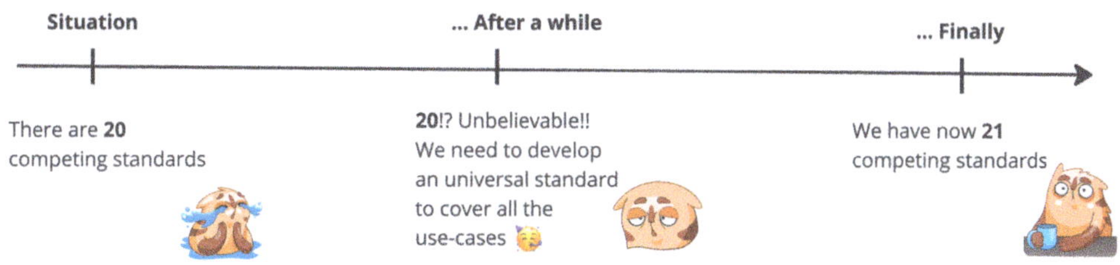

Figure 8.6: *Standards*

Jokes aside, there are indeed well-established standards when it comes to conventions, design guidelines, implementation, and maintenance of APIs. While we will not aim to cover all of them in this section, some directly impact the architecture of the clients (micro frontends) that consume them. We will address these next.

It is important to emphasize that while the choice of a specific API standard directly influences the application design of a given micro frontend–and possibly the tooling used in various implementations–the more heterogeneous the systems are, the more complex the tooling required to maintain them becomes. However, this does not apply to the micro frontend architecture of the system as a whole, which, as explored in earlier sections, can easily handle technological and architectural standard variations. For more details, see: *Chapter 3, Frontend Architectural Patterns.*

RESTful APIs and GraphQL

When it comes to API standards, we need to start our conversation with two "siblings" of contrasting behaviors: the talkative one, always providing everything it has available–RESTful API–and, on the other side, the straightforward one–GraphQL–that only gives us what we explicitly request.

Countless debates, often heated, have taken place between advocates of these two standards. Today, more than a decade since its emergence at Facebook in 2012, GraphQL finds its place in more specific use cases, particularly where the frontend application requires complex data manipulation, often in response to highly customizable interfaces. Imagine those dashboards where users can tweak various details about what will and will not be displayed.

The major challenge of using GraphQL lies in its implementation cost–specifically in terms of complexity. This is mainly due to the resolvers, the backend functions responsible for returning the data requested by the consumer. The cost arises from the producer not knowing in advance which data the consumers will request, leading to a multitude of possibilities. In contrast, the RESTful standard operates with fixed resources, simplifying this process.

In this context, the use of GraphQL should be seen as an exception and adopted only in scenarios where its use is truly indispensable.

Note: *It is beyond the scope of this book to provide detailed definitions of the two standards. Instead, our focus is on establishing general guidelines for their adoption.*

RPC: gRPC and tRPC

The idea of abstracting application details related to data transmission over the network is almost the holy grail of distributed systems. The hypothetical scenario where remote function calls could be executed in the same way as local functions would significantly reduce the complexity of such systems and that is the main concept behind RPC - Remote Procedure Calls: a communication pattern where a client calls a function that appears local but is actually executed on a remote server.

Although this ideal remains aspirational, considerable progress has been made since the first studies in the 1970s to the present day.

Among current technologies, one that has gained significant traction is gRPC (Google Remote Procedure Call–currently, the "g" in the name is somewhat open to interpretation due to the technology's open-source nature). Introduced by Google in 2015, gRPC is an open-source, high-performance framework for building remote procedure call (RPC)-based applications. It is designed to simplify communication between distributed systems, allowing client and server applications to interact as though they were calling local methods, even if they are running on different machines or networks. By leveraging modern technologies for speed, scalability, and efficiency, gRPC has become a popular choice for microservices and cloud-native architectures.

In the context of micro frontend architecture, gRPC is particularly compelling for communication between server-side services. For instance, consider a Server-side Template Composition integration, where multiple micro frontends exchange information seamlessly. gRPC's efficiency and high performance make it an excellent fit for such scenarios, ensuring robust and streamlined communication.

It is important to highlight, however, the coupling that this approach entails. Whenever possible, and where eventual consistency is acceptable, communication methods with lower levels of coupling should be preferred (for example, through event sourcing and similar approaches). However, in scenarios where consistency is critical, the use of gRPC as a communication protocol has proven to be a more performant option in various benchmarks. References to some of these benchmarks can be found at the end of the chapter (*References* section).

The protocol can also be used for communication between the client (browser) and server. However, browsers currently cannot interpret the Protocol Buffers data traffic standard (more details in the next section). In such contexts, a proxy agent–gRPC-

Web–acting on both the client and server is required, as shown in the following diagram:

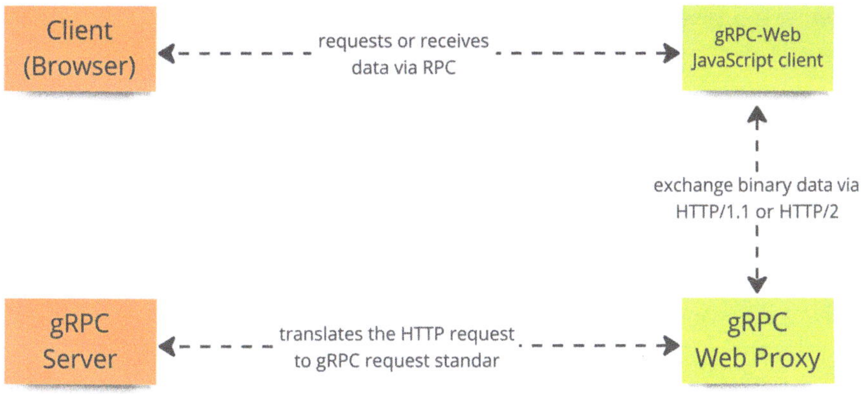

Figure 8.7: *gRPC-Web*

Note: *gRPC-Web is a JavaScript client library and a proxy server that enables gRPC communication between a web browser and a backend server.*

Although promising, the use of gRPC for communication between clients (browsers) and servers should be carefully considered. Several factors work against its adoption, including the fact that it is a relatively recent standard, resulting in less tooling, community support, and a generally more complex setup. Overall, its use is recommended in scenarios where performance is critical and minimizing the amount of data transmitted over the network is desirable.

Another RPC-based technology that has emerged more recently, particularly within the TypeScript ecosystem, is tRPC. Unlike gRPC, which is language-agnostic and relies on *.proto* files and code generation, tRPC embraces a code-first philosophy tightly coupled to the TypeScript environment. It allows developers to define server-side functions that can be called directly from the client as if they were local, without requiring any schema definition or code generation. The key innovation lies in its end-to-end type safety: the types used on the server are automatically inferred on the client, drastically reducing the risk of runtime errors and improving developer productivity. While gRPC is ideal for cross-language, high-performance service communication (especially among backends), tRPC is purpose-built for fullstack TypeScript applications, typically within a monorepo or tightly integrated architecture. This makes tRPC particularly attractive for web applications using frameworks such as Next.js or Vite, where client and server code live side by side.

The trade-off, however, is that tRPC is not suitable for cross-language environments and does not offer the same level of tooling or maturity found in gRPC. Moreover, while gRPC emphasizes performance and transport efficiency (using HTTP/2 and Protocol Buffers), tRPC favors simplicity and development speed, transmitting data as JSON over standard HTTP. In terms of micro frontends, tRPC excels in client-server communication within a controlled ecosystem, such as admin panels, internal tools, or dashboards where TypeScript is used throughout the stack, for instance, a scenario where a given team owns a particular micro frontend and a BFF based on Typescript.

It does not replace gRPC but complements it in use cases where developer experience, rapid iteration, and strong typing within a single-language system are prioritized over raw performance or interoperability.

Data Formats

And finally, as a consequence of the adopted API Standard, the data format and, consequently, the API used to manipulate this data by the frontend application are defined.

Among the main standards, we have the de facto one: the JSON format, which is currently used almost ubiquitously in browser-based applications, largely due to the JavaScript language. In all cases, the developer experience is ensured given the familiarity web developers have with this specification.

An alternative, also with significant advantages in terms of developer experience, is the use of Protocol Buffers.

Protocol Buffers (Protobuf) are a language-neutral, platform-neutral, extensible mechanism for serializing structured data.

The improvement in developer experience comes mainly from the unification of interfaces between the producer and consumer, making it easier to understand how a given API should be consumed—assuming, in this case, that the development team is familiar with the producer and consumer structures.

Lastly, although still widely used, primarily in legacy systems, there is the XML data format and technologies based on it (SOAP, XSLT, XPath, XQuery, among others). Generally, its use is discouraged, mainly due to the low level of developer experience and the declining maintainability of the ecosystem around these technologies in recent years.

Client SDK Generation

The Client SDK Generation refers to the process of creating client-side Software Development Kits (SDKs) based on a server-side API. These SDKs provide pre-built methods, functions, and utilities that make it easier for developers to interact with an API, reducing the need to manually handle HTTP requests or responses.

One of the major challenges for client applications when consuming APIs is the lack or inconsistency of typing in those APIs. Who has not, when dealing with a specific API, struggled to define its structure? Whether it is attempting to generate SDKs only to encounter specification errors or dealing with documentation that contradicts the actual responses received.

In this context, it is crucial to be integrated into the deployment process of these APIs, regardless of the standard adopted. Ensuring the integrity of generated documentation (such as OpenAPI Specification) and its corresponding types is essential. When there is no control over the deployment process, adopting external services for instance, anti-corruption API layers, or equivalent mechanisms to abstract these inconsistencies from various clients becomes a strategic move.

Such an approach will undoubtedly enhance the structure of client applications (micro frontend applications and other dependent APIs).

Conclusion

In this chapter, we aimed to explore the key architectural patterns—Backend For Frontend, API Gateway, and API Aggregation—alongside API standards such as RESTful APIs, GraphQL, and gRPC, as well as data transfer formats such as JSON, XML, and Protocol Buffers, which frontend implementations may need to interact with while consuming backend services. Concluding with general recommendations for their adoption.

In the following chapter, we will check the testing strategies tailored to the demands of micro frontend architectures. We will explore a range of testing methodologies, from foundational techniques such as unit and component tests to advanced practices such as contract and end-to-end testing. Additional focus will be given to visual regression, performance, and usability testing to maintain quality at scale. Moreover, we will discuss critical considerations for versioning, compatibility, and security to ensure that micro frontends remain cohesive, reliable, and future-proof in a rapidly evolving ecosystem.

References

1. https://grpc.io/
2. https://protobuf.dev/
3. https://blog.shiftasia.com/grpc-vs-rest-speed-comparation/
4. https://medium.com/%40i.gorton/scaling-up-rest-versus-grpc-benchmark-tests-551f73ed88d4
5. https://medium.com/%40EmperorRXF/evaluating-performance-of-rest-vs-grpc-1b8bdf0b22da

CHAPTER 9
Testing Strategies

Introduction

Paraphrasing some statements commonly heard not too long ago:

"*Testing is for the backend; frontend doesn't really apply...*"

Or something along the lines of:

"*Let's focus our tests on the most important parts of the system.*" (Assuming frontend applications do not fall into that category.)

In this chapter, we will focus on the key aspects of testing frontend applications, with an emphasis on micro frontend architecture. Our focus will not be so much on defining each practice but rather on their applications, best practices, pitfalls, and common "*bad smells*" encountered by practitioners when implementing micro frontend architecture.

Structure

In this chapter, we will cover the following topics:

- Unit and Component Tests
- Contract Testing
- Integration Testing
- End-to-End Testing
- Visual Regression Testing
- Versioning and Compatibility
- Performance Testing
- Accessibility Testing
- Security Testing

Unit and Component Tests

When it comes to Unit and Component testing, there are not many changes in practice when comparing the micro frontend implementation to the traditional frontend architectures (More details in *Chapter 3, Frontend Architectural Patterns*). Generally speaking, the main difference lies in the number of tests required for each implementation. Since each micro frontend has a reduced scope, the number of Unit and Component tests needed to meet predefined minimum standards (also known as minimum code coverage) is also reduced.

As with other aspects of application maintainability, the reduced scope once again simplifies maintenance. Who has not struggled with updating major releases of unit testing libraries–such as Jest–working on codemods, and losing their sanity trying to understand false negatives?

Note: *Jest is a JavaScript testing framework developed by Facebook, primarily used for testing JavaScript and TypeScript applications. It is widely used in the React ecosystem but can also be used with Node.js and other JavaScript frameworks.*

In distributed architectures, the effort required for such modifications is significantly reduced–not to mention the flexibility that each team will have in defining minimum code coverage, technologies, approaches, and more.

Note: *Code coverage is a software testing metric that measures how much of the codebase is executed during testing. It helps assess the effectiveness of test cases and identify untested parts of the code.*

Contract Testing

Some desired characteristics in tests have particular relevance and complexity in distributed systems, namely:

- **Reliability**: Tests should produce consistent results when run repeatedly under the same conditions. Flaky tests (tests that pass or fail inconsistently) should be avoided, as they undermine trust in the test suite.
- **Determinism**: Tests should produce the same result every time they are run, regardless of the environment or timing. Avoid relying on external factors such as network calls, system time, or random data unless explicitly tested.

Basically, we want to have tests that consistently produce the same results and are not affected by external factors.

Therefore, with these objectives in mind, we employ a myriad of techniques: stubs, mocks, fakes, dummies, and other things to stub out parts of a system for testing. (All these techniques are referred to in various literature as TestDouble, a term we will use from now on.) We then abstract details related to other services (other micro frontends and/or microservices, external APIs, environment details, and the like).

But the question that remains is whether the assumptions we have, and which are implemented by these TestDoubles, are true and remain true over time.

What happens if the external service changes its contract?

This is the central idea of Contract Testing: to validate from time to time, or under certain conditions, that the assumptions adopted by the TestDoubles remain true.

The following figure schematically illustrates this idea:

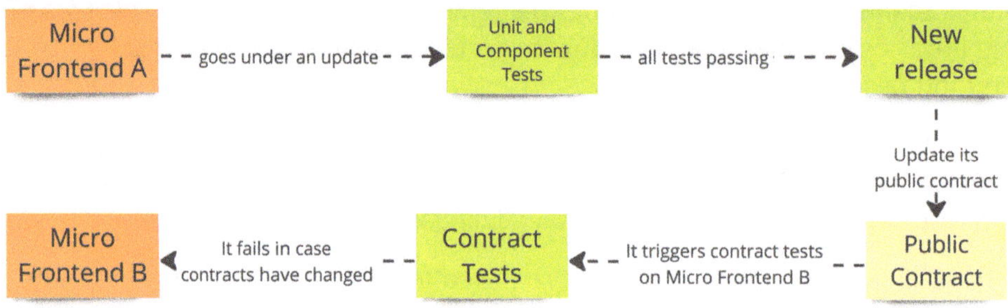

Figure 9.1: *Contract Tests*

In this scenario, releases made in Micro Frontend A trigger contract tests in Micro Frontend B. If the update to the Public Contract somehow breaks the assumptions of the TestDoubles in Micro Frontend B (often due to non-backwards compatible changes, though not exclusively limited to these), the team of Micro Frontend B or even the team of Micro Frontend A is alerted, and the appropriate action can be taken (such as a probable rollback of the release in Micro Frontend A, disabling feature flags related to the new functionality, or any other necessary measures).

Note: *More details related to feature flags in Chapter 10, Deployment Strategies.*

Consumer-Driven Contracts

The previously discussed context starts with changes in the provider triggering checks in the consumers. However, in these scenarios, the providers themselves have no idea who their consumers are or what exactly they consume. This essentially leaves them in a situation where any release made needs to be treated as a public contract and maintained as such. Now, let us imagine the following situation:

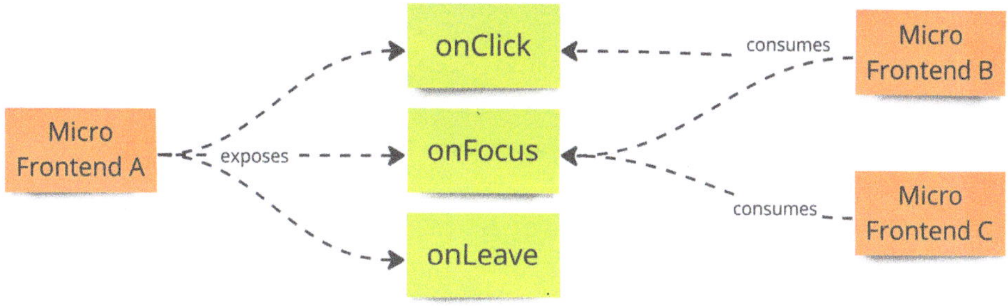

Figure 9.2: *Consumer-Driven Contract*

In this structure, Micro Frontend A (provider) has Micro Frontends B and C as consumers. However, neither of them consumes the **`onLeave`** method. In this context, if necessary, this method could undergo non-backwards compatible changes without causing side effects for any of the consumers.

And this is the basic idea of the Consumer-Driven Contracts pattern, as illustrated in the following diagram:

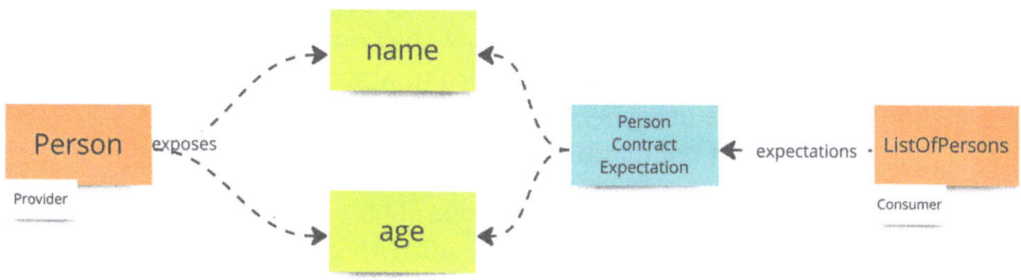

Figure 9.3: *Contract Expectations*

In this diagram, we have the relationship between the provider **`Person`** and the consumer **`ListOfPersons`**, where the consumer establishes a set of expectations (also referred to in some literature as a pact) regarding its provider.

In the following example, we have a TypeScript code snippet implementing the mentioned contract:

```
export interface PersonContract {
  name: string;
  age: number;
}

/** Expectations that the ListOfPersons component has in regards to the Person component */
export const personContractExpectations = {
  name: expect.any(String),
  age: expect.any(Number),

  validatePerson: (person: PersonContract) => {
    // set expectations in regards to the name being defined and not empty
    expect(person.name).toBeTruthy();
    expect(person.name.length).toBeGreaterThan(0);

    // set expectations in regards to the age being defined and between 20 and 70 range
    expect(person.age).toBeTruthy();
    expect(person.age).toBeGreaterThanOrEqual(20);
    expect(person.age).toBeLessThanOrEqual(70);
  },
};
```

***Figure 9.4:** Person Contract Expectations*

With this contract, we make it clear what is actually being used from the provider's interface, leaving it free to make modifications that do not impact its consumers. Imagine a future where the provider introduces a new attribute, let us say **`birthDate`**. Until a consumer establishes an expectation regarding this attribute, the provider is free to make non-backwards compatible changes.

We can then effectively validate these assumptions in tests. For this, we will use the Jest framework. In this implementation, each of the entities (**`Person`** and **`ListOfPerson`**) are implemented using the Run-time Integration via WebComponent (for more details, please refer to: *Chapter 5, Integration Strategies - Client-side Composition*).

The following test checks whether a hypothetical **`ListOfPersons`** WebComponent renders a fixed list of **`PersonComponent`** (this part is not super relevant, it simulates an implementation unit test) and whether each of them matches the expectations established in the **`personContractExpectations`** contract.

```
import "../components/person";
import "../components/list-of-persons";
import { personContractExpectations } from "../contracts/person.contract";

describe("Component Contract Tests", () => {
  beforeEach(() => {
    document.body.innerHTML = "";
  });

  test("ListOfPersons should create 5 Person components with valid data", () => {
    const listComponent = document.createElement("list-of-persons");
    document.body.appendChild(listComponent);

    const persons = document.querySelectorAll("person-component");
    expect(persons.length).toBe(5);

    persons.forEach((person) => {
      const personData = {
        name: person.getAttribute("name") || "",
        age: Number(person.getAttribute("age")),
      };

      personContractExpectations.validatePerson(personData);
    });
  });

  test("Person component should correctly render received data", () => {…
  });
});
```

Figure 9.5: *Consumer-Driven Contract Test*

For a complete implementation, refer to: *https://github.com/ava-orange-education/-Micro-Frontends-Architecture-for-Scalable-Applications/tree/main/contract-integration-testing*

Note: *The* **`ListOfPerson`** *as consumer only (for this use-case) has no contract expectations, meaning there are no consumers of it expecting certain behavior.*

Integration Testing

At a certain point in the testing scale of our architecture, we need to ensure that our service (micro frontend) works as expected when integrated with other systems: APIs, DBs, queues, other micro frontends, and so on.

Integration tests are meant to actually test the integration, not just its contracts. However, this approach should be used in moderation due to its potential side effects, particularly in terms of execution cost compared to previously discussed techniques, as well as issues related to determinism and reliability in tests.

The exact ideal number of integration tests, just like other types of tests, is highly dependent on the specific context, and any referenced values here would be mere speculation.

In general, we can adopt a less conservative stance regarding integration testing and test a core method of other micro frontends. For example, continuing the previous case, we could test whether the web component is rendered on the page as expected.

```
test("Person component should correctly render received data", () => {
  const person = document.createElement("person-component");
  person.setAttribute("name", "Test Name");
  person.setAttribute("age", "25");
  document.body.appendChild(person);

  const shadowRoot = person.shadowRoot;
  expect(shadowRoot?.querySelector(".person")).toBeTruthy();
  expect(shadowRoot?.textContent).toContain("Test Name");
  expect(shadowRoot?.textContent).toContain("25");
});
```

Figure 9.6: *Integration Testing*

We test whether the WebComponent of the micro frontend we are consuming renders the provided values (name and age) within a given environment–in this use-case, the browser. More extensive tests could naturally be conducted, but they would be much more specific to the particular integration.

It is pertinent to highlight that, within this use-case, a given web component should be viewed as a separate micro frontend. From this perspective, tests of a web component that reference another are, in essence, testing the integration of external systems.

From the perspective of integration tests, it becomes more important to ensure the stability of the infrastructure where the service is running (potentially executing tests within containers–Docker and similar technologies) and to guarantee idempotency when consuming the service.

Note: *Idempotent refers to an operation that produces the same result no matter how many times it is executed, given the same input and system state. In the context of integration testing for micro frontends, it is crucial to ensure that the state of micro frontends is always reset before test execution.*

End-to-End Testing

End-to-End (e2e) testing refers to the practice of testing a system from the beginning to the end. However, many discussions around this practice, especially in distributed architectures, introduce a certain degree of confusion. Misunderstandings regarding the definition of what constitutes end-to-end testing are common. Who has not participated in the creation of e2e tests for a specific domain of an application–tests that, while possible, do not always faithfully reflect the user journey?

E2E should be understood as the user journey or customer journey, meaning the visual or narrative representation of the steps a user takes to achieve a specific goal within a product, service, or website. It maps out the entire experience from the user's perspective, including their interactions, pain points, and touchpoints with the interface or system.

It is important to note that "*user*" should not be understood exclusively as a person–other systems can (and should) also be seen as users, even if this perspective is less relevant in frontend development.

Ideally, e2e development should be oriented around this user journey, which should not necessarily be reflected in the distributed system architecture. In other words, while some user journeys may be exclusive to a specific domain (such as a particular micro frontend implementation), the relationship between the two should not be constrained by one another.

User journeys can involve multiple micro frontend implementations, and a single micro frontend implementation can be part of various user journeys.

With this understanding, implementing these tests typically requires the formation of functional teams dedicated to establishing and maintaining them.

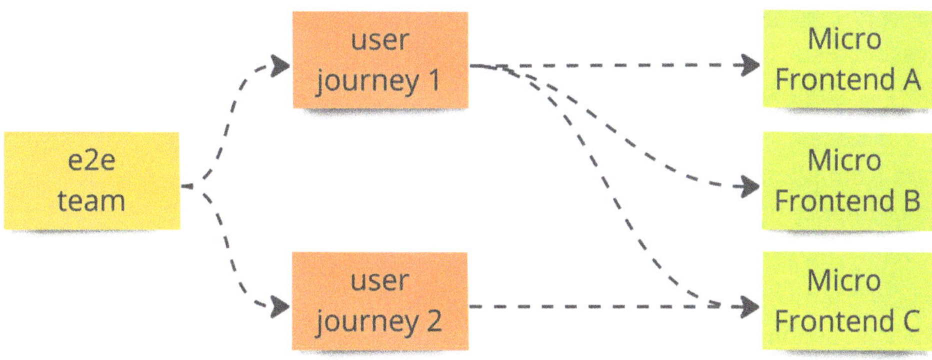

Figure 9.7: *e2e tests*

In this scenario, an e2e team, based on predefined user journeys, implements the tests. From their perspective, the complexity of the distributed system is abstracted–just as it should be for the end user.

In summary, from the standpoint of e2e tests, the micro frontend architecture implementation should be abstracted away. These tests should be seen as a final quality gate, used in moderation, considering their operational costs related to maintenance and execution (low performance).

Last but not least, through tracing techniques, failures in these tests should be able to report the origin (micro frontend) responsible for the issue.

More details on tracing strategies and techniques will be covered in *Chapter 11, Observability - Tracing.*

Visual Regression Testing

Visual Regression Testing aims to test visual regressions in the application. Unlike snapshot testing, where the test verifies the DOM (Document Object Model) structure of the page, here we want to visually verify what is actually rendered by a given client (browser).

Simply put, visual regression testing compares screenshots (images) of your system taken before and after a change. It flags errors or warnings based on the visual differences detected. Snapshot testing, on the other hand, generates a text-based representation of the page's structure (the DOM) and compares the versions before and after the modification.

Such tests usually take a significant amount of time, which results in lower adoption of this kind of testing. Therefore, it is common to focus only on the critical parts of the system.

Despite common practices, each case may be unique in nature and requirements; moreover, the development of tooling may increase the performance of visual regression tests. In a distributed system, a team that is responsible for the given micro frontend should also make decisions regarding the usage and amount of various types of tests.

A good example may be a payment component. The way it looks and functions has a direct impact on user conversion–a critical KPI for the business, and is therefore susceptible to a broader coverage of visual regression testing.

Note: *User conversion, in the context of digital marketing and product development, is the specific action a user performs that indicates they have become a customer, lead, or achieved a valuable outcome.*

In general, teams should, whenever possible, avoid running visual regression tests in a centralized way. When functional teams take full ownership of all end-to-end tests, it introduces a level of centralization that can limit the autonomy of other teams. The more we centralize, the fewer benefits we gain from the architecture. In the end, we risk working against our main goal: giving teams full ownership of their implementation.

Versioning and Compatibility

Versioning and Compatibility refers to tests conducted to ensure that the application behaves as expected across different clients (browsers, Node.js versions, operating systems, screen sizes, aspect ratio, and resolutions) and different versions of itself.

The first challenge in achieving this is defining which clients the application should support—specifically, which browsers and platforms must be compatible, particularly in terms of backward compatibility. Generally, this is a business decision, as the business understands its target audience. However, this decision should naturally be supported by data from the technical team.

A great advantage in this regard is the tooling available today. Tools like browserslist, which rely on constantly updated databases from sources such as **Can I use:** (*https://caniuse.com*) and **StatCounter** (*https://gs.statcounter.com*), provide a powerful API for specifying requirements regarding client versioning and compatibility.

From an architectural perspective, it is crucial that these definitions are enforced across all micro frontend implementations. Otherwise, the risk of inconsistencies and errors arising in less frequently tested clients increases.

A commonly used implementation pattern is to have an external library (NPM package) integrated via build-time integration which would enforce such guarantees. The referenced library would then be available to use in any of the micro frontend integration strategies. More details in *Chapter 5, Integration Strategies*.

Something like the following diagram:

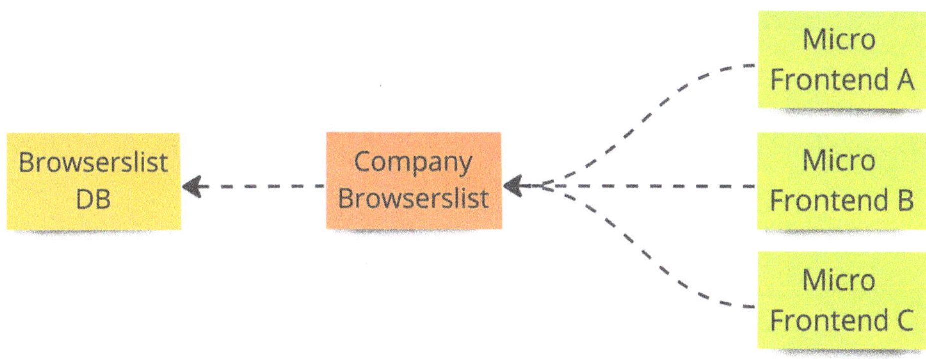

Figure 9.8: *Versioning and Compatibility*

In this implementation, an npm package **`CompanyBrowserslist`** defines the set of queries specifying the clients that the company aims to support, something like:

```
/**
 * Company browser support definitions.
 */
module.exports = {
  production: [
    "> 1%",
    "last 2 versions",
    "not dead",
  ],
  development: ["last 1 chrome version", "last 1 firefox version", "last 1 safari version"],
};
```

Figure 9.9: *Company Browserslist Configuration*

More info about **`browserslist`** and its queries can be found in: *https://github.com/browserslist/browserslist*

And then, the various implementations consume this setup as an npm dependency, ensuring uniformity across them.

Once this setup is defined, further tooling improvements regarding linting, transpiling, and so on become additionally necessary.

Also, these definitions provide great guidance for defining e2e testing strategies.

Let us assume a hypothetical scenario of an application whose target audience is located in Europe. Insights from **`StatCounter`** can help define priorities for focusing end-to-end (E2E) tests:

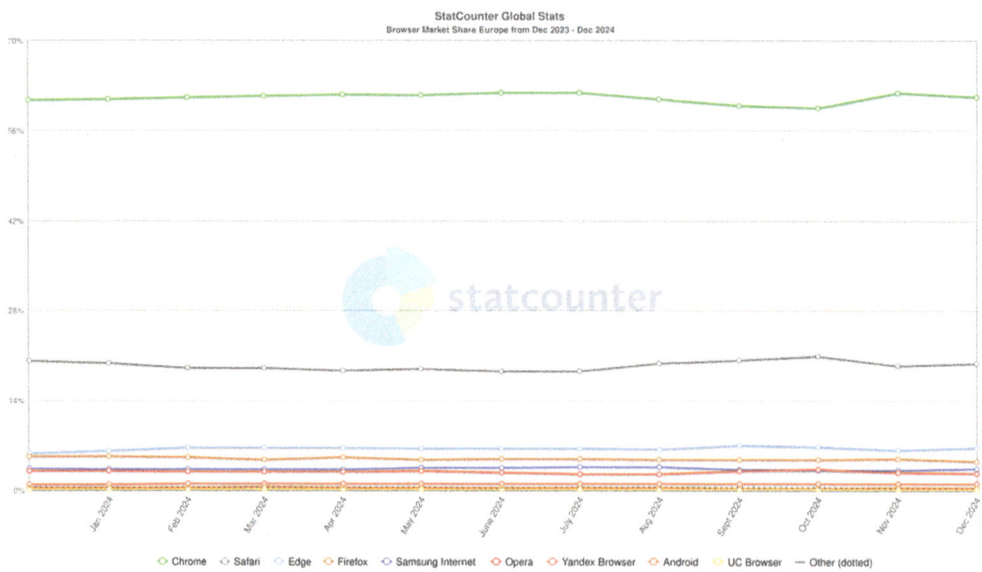

Figure 9.10: *Browser Market Share in Europe - December 2024*
Source: Statcounter

The chart provides strong indications of which browsers we should prioritize in our E2E testing efforts.

Performance Testing

Performance has been, it is, and will most likely remain the "*hot topic*" in IT. Who has not engaged in heated discussions on the subject, deciphered code that looks like ancient hieroglyphs or archaeological findings from unknown civilizations that claim to be the most performatic algorithm of all times? Terms like this (as well as architectural and design) carry an aura of "*divinity*," intelligence, and significance in software development cycles.

Jokes aside, we dedicate this section to the much-discussed topic. Even though these practices rarely change, when introducing micro frontend architecture, the consequences of neglecting them become more evident.

Although it is not the primary focus, it is important to define performance. In our context, we refer to it as the set of metrics for testing aspects such as loading performance, interactivity, rendering, network performance, and perceived performance of a given micro frontend implementation or a set of them running within a Shell Application.

A brief explanation of each of these metrics follows:

Loading Performance Metrics shows how quickly a page loads and becomes usable.

- **Time to First Byte (TTFB):** Measures the time taken for the server to respond with the first byte of data.
- **First Contentful Paint (FCP):** Captures when the first piece of content is rendered on the screen.
- **Largest Contentful Paint (LCP):** Measures when the largest visible content is loaded.
- **Speed Index (SI):** Measures how quickly content is visually displayed.
- **Onload Time:** The time when the browser has loaded all resources (but may not be fully rendered).
- **DOMContentLoaded (DCL):** Measures when the HTML is fully parsed and ready.

Interactivity and Responsiveness Metrics indicates how quickly a webpage responds to user input.

- **First Input Delay (FID):** Measures how long it takes for the page to respond to the first user interaction.
- **Total Blocking Time (TBT):** The total time JavaScript blocks the main thread and prevents interactions.

- **Interaction to Next Paint (INP)**: Measures overall responsiveness to user interactions (will replace FID).
- **Time to Interactive (TTI)**: Measures when a page becomes fully interactive (event handlers are registered, and UI is stable).

Visual Stability Metrics measure how stable the layout remains during page load.

- **Cumulative Layout Shift (CLS):** Measures unexpected layout shifts (for example, images or ads pushing content down).
- **Layout Instability API:** Tracks element movement on the page.

Network and Resource Performance Metrics focus on server, connection, and resource load performance.

- **DNS Lookup Time:** Measures how long the DNS resolution takes.
- **TCP Connection Time:** Measures how long it takes to establish a connection.
- **TLS Handshake Time:** Measures SSL/TLS negotiation time.
- **Resource Load Times**: Measures how long each resource (CSS, JS, images) takes to load.

Perceived Performance Metrics analyze how users feel about the performance of a site.

- **Perceived Load Time**: How fast users think the page has loaded.
- **User Timing API:** Allows developers to set custom marks and measures in JavaScript.
- **Hero Element Timing**: Measures how long it takes for key elements (for example, product images, CTA buttons) to load.

The tooling used for such tests is quite extensive. In the context of web standards, the `PerformanceObserver` API provides a powerful interface for implementing custom metrics specific to an application, such as the *Hero Element Timing metric.*

For more general performance metrics such as *Loading Performance, Interactivity & Responsiveness, and Visual Stability*, Web Vitals-based implementations have gained widespread industry adoption.

Note: *The* ***`PerformanceObserver`*** *API is a browser API that allows you to observe and collect performance metrics in real time. It listens for performance events (like layout shifts, resource loads, or long tasks) and helps developers analyze web performance without relying on external tools.*

Web Vitals is a set of performance metrics defined by Google to measure user experience on the web. These metrics focus on key aspects of web performance, particularly loading speed, interactivity, and visual stability.

More on the topic in: *https://web.dev/articles/vitals*

Lighthouse is a widely adopted and highly relevant tool for Web Vitals checks. It can be integrated into CI/CD pipelines to enforce predefined performance thresholds, similar to how code coverage thresholds work for unit tests.

More on Lighthouse:

- **Overview**: *https://developer.chrome.com/docs/lighthouse/overview*
- **CLI integration for CI/CD pipelines**: *https://github.com/GoogleChrome/lighthouse*

The execution cost (in terms of time and required resources) of such tests can often be high, similar to end-to-end (e2e) tests. However, their results are crucial and, in many cases, serve as selling points–a competitive advantage in negotiations with stakeholders particularly interested in the system's performance attributes.

A performance testing implementation in a micro frontend environment could follow this general structure:

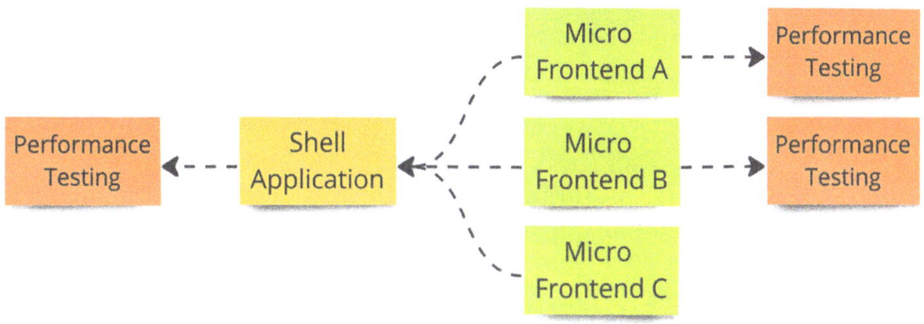

Figure 9.11: *Performance Testing*

In this scenario, each micro frontend implementation defines its own performance requirements as well as when to execute these tests–whether on the developer's machine, as a Git hook, and/or within a CI/CD pipeline, among other options. The execution mode, synchronous or asynchronous, largely depends on Developer Experience (DX), given the time these tests may take.

Finally, and most importantly, performance testing is conducted at the shell application level, ensuring the desired performance standards for the application as a whole.

It is essential to emphasize that the primary goal here is to guarantee performance adherence to predefined metrics before release, thereby preventing performance degradation throughout the application's lifecycle.

More on performance monitoring will be covered in *Chapter 11, Observability*.

Accessibility Testing

The first effort regarding accessibility testing (accessibility also referred to as a11y, it is a numeronym, with 11 representing the count of letters between the letter *a* and the letter *y*) is related to its definition and mainly the establishment of a set of metrics to validate this predetermined definition.

There is a lot of confusion between poor UI/UX and poor accessibility, and although the first can have a side effect on the second, they should not be confused.

The WCAG (Web Content Accessibility Guidelines) is a set of internationally recognized standards for making web content more accessible to people with disabilities. It is developed by the W3C's Web Accessibility Initiative (WAI) and provides guidelines to ensure websites, apps, and digital content are usable by people with visual, auditory, cognitive, and motor impairments.

And although other standards, in many cases oriented to specific niches, can be used, the WAI has a powerful tooling supporting these metrics and as mentioned before, international recognition.

Its tests do not actually require the full rendering of the application, and depend only on the DOM of the application. Therefore execution costs are not as relevant when compared to other tests such as e2e and visual regression testing.

Mixed setups, with local tests (tests executed within the context of a given micro frontend) and global tests, performed by a functional test team aiming to check accessibility issues in the application as a whole are interesting.

Many of the accessibility problems result from the final structure of the DOM of the page; therefore, tests that consider the entire application are relevant.

Imagine an integration of a certain micro frontend that renders an HTML element <H3> for example, being integrated into the shell application and the same not having the counterparts `<h1>` and `<h2>`, this integration would cause an accessibility problem that would not be seen by local tests in the frontend.

Note: *Heading hierarchy (<h1> through <h6>) creates a document outline that helps users, especially those using screen readers, understand the structure and importance of content. And the lack of them is considered following WAI metrics an accessibility issue.*

A setup with accessibility tests could be implemented in the following way:

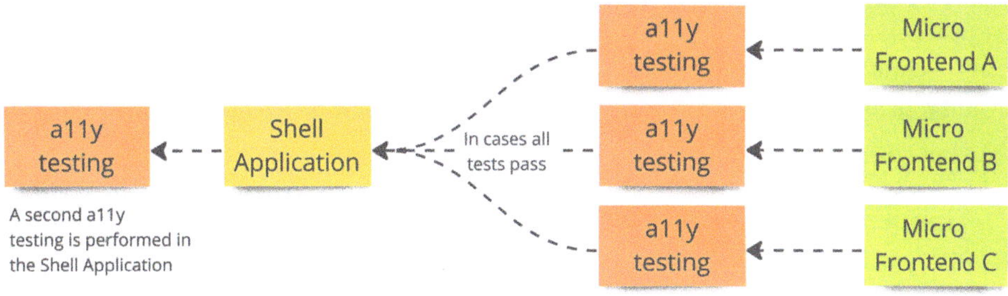

Figure 9.12: *a11y Testing*

In this specific scenario, accessibility testing is conducted in two phases. The first phase involves testing each micro frontend independently. The second phase takes place after the micro frontends are integrated into the Shell Application, allowing for a comprehensive assessment of the overall accessibility.

Security Testing

Understanding DevSecOps (development, security, and operations) extends the DevOps initiative by emphasizing the integration of security practices and tools at every stage of the software development lifecycle–from planning and design to development, testing, deployment, and operations. As such, frontend development cannot be separated from this. With that in mind, the question that arises and which we aim to explore and answer in this section is: how much does the micro frontend architecture change frontend development efforts towards ensuring security standards in the application?

We will use the OWASP Application Security Verification Standard (ASVS) Project as a guideline, which aims to:

Normalize the range of coverage and level of rigor available in the market when it comes to performing web application security verification using a commercially viable open standard.

More info: *https://owasp.org/www-project-application-security-verification-standard/*

This framework is widely recognized in the development industry and provides us with a solid foundation for implementing security testing. In addition, there is a wide range of existing tools for conducting these tests based on this standard.

Regarding micro frontend architecture, the main points of interest focus on: secure architecture and design, secure coding practices, and secure development lifecycle integration.

The architectural and design security definitions of the micro frontend architecture aim to establish a minimum set of requirements for each implementation, thereby reducing some of the existing flexibility—potentially limiting the scope of tool, technology, and similar choices—with the goal of minimizing the attack surface.

Concepts like the following should be considered in this context:

- **Threat Modeling**: Analyze potential threats throughout the application's lifecycle. This includes identifying assets, vulnerabilities, and attack vectors. Techniques such as STRIDE (Spoofing, Tampering, Repudiation, Information Disclosure, Denial of Service, Elevation of Privilege) can be helpful.
- **Defense in Depth**: Implement multiple layers of security controls to provide redundancy and minimize the impact of a single point of failure.
- **Least Privilege**: Grant users only the minimum necessary permissions to perform their duties.
- **Technology choice**: Considering security implications when choosing technologies and frameworks.

Secure coding practices do not change significantly compared to traditional architectures, or what we might call non-distributed architectures. The same well-known techniques should be applied in this context in the same way. These include input validation and sanitization, authentication and authorization, data encryption, secure session management, error handling and logging, automated tools to analyze code and dependencies for vulnerabilities, among others.

Secure Development Lifecycle integration is one critical aspect in the micro frontend architecture when it comes to security testing efforts.

While a monolithic frontend also exposes an attack surface, micro frontend architectures may increase the complexity of securing the application due to their distributed nature. Each independently deployed micro frontend can introduce variability in how security controls are implemented or enforced, especially when different teams are responsible for different parts. This operational fragmentation can unintentionally expand the effective attack surface if not managed carefully.

Note: *The Secure Development Lifecycle (SDLC), also known as SSDLC, is essentially the traditional Software Development Lifecycle with security considerations integrated into each and every phase. The goal of a Secure SDLC is to build security into the software from the ground up, rather than bolting it on as an afterthought.*

Another relevant point, already explored in other sections (*Chapter 5, Integration Strategies - Client-side Composition* and *Chapter 6, Communication and Routing - Shared Dependencies*), is related to Data Isolation and Sharing. From a strictly security perspective, the more we share, the better it is, and therefore shared data or dependencies must be monitored, frequently reviewed, and tested.

The following diagram demonstrates a possible implementation of a micro frontend architecture with security testing integrated:

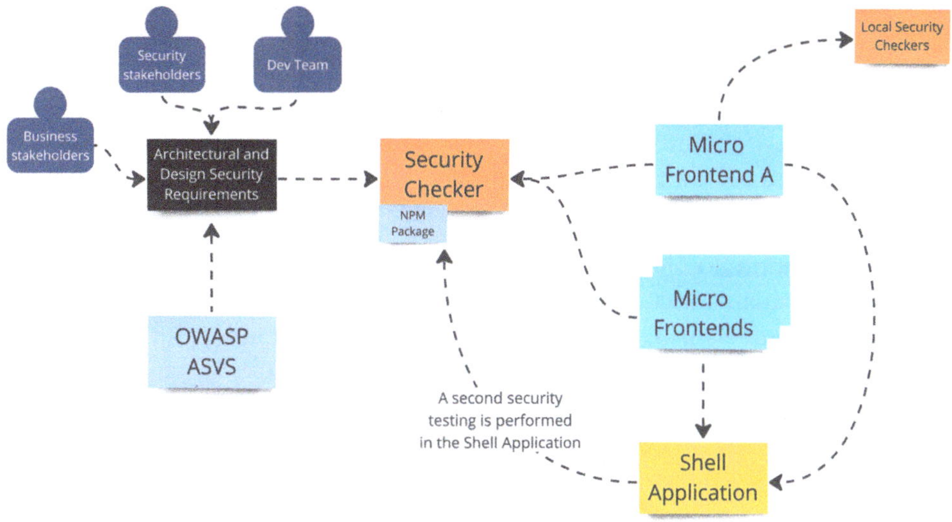

Figure 9.13: *Security Testing*

In the proposed diagram, we have:

The business team, a functional security team, and the development team, based on the best practices of the OWASP ASVS framework, work together to define a minimum set of requirements for the micro frontend implementations.

This document consequently establishes the requirements for creating a tooling solution (in this example, an NPM package) to ensure these definitions are met.

Note: *Although not strictly necessary, in our practice, we have seen many scenarios where such documents, when not supported by a tool, tend to become outdated or, in many cases, simply ignored by development teams.*

Once implemented, the aforementioned tool should be used in the development process, validated either in CI/CD pipelines or through git hooks on the developer's local machine—or both.

Naturally, each micro frontend implementation has the flexibility to implement its own local security checkers, meaning extensions to the company's Architectural and Design Security requirements that are necessary for specific cases.

Finally, similar to checks related to accessibility, a second security check is performed in the Shell Application, ensuring that the various micro frontends, when integrated, still satisfy the security requirements.

It is important to emphasize that the diagram shown is not intended to be a definitive guide but rather a model that organizations can use as a reference and adapt to their specific scenarios.

Conclusion

In the discussions of this chapter, we first aim to introduce a general concept regarding the most common testing practices in frontend applications, examples of implementations, and how the architecture of micro frontends fundamentally impacts these practices.

The core architectural concern lies in defining clear responsibilities among various cross-functional teams focused on developing different micro frontends, as well as dedicated teams specializing exclusively in testing (for example, end-to-end testing, visual regressions, performance, and accessibility testing).

In the next chapter, as an extension of testing practices, we will explore deployment strategies for systems, covering techniques such as Continuous Integration/ Continuous Deployment (CI/CD), Blue-Green Deployment, and Canary Releases.

References

1. https://github.com/ava-orange-education/-Micro-Frontends-Architecture-for-Scalable-Applications
2. https://jestjs.io/
3. https://caniuse.com/
4. https://gs.statcounter.com/
5. https://github.com/browserslist/browserslist
6. https://web.dev/articles/vitals
7. https://developer.chrome.com/docs/lighthouse/overview
8. https://developer.mozilla.org/en-US/docs/Web/API/PerformanceObserver
9. https://www.w3.org/WAI/
10. https://owasp.org/www-project-application-security-verification-standard/

Chapter 10
Deployment Strategies

Introduction

Throughout our analysis of various aspects related to developing Scalable Applications using the micro frontend architecture, we have frequently referenced deployment strategies and Continuous Integration / Continuous Deployment (CI/CD), especially in the context of testing techniques.

We began our discussions in *Chapter 7, UI/UX and Design System* with a more philosophical and conceptual argument about the need for independent deployment, followed by technical implementations using CI/CD to ensure quality–covered in *Chapter 9, Testing Strategies.*

In this chapter, we will focus on implementing Continuous Integration / Continuous Deployment and exploring potential features such as Blue-Green Deployment and Canary Releases for the micro frontend architecture.

Structure

In this chapter, we will cover the following topics:

- Continuous Integration / Continuous Deployment (CI/CD)
- Blue-Green Deployment
- Canary Releases

Continuous Integration / Continuous Deployment (CI/CD)

Definitions-wise, Continuous Integration / Continuous Deployment (CI/CD) refers to a set of software development practices that automate the process of integrating code changes, testing them, and deploying them to production.

In the distributed architecture of micro frontends, this process is consequently distributed across each implementation as well as the shell application, following a structure similar to the diagram:

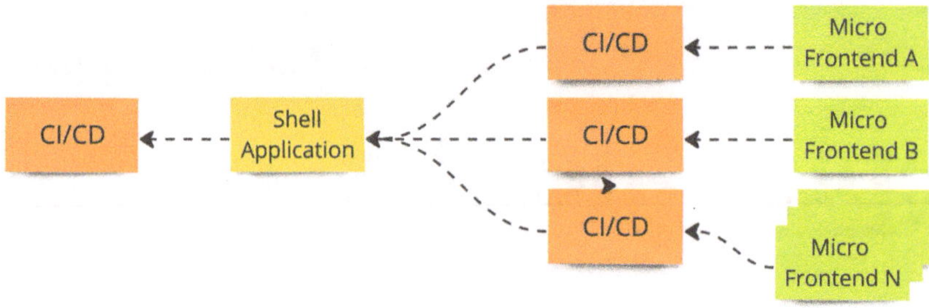

Figure 10.1: CI/CD

This simplified diagram illustrates the relationship between multiple micro frontends and their respective CI/CD pipelines. In some cases, changes to a micro frontend may trigger a CI/CD process in the shell application for additional integration testing. This is an optional step, dependent on the specific implementation.

When discussing CI/CD in the context of micro frontend architecture, the primary focus is on determining the necessary guarantees for each implementation. We refer to this as CI/CD design.

While the architecture provides deployment independence, it is essential to establish minimum quality standards.

In the following sections, we will outline a set of best practices. These guidelines are not rigid rules but rather recommendations based on successful micro frontend implementations.

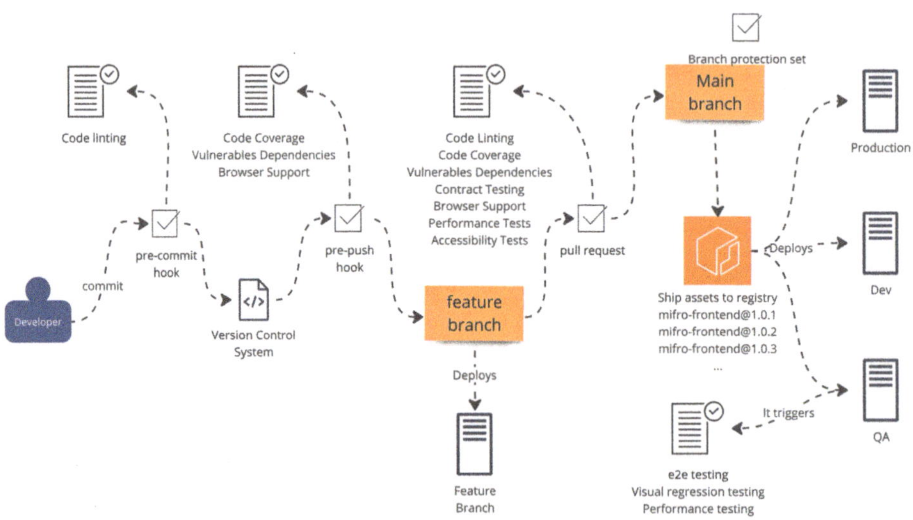

Figure 10.2: CI/CD Design

In this scheme, we have established a CI/CD design that begins with the developer making a commit on their machine to a version control system (git in most cases). This action triggers a code linting check, ensuring company-wide definitions regarding code style and formatting (if applicable).

Note: *Code linting is the process of analyzing source code to identify potential errors, bugs, stylistic inconsistencies, or suspicious constructs.*

This process continues until the developer decides to publish its local changes (from a local feature branch) into a remote feature where the following tests are performed: unit tests, code coverage, dependency vulnerabilities, and browser support. With this setup, we ensure faster feedback to the development team regarding common errors.

An important note about code coverage: as a general rule, unit tests are quick to execute and therefore suitable for running directly on the developer's computer. However, in some scenarios, this assumption may not hold true, potentially causing some friction in the developer experience. Nonetheless, this scenario would be considered an exception, and improvements to the unit tests would therefore be necessary.

Once these checks are completed and accepted, creating a new feature branch on the remote triggers the provisioning of an on-demand environment, (more details of the upcoming section: *On-demand Environments*) where the feature can be tested by the quality team and interested stakeholders even before merging into the main branch. This approach is particularly useful in the context of trunk-based development, aiming to keep the main branch more stable.

Note: *Trunk-Based Development (TBD) is a branching strategy where all developers work in a single main branch (the trunk) rather than using long-lived feature branches. Changes are integrated frequently, usually multiple times a day, to maintain a continuously deployable codebase.*

Once a feature is considered complete and ready to be merged into the main branch, a pull request is created. It is crucial to ensure the protection of this main branch, guaranteeing that no code is added without going through the proper pull request process. Otherwise, the guarantees provided by the CI/CD pipeline are compromised.

This pull request process triggers checks for the following: code linting, code coverage, vulnerable dependencies, contract testing, browser support, performance testing, and accessibility tests. To ensure that all frontends follow the same CI/CD process, and all the checks are performed across the whole micro frontend ecosystem, a parameterized pipeline, such as GitHub's workflow, can be used.

Once these checks are satisfied, along with other branch protection requirements—potentially including a minimum number of approvals from peer developers, among others—the process of releasing the generated assets (container image or static files in some cases) begins.

The different versions are stored in the specific registry (enabling, as we will see next, Blue-Green Deployment) and later used in the different environments.

The process by which these artifacts are deployed to their respective environments (QA, staging, production, and so on) is not detailed here, but GitOps practices are commonly used.

Note: *GitOps is a set of practices that use Git as the single source of truth for managing infrastructure and application deployment. It involves storing declarative infrastructure and application configurations in a Git repository, which are then automatically applied and maintained by a* Continuous Delivery (CD) tool *(such as* Argo *CD or Flux). More info: https://about.gitlab.com/topics/gitops/*

Lastly, among the various environments, it is expected to have one that is different from both the development and production environments, with the purpose of not impacting the development team or the system's users, respectively. In the scheme, this is referred to as the QA environment, where more extensive and demanding tests, such as end-to-end testing, visual regression testing, and performance testing, can be carried out. This environment is expected to have data closely resembling the production environment to make these tests as realistic as possible.

The scenario described outlines a process commonly found in scalable application setups. Although micro frontend architecture does not prescribe a specific approach, the closer the deployment processes are across the various micro frontends, the easier it will be to maintain them.

On-demand Environments

An on-demand environment (also known as a preview deployment environment) is a temporary, automatically provisioned runtime environment that reflects the current state of a feature or code branch. These environments are typically created dynamically in response to specific events–such as the creation of a pull request or a feature branch–and are used to preview, test, or validate changes before they are merged into the main branch.

In distributed systems architectures, preview environments ideally should include only the changed components (for example, a micro frontend and its backend) or a combination of multiple components, needed in order to have the feature properly tested, and deployed together in specific versions. This strategy allows for faster iterations and reduces the cognitive overhead of full system deployment.

Therefore on-demand environments must support branch pairing or matrix-based deployments, where a combination of branches from different services are deployed together in a single environment.

Some teams address this by tagging related feature branches with metadata or using custom CI/CD pipelines that allow defining a set of repositories and branches to be deployed together. Others adopt manifest-based deployment descriptors or shared configuration files that describe which versions of each service should be used in a given preview. These solutions enable more realistic end-to-end (E2E) testing in pre-merge stages, improving the feedback loop while reducing the risk of integration failures later.

Blue-Green Deployment

Blue-Green Deployment is a deployment strategy that reduces downtime and risk by running two production environments, called Blue and Green. One environment (for example, Blue) is the active version currently serving users, while the other (for example, Green) is the new version of the application ready for deployment.

When working with the micro frontend architecture, an important nuance is that releases are typically limited in scope to a specific micro frontend, which inherently reduces the risk of downtime across the system. This architectural trait opens the door for blue-green deployments at both global and local scopes.

In tightly coupled systems–where the shell application and micro frontends are versioned and deployed together–blue-green deployment often applies to the full application stack. In contrast, with runtime composition strategies (More details in *Chapter 5, Integration Strategies*), teams can manage blue-green deployments for their micro frontends independently. Each team can maintain its own Blue and Green environments and control traffic routing at the CDN, service discovery, or manifest level. This independence enhances team autonomy and limits the blast radius of a failed release.

In the specific case of implementing blue-green deployment, these two environments should be seen from a development perspective as an additional environment in the release process. In the following figure, we focus on the artifact distribution workflow generated in each of the environments:

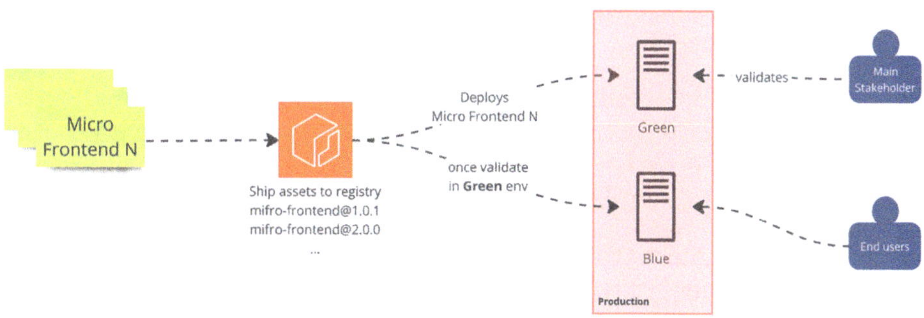

Figure 10.3: *Blue-Green Deployment*

The artifact registry, as previously mentioned, stores the various versions of a given micro frontend. In the blue-green deployment process, the artifact is first made available on a "Blue" server, which is identical to the "Green" server.

This deployment is validated by a group of stakeholders, QA teams, and other interested parties. Only after their review and approval is the release made available on the "Green" server and consequently to end users.

A side benefit of this strategy is redundancy in case of failures. In the event of an outage on the green server, the blue server takes over, thus reducing the chances of system downtime.

Canary Releases

A Canary Release is a deployment strategy that gradually rolls out a new version of an application to a small subset of users before fully deploying it to the entire user base.

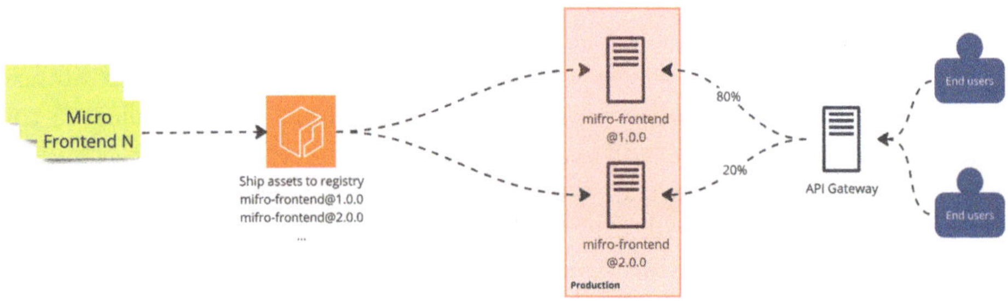

Figure 10.4: *Canary release*

In the scenario above, we have a diagram similar to Blue-Green Deployment but with quite different approaches. In the production environment, we have both versions of the software available: micro-frontend@1.0.0, the stable version, accessible to most users (80%), with this control being managed by an API gateway, and the "canary" version micro-frontend@2.0.0, where new features are gradually introduced, in this specific case to 20% of users.

Naturally, the criteria for distributing the canary release are not limited to traffic percentages; any other criteria the team feels comfortable with can be used. The key aspect of this approach is to define criteria that allow for efficient monitoring of the feature. More on this topic in *Chapter 11, Observability*.

The canary release, combined with the feature flags technique, enables more targeted testing, focusing on specific features or user groups within the canary release and better controlling the exposure of new features within the canary release. This is achieved by enabling certain features only for the canary group, allowing for more granular control.

Ultimately, it enables issue isolation–if a specific feature within the canary release causes problems, it can be quickly disabled using the corresponding flag, minimizing the impact on the overall release.

Note: *Feature flags are a software development technique that allows developers to control the availability of specific features or functionalities within an application at runtime, without requiring a new code deployment, an approach strongly encouraged by trunk-based development. More details at: https://trunkbaseddevelopment.com/feature-flags/*

The following diagram illustrates the approach:

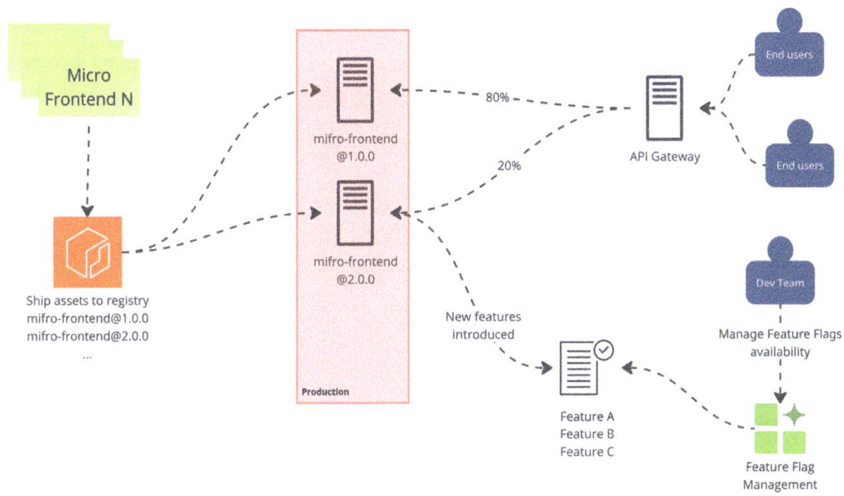

Figure 10.5: *Canary Release + Feature Flags*

In this scenario, a feature flag management platform is introduced, responsible for managing the various feature flags within the system. Specifically, in the case of the canary release, three new features (A, B, and C) have been added, which can be managed by the dev team or any other responsible stakeholder, allowing for gradual control of each feature. This adds an extra layer of safety to the deployment.*

Note: A *feature management platform is a software system that provides a centralized and controlled way to manage the release and delivery of software features. It leverages feature flags to allow developers to control the availability of specific features within an application at runtime. Some relevant platforms in the field worth mentioning: LaunchDarkly, Flagsmith, Split.io, Unleash.*

Regarding the use of feature flags, it is highly recommended, especially in distributed architectures, to use a feature flag management platform since managing these feature flags can easily get out of control. Proper processes related to their management lifecycle should be well established, and their usage be standardized.

We have participated in many discussions where a thorough investigation was necessary to determine the total number of feature flags required for a specific system module to function correctly. This often stems from a lack of visibility and control over the feature flag lifecycle. Flags are frequently added for temporary purposes–such as experiments, rollouts, or hotfixes–but without clear processes for their documentation, ownership, and removal, they tend to accumulate. This creates "flag debt," where outdated or unused flags linger in the codebase, increasing complexity and making it harder to reason about system behavior. In distributed architectures, where multiple teams may interact with the same modules, this becomes even more problematic. A feature flag management platform can provide tooling support, but it is not a silver bullet–teams must also establish and follow strong lifecycle governance practices to ensure flags remain useful and do not become liabilities.

Not to mention testing the feature flags themselves–it is important to ensure that they are truly toggling functionality as intended. One common issue is that a flag may appear to be off, yet parts of the feature might still be accessible due to incomplete guarding (for example, UI elements hidden but APIs still callable). In larger systems, this can lead to inconsistent behavior, hidden bugs, or even security issues. This makes it essential to test not just the feature, but the flag's behavior across all relevant environments, user roles, and entry points. In other words, the flag becomes a part of the system's logic and needs the same level of validation as any other code path. As always in life, there is no free lunch, and their introduction should be considered with moderation.

Finally, a beneficial side effect of this deployment strategy is the possibility of A/B testing (also known as split testing or bucket testing), which is a method used to compare two versions–the stable and the canary versions of a given app (in our case, micro-frontend)–to determine which one performs better. This deployment strategy, combined with a proper observability setup, can provide great insights into the released feature.

Conclusion

With these analyses, we conclude our chapter. Although deployment approaches for systems–and more specifically for frontend and micro frontend applications–are diverse, we understand, through a constant examination of successful and unsuccessful cases in the software industry, that these approaches enable the effective implementation of micro frontend architecture.

These approaches provide a valuable toolbox for practitioners to use as a guide and to adjust practices according to the specific needs of the system. They foster a robust deployment pipeline that balances speed and stability. They empower teams to continuously deliver value to users while mitigating risks associated with distributed deployments. By adopting these strategies, organizations can enhance their delivery velocity, minimize disruptions, and maintain a high standard of software quality, ultimately achieving a more resilient and adaptable micro frontend architecture.

In the next chapter, we will continue with an analysis of post-release techniques—that is, actions that, supported by a solid deployment process, aim to provide insight into the system's behavior in production. We will explore the main observability techniques for micro frontend architectures.

References

1. https://about.gitlab.com/topics/gitops/
2. https://trunkbaseddevelopment.com/feature-flags/
3. https://launchdarkly.com/
4. https://www.flagsmith.com/
5. https://www.split.io/
6. https://www.getunleash.io/

CHAPTER 11
Observability

Introduction

In this chapter, we will expand on the discussions initiated in *Chapter 4, Micro Frontend Foundations - Highly Observable*, focusing on techniques and tools to achieve the desired level of observability in distributed systems–in our case, micro frontends.

As a reference, we use the previously established definition:

"Observability is a measure of how well **internal states of a system** can be inferred from knowledge of its **external outputs**" - R.E. Kálmán, 1960

Therefore, we will analyze approaches to having external outputs that enable the later inference of a system's internal states.

Structure

In this chapter, we will cover the following topics:

- Context
- Application Metrics
- Logging
- Tracing
- Error Tracking

Context

Before we dive into definitions, implementation details, and finally the specifics concerning micro frontend architecture, it is important to understand where our discussion stands on this long and winding path of developing scalable frontend systems.

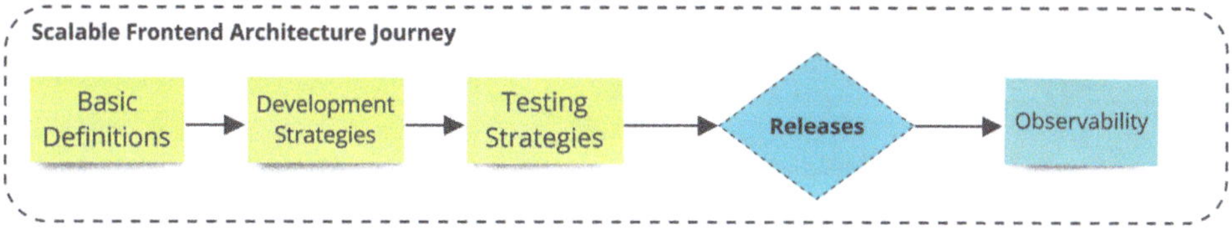

Figure 11.1: *Scalable Frontend Architecture Journey*

Our discussions so far have been centered around the process, specifically the pre-release phase. In other words, all the necessary activities (architectural definitions, development and testing strategies, and implementations, among others) are required before releases begin to happen.

It is important to highlight the multifaceted nature of the release process, which is a fundamental characteristic of micro frontend architecture. Although the diagram described above appears linear, this process is cyclical (considering the scope of a given team that performs multiple iterations, producing and requiring various release processes) and parallel (considering that, at a given moment, multiple teams work on different features simultaneously).

Therefore, the content discussed regarding observability refers to monitoring the system at run-time, in the wild, aiming to provide feedback that can feed back to development teams with relevant data about system performance–specifically, the performance experienced by end-users rather than in isolated environments, such as those used in the various types of testing explored in *Chapter* 9, *Testing Strategies*.

Application Metrics

Application metrics are quantitative data points that provide insights into the behavior, performance, and health of an application. They are typically numerical values collected over time, enabling teams to monitor, analyze, and understand the application's internal state and performance characteristics.

We see them as the most basic observability building blocks, just as companies establish Objective Key Results (OKRs) to know how well the 'health' of the company is doing. The same reasoning is applied to systems and (for better and for worse, the same difficulties). Who has never witnessed managers "adjusting perspectives" around certain OKRs to reflect a supposed desired performance?

Nevertheless, a similar situation is often found with certain application metrics, which due to a lack of clear definition or in many cases, their absence, or rather, the absence of mechanisms that enable the collection of such metrics, generate situations of uncertainty regarding the state of a particular system or component thereof.

These application metrics can be categorized based on their applicability into 4 categories:

Performance Metrics

Metrics that measure the speed and efficiency of the application. They focus on how quickly and smoothly the application responds to user requests and processes data.

Examples:

- **Response Time**: How long it takes for the application to respond to a user action (for example, clicking a button, submitting a form).
- **Latency**: The delay before a transfer of data begins following an instruction for its transfer.
- **Throughput**: The amount of data or number of transactions processed by the application in a given time.
- **CPU Utilization**: The percentage of processing power being used by the application.
- **Memory Usage**: The amount of memory the application is consuming.

Availability and Reliability Metrics

Metrics that measure the uptime and stability of the application. They indicate how often the application is accessible to users and how well it performs without errors or crashes.

Examples:

- **Uptime**: The percentage of time your application is running and available.
- **Downtime**: The amount of time your application is unavailable.
- **Error Rate**: The percentage of requests that result in errors.
- **Crash Rate**: How often the application crashes or becomes unresponsive.
- **Mean Time To Failure (MTTF)**: The average time a system or component functions before failing.

Business Metrics

Metrics that track how the application contributes to the business goals. They provide insights into user behavior, conversions, and revenue.

Examples:

- **Conversion Rate**: The percentage of users who complete a desired action (for example, making a purchase, signing up for a newsletter).

- **User Engagement**: How users interact with your application (for example, time spent on site, pages visited).
- **Customer Churn**: The rate at which customers stop using your application.
- **Revenue**: The amount of money generated by your application.
- **Number of Active Users**: The count of users actively engaging with the application.

These metrics are mainly driven by product teams, and quite often used in distinct tools, they are not much concerned with the system internals and their individual components, but rather with the system general adoption.

Custom Application Metrics

Metrics that are defined specifically for the application's (or micro frontend application) unique needs and characteristics. They may not fall into the other categories and are tailored to track specific aspects of your application's behavior or performance.

Examples:

- **Number of API calls**: If your application relies on APIs, you might track the number of calls made to those APIs.
- **Queue Length**: If your application uses queues for processing tasks, you might track the length of those queues.
- **Specific feature usage**: You might track how often users utilize a particular feature of your application.
- **Game-specific metrics**: If it is a game, you might track player levels reached, items collected, and so on.

With respect to Performance Metrics and Availability and Reliability Metrics, their numbers may differ (likely the user-facing micro frontend application that users use to make payments will have higher performance, availability, and reliability requirements than a micro frontend responsible for internal system controls, for example). However, these are metrics necessary for all implementations.

As for Business Metrics, in most implementations, the main concern is to provide features to the software that allow it to be monitored by external applications.

Last but not least, the definition of Custom Application Metrics based on the specific needs of a given micro frontend is naturally the responsibility of the team.

The relationship between these different metrics and the micro frontend architecture can be outlined as shown in the following figure:

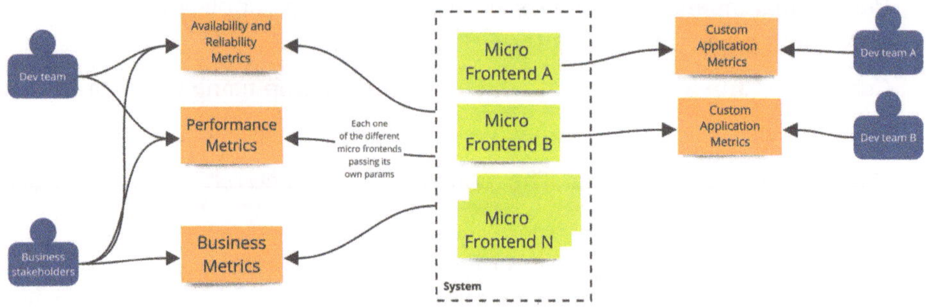

Figure 11.2: *Application Metrics*

Based on a set of defined availability and reliability, performance, and business metrics, and potentially some custom metrics required by individual micro frontends, the running micro frontend instances are expected to provide these metrics. Some of them, mostly the ones belonging to the availability and reliability metrics, can be automatically inferred based on the environment; for instance, an error rate metric could be collected automatically by a generic error handling available in the Shell Application, more on that in the *Error Tracking* section, while some others, mainly the business related metrics, will require active team's efforts, mostly for integrating with some web analytic software but not restricted to the same.

Note: *Web analytics software is a type of software that collects, measures, analyzes, and reports data about how users interact with websites or web applications.*

Logging

It is still memorable how Redux's time travel debugging showcased the ability to inspect and replay a sequence of user actions—effectively traveling back and forth in an application's state history. This was particularly impactful for understanding how a specific outcome resulted from a chain of interactions.

In distributed systems, achieving similar visibility is far more complex. One key challenge is consolidating user actions that span multiple independently deployed components. Client-side composition via run time integrations, for instance, by enabling teams to integrate independently built micro frontends at runtime, can facilitate cross-component user experiences. However, tracking and coordinating state across federated modules is non-trivial. Unlike Redux in a monolith, there is no built-in mechanism for time travel or unified state inspection. Developers must implement custom event tracing or shared telemetry pipelines, which can increase complexity and reduce reliability.

Other integration strategies, such as build-time or edge-side composition, offer different trade-offs. For example, server-side rendering can more easily centralize logs and user interactions, but at the cost of runtime flexibility. Each approach must balance observability, performance, and decoupling, depending on the system's requirements.

Note: *Redux is a predictable state container for JavaScript applications, commonly used with libraries such as React. It helps manage the state of an application in a centralized way, ensuring that state updates are predictable and traceable.*

Regarding log collection between backend services, the current practices are generally much more advanced. In contrast, client-side user monitoring is often limited–sometimes even nonexistent–primarily due to privacy regulations such as GDPR and data minimization principles. These legal constraints restrict the collection of user-specific data (such as IP addresses, click behavior, or device identifiers), making it harder to gather the same depth of telemetry. As a result, client-side logs usually focus on capturing only essential information, such as runtime errors or performance issues.

This scenario, while not exclusive to micro frontend architecture, tends to become more complex in this context due to its distributed nature. Therefore, establishing a clear policy that defines what, when, and how data can be collected is essential to prevent the previously mentioned issue–the complete absence of logs.

Note: *While backend applications are typically instrumented to produce logs for system-level observability, frontend applications are more focused on producing user monitoring data – giving insight into real-world user interactions and experience.*

Best Practices for Data Privacy and Security:

- Implement robust masking and redaction techniques to prevent the capture of Personal Identifiable Information (PII).
- Anonymize user behavior data to prevent it from being linked back to individual users.
- Store logs data securely, with appropriate access controls and encryption.
- Implement clear data retention policies.
- Ensure compliance with relevant data privacy regulations.
- Be transparent with users about the use of logs and provide them with the option to opt-out.
- Conduct thorough due diligence on third-party vendors and ensure that they have strong data privacy and security practices.

Lastly, regarding the log format itself, although it is of lesser importance compared to log collection, having a well-structured format greatly facilitates log tracing and comprehension.

The following schema proposes an implementation of the aforementioned components:

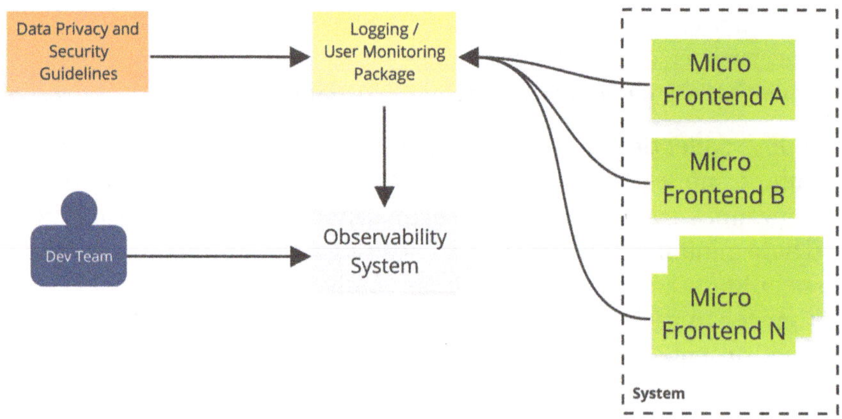

Figure 11.3: *Logging*

The core concept is: based on a set of data privacy and security guidelines, a Logging Package, in the context of Server-side Template or Edge-side Composition, or a User Monitoring Package, in the context of Client-side composition–for example, an npm package–exposes an API to its consumers (micro frontends), allowing them to record logs. This package then handles all the necessary data privacy and security requirements, ensuring standardization and security in log collection across multiple teams working on micro frontends.

A similar pattern is commonly found in microservices architectures, meaning this is not necessarily a new idea. The novelty here lies in its application within frontend development.

These logs are then made available in an observability system, where they can be leveraged by the development team.

It is important to note that this is a common scenario in scalable systems, and as a result, a wide range of tools exist to address it. Solutions such as *Datadog*, AWS *Cloudwatch*, and *Grafana Loki* provide extensive capabilities not only for logging but also for the overall observability of distributed systems. Consequently, custom-built solutions should generally be avoided.

Tracing

Tracing refers to the technique used to track the flow of a request as it travels through different services in a distributed system. As for the micro frontend architecture context, tracing focuses on tracking the flow of a user request or event across multiple services or components – in this case, across different micro frontends and potentially their corresponding backend services.

It is the usage of the logs and the user monitoring data collected from the various microservices and/or micro frontends to track how the end user interacts with the system. Allowing therefore a 360° view of the system, enabling teams to trace a user click through micro frontends and into backend microservices – and back again when things go wrong.

Another technique that has proven valuable in distributed systems, in the context of user monitoring, is session replay collection. It essentially records a user's session, capturing everything from mouse movements and clicks to form inputs, scrolling, and network requests. This recording can then be played back later, providing a detailed view of the user's experience.

What they capture:

- **User interactions**: Mouse movements, clicks, taps, scrolls, form submissions, and other user inputs.
- **DOM state**: The structure and content of the web page as it changes over time. This includes HTML, CSS, and JavaScript modifications.
- **Network requests**: API calls, resource loading (images, scripts, and so on), and their responses.
- **Console logs**: JavaScript errors, warnings, and other messages logged in the browser's console.
- **Timing information**: Performance metrics such as page load time, interaction latency, and resource loading times.
- **User metadata**: Information about the user's browser, operating system, device, and location.

When used together, these three techniques (logging + user data monitoring + session replay collection) provide a distinct level of system tracing capability, and we have seen several successful cases of their implementation.

Relevant factors to consider when using them once again relate to data privacy and security, as discussed in the previous section. Additionally, regarding session replays, there are concerns about performance impact due to the large volume of collected data. Storage costs should also be taken into account, making it essential to define an appropriate data retention period.

Error Tracking

Error tracking is the process of monitoring, capturing, and analyzing errors that occur in software applications, whether they are web applications, mobile apps, desktop software, or backend services. It can be seen as a specialized subset or byproduct of logging, focused specifically on the detection and management of error-level events. While logging records a wide range of application activity across various levels (such as debug, info, warn, and error), error tracking specifically focuses on the error-related entries within the broader set of logs, extracting structured insights–such as stack traces, user context, and frequency–to help developers prioritize and resolve critical issues efficiently.

Definitions understood, error tracking is the de facto concern of engineering. In its most basic implementation, we rely on our users as the primary "tool" for error tracking–who has not worked on systems where bug reports, often from end users, were the main source of issue detection?

As crazy as it may sound, this scenario is not an exception–just like jQuery is still not an exception today (jokes aside). However, the focus here is not to argue the importance of error tracking but rather, in the context of micro frontend architecture, to ensure proper handling so that the responsible teams are alerted when such incidents occur.

At a given moment, User X, while using Application Y, encounters an error. If this application follows a horizontal slicing approach, multiple micro frontends may coexist at that moment. When it comes to error handling, some key characteristics are desirable:

- **Scoping**: An error generated by Micro Frontend A should clearly reflect its origin. Otherwise, we risk a chaotic situation where multiple teams investigate the same error without sufficient information about its source. This is definitely something we want to avoid.
- **Isolation**: Ideally, an error in one application should not cause errors in another.

The micro frontend architecture integration strategy (for more details, please refer to *Chapter 5, Integration Strategies*) significantly influences the approach and complexity of error tracking.

Vertical Slicing inherently creates an isolated environment between different micro frontends. Each page in the system may generate an error, which is captured by an error tracking system and easily reported.

As for Horizontal Slicing, the Run-time Integration via iFrames also provides strong isolation guarantees. Since each micro frontend runs within its own iframe, errors can be easily traced back to their source. However, integration with Run-time Integration via JavaScript, Run-time Integration via Web Components, and Client-side Composition in Native Apps introduce significant complexity in terms of error scoping and isolation.

Because from the perspective of the client (browser or native application), all micro frontends appear as a single application, so distinguishing them relies on each micro frontend properly handling errors.

Tooling wise, we are well-equipped in this area, as most modern frameworks provide error boundary implementations. For example, in React, we can use the following implementation:

```
import { useEffect } from "react";
import { ErrorBoundary } from "react-error-boundary";

function fallbackRender({ error, resetErrorBoundary }) {
  // Call resetErrorBoundary() to reset the error boundary and retry the render.

  useEffect(() => {
    logError({
      error,
      extra: {
        microFrontend: "micro-frontend-b",
        version: "2.0.0",
        // ... other context
      },
    });
  }, [error]);

  return (
    <div role="alert">
      <p>Something went wrong:</p>
      <strong>{error.message}</strong>
    </div>
  );
}

<ErrorBoundary
  fallbackRender={fallbackRender}
  onReset={(details) => {
    // Reset the state of your app so the error doesn't happen again
  }}
>
  <ExampleApplication />
</ErrorBoundary>;
```

Figure 11.4: *React Error Boundaries*

In this example, the application is encapsulated by an *ErrorBoundary* React component, which logs the error while adding information about the specific micro frontend–in this case, *micro-frontend-b*.

However, the challenge becomes more intriguing when dealing with JavaScript and, consequently, browser clients, due to the Event Loop. This means that all asynchronous operations, such as network requests, timers, user inputs, and element events (for example, clicks, mouseover, keydown, and so on), are affected.

Errors occurring in these events are not captured by React's error boundaries. Although there is an interface available to detect them (Window: error event), it provides limited information regarding the origin of the error.

Note: *The Event Loop is a crucial mechanism in JavaScript (and environments such as Node.js and browsers) that allows it to be asynchronous and non-blocking. JavaScript is single-threaded, meaning it can only execute one piece of code at a time. However, many operations (such as network requests, timers, user input) are inherently asynchronous – they take time to complete. The Event Loop manages these asynchronous operations so that the main thread is not blocked while waiting for them.*

```
const microFrontends = [
  {
    name: "micro-frontend-a",
    source: "micro-frontend-a.bundle.js",
  },
  {
    name: "micro-frontend-b",
    source: "micro-frontend-b.bundle.js",
  },
];

window.onerror = (message, source, lineno, colno, error) => {
  let microFrontend = undefined;

  for (const mf of microFrontends) {
    if (source.includes(mf.source)) {
      microFrontend = mf.name;
      break;
    }
  }

  logError({
    error,
    extra: {
      microFrontend: microFrontend, // Best guess
    },
  });
};
```

Figure 11.5: *Event Loop Error tracking*

In this implementation, based on the source parameter available in the *window.onerror* event interface, we infer which micro frontend generated the error.

It is important to highlight that this approach is not highly reliable, as errors may originate from shared dependencies. Still, it can be used as a last resort, assuming that each micro frontend has implemented the expected exception handlers using *try-catch* structures—though this assumption also does not provide strong guarantees.

```
// In micro-frontend A:
try {
  // ... code that might throw
} catch (error) {
  logError({
    error,
    extra: {
      microFrontend: "micro-frontend-a",
      version: "1.2.3",
      // ... other context
    },
  });
}

// In micro-frontend B:
try {
  // ... code that might throw
} catch (error) {
  logError({
    error,
    extra: {
      microFrontend: "micro-frontend-b",
      version: "2.0.0",
      // ... other context
    },
  });
}
```

Figure 11.6: *Exception Handling in Each Micro Frontend*

The preceding scenario highlights some key premises for error handling implementations in each micro frontend.

The diagram that follows outlines a general approach to error tracking:

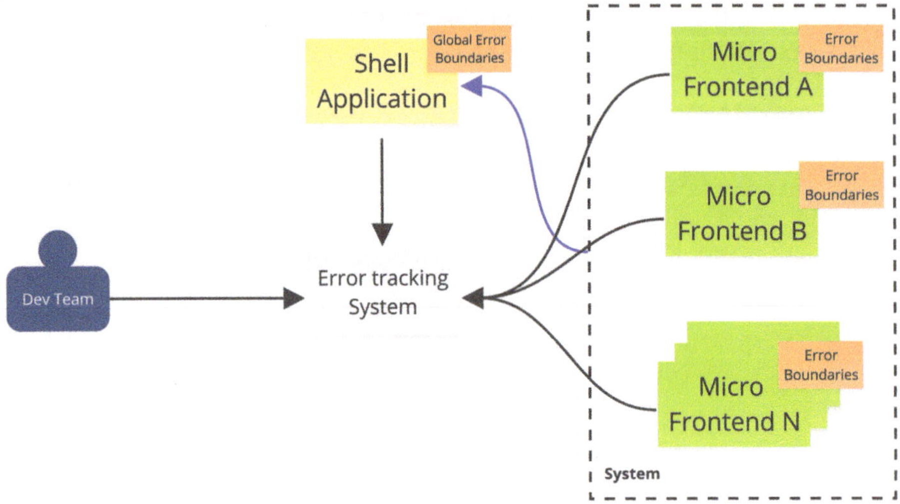

Figure 11.7: *Error Tracking*

In this scenario, each micro frontend implements its respective error boundaries and error tracking, for example, through React *ErrorBoundaries* or any other mechanism available in the respective framework, or by using try..catch structures. If an error is not handled by the specific micro frontend, it propagates to the Shell Application, which, through a "global error boundary"–such as the *window.onerror* event interface (or any other similar mechanism available on the platform, such as *Thread.setDefaultUncaughtExceptionHandler* on Android, *NSSetUncaughtExceptionHandler* on iOS applications, and so on)–attempts to filter the error's origin (*Figure 11.5*) and then report it to the error tracking system.

However, it is important to emphasize that this approach mainly applies to integration with horizontal slicing. For vertical slicing, the approach would be much simpler, considering that at any given time, only a single micro frontend can be running, and therefore, there is only one possible error origin.

Note: *An error tracking system (also called an application monitoring system or exception tracking system) is a tool that helps developers detect, log, analyze, and resolve errors in software applications. These systems provide insights into application failures by capturing stack traces, error messages, affected users, and environmental details. Well-known systems are: Sentry, Datadog Error Tracking, and New Relic Errors Inbox.*

Conclusion

With these considerations regarding error tracking in micro frontend architectures, we come to the end of another chapter. These points should provide a checklist of relevant items to review when implementing error handling in the system.

With this chapter, we also conclude the main themes related to the implementation of micro frontends in scalable systems. While this is not an exhaustive list, based on market observations, we understand that these points are critical to the success of both the architecture and the system as a whole.

Next, we will conclude our work with a case study on a micro frontend implementation, taking into account: Context, Business Requirements, Organization Structure, Tech Stack, Architectural Considerations, Implementation Strategies, Challenges Faced, and Main Outcomes. This will allow us to analyze and understand the concepts explored so far and provide the reader with a more practical understanding of the architecture.

References

1. https://www.datadoghq.com/
2. https://grafana.com/oss/loki/
3. https://aws.amazon.com/cloudwatch/
4. https://developer.mozilla.org/en-US/docs/Web/API/Window/error_event
5. https://developer.android.com/reference/java/lang/Thread.UncaughtExceptionHandler
6. https://developer.apple.com/documentation/foundation/1409609-nssetuncaughtexceptionhandler
7. https://sentry.io/
8. https://www.datadoghq.com/product/error-tracking/
9. https://docs.newrelic.com/docs/errors-inbox/errors-inbox/

CHAPTER 12
A Micro Frontend Adoption

Introduction

Having understood the key concepts, implementation strategies, and supporting disciplines necessary for the micro frontend architecture, let us imagine that in the past few weeks, you have worked tirelessly to promote these concepts, explaining to key stakeholders how crucial and essential the micro frontend architecture will be for the evolution of your company's system. Finally, you received approval from the C-level executives to move forward with its implementation.

The next question is about the necessary steps for this implementation. What actions must be taken for this adoption? How detailed should the overall implementation strategy be? What commitments should be established between teams? What expectations should be managed? What risks should be mitigated? And many other questions that typically arise along the way.

While it is neither feasible nor realistic to attempt to answer all these questions in this brief analysis, this chapter aims to provide a real-world context for implementing the architecture. It will demonstrate the previously explored concepts in a practical scenario, contrasting theory and practice, the ideal versus the feasible, and the conceptually expected against the constraints of time, budget, and all other factors typically present in large corporations.

Note: *To ensure the confidentiality and privacy of the individuals, companies, and projects referenced throughout this chapter, all sensitive information has been anonymized. Names, organizational structures, timelines, technologies, and other identifying details have been altered or generalized. In some cases, scenarios have been synthesized or merged from multiple sources to illustrate key points without revealing proprietary information. While the experiences are inspired by real-world situations, the representations here are fictionalized and intended solely for educational and illustrative purposes.*

Structure

In this chapter, we will cover the following topics:

- Context
- Business Requirements
- Organization Structure
- Tech Stack
- Architectural Considerations
- Challenges Faced
- Main Outcomes
- Other Relevant Use Case
- Future of Micro Frontends
- Artificial Intelligence and Micro Frontends

Context

Acquisition processes, especially in dynamic sectors such as technology, are nothing new–they are relatively common. Large corporations frequently use acquisitions as a strategy for continuous growth. Such processes bring significant challenges and opportunities, particularly in the field of software development.

To illustrate these challenges, consider a scenario in which a company has recently formed a new group by acquiring three different software platforms. Each platform aims to help businesses manage reservations, appointments, and bookings for their services through features such as online booking, calendar management, payment integrations, customizable workflows, reporting, and analytics.

Although their goals were similar, the systems differ significantly in their approaches, strategies, user interfaces, and architectures. The newly formed group now faces the complex task of unifying these distinct systems. Achieving technological convergence across the platforms is essential for the group's success – and highlights the typical challenges that arise during software integration after an acquisition.

Business Requirements

Among the main business requirements, we can list:

Unified Booking Experience

- Ensure a consistent user experience across all customer-facing platforms.
- Develop a decentralized booking system that supports all core functionalities (for example, calendar management, payments, reporting).

- Allow for multi-brand theming and customization to maintain brand identity for existing customers.

Consistent and Intuitive User Experience

- Maintain a cohesive design language while allowing some customization for different brands.
- Ensure intuitive navigation across all user types (business owners, staff, and customers).

System Interoperability and Data Consolidation

- Establish a data migration strategy to unify customer, booking, and payment data without disruption.
- Implement data deduplication and synchronization mechanisms to prevent inconsistencies.

Modular and Scalable Architecture

- Design a modular architecture to allow incremental migration of features.
- Ensure high availability and fault tolerance to maintain uptime during the transition.
- Support multi-tenant capabilities to serve businesses of different sizes and needs.

Harmonized User Roles and Permissions

- Define a common user management system with Role-Based Access Control (RBAC).
- Ensure smooth authentication and authorization mechanisms, including SSO and OAuth support.

With these requirements established, the development team can set a direction to guide their actions and priorities, aligning these requirements with non-functional aspects and time-to-market goals.

Regarding project deadlines, quarterly milestones have been defined to ensure continuous deliveries, initially focusing on a basic product for new users and later on migrations for existing users.

Organization Structure

Given the diverse geographical locations of the development teams (spread among three different continents) and the technological divergence among the systems (monolith vs. distributed architectures at different migration stages), the organization structure aimed to facilitate collaboration, efficiency, and alignment while accounting for time zones, cultural differences, and varying levels of system maturity.

Teams were distributed along the regions together with business domains so that they could have maximum autonomy in their decisions.

A Platform Team spanning all the regions was established to provide foundational services (authentication, APIs, observability, CI/CD pipelines, and so on) as well as maintenance of the pre-existing platforms.

A Quality Assurance also spanning all the regions was established in order to guarantee that all integrations work as expected and lead the efforts on testing and quality checks across all the platforms.

Regional Autonomy with Global Alignment:

While teams in each region may work semi-autonomously on specific aspects of the system, a shared governance structure, as the following was defined:

- Architecture Review Board to standardize patterns and practices;
- Tech Leads Sync meetings to align on challenges and progress;
- Shared Engineering Principles to maintain consistency despite regional differences.

Lastly, UI/UX representatives were delegated to each one of the team, so the global initiatives, mainly related to design system definitions were easily propagated.

The organization structure, focusing on the development teams, can be depicted as the following:

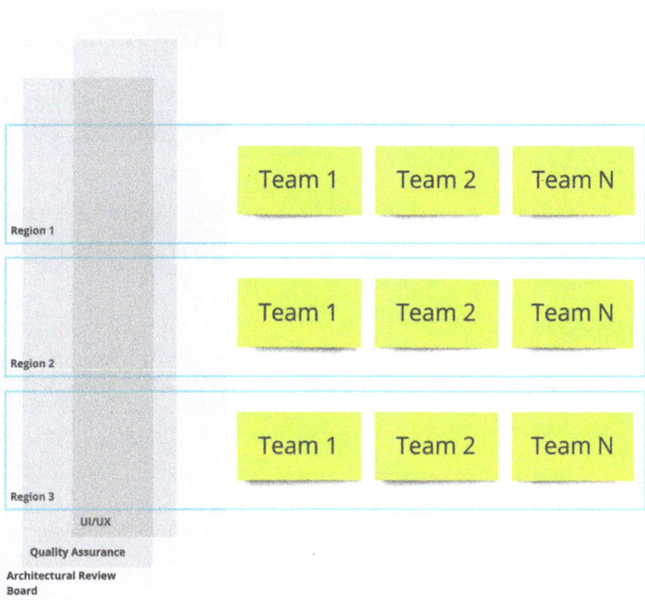

Figure 12.1: *Organization Structure*

Basically, we have business-focused teams distributed per region with intersecting points with UI/UX, Quality Assurance, and Architectural functional teams.

Communication and Collaboration Challenges

Due to the time zone differences, asynchronous communication was heavily enforced, with reliance on documentation, RFCs (Request for Comments)), and decision logs.

Tech Stack

As one might expect, the technology stacks across regions were varied, though some patterns emerged. The following is a generalized breakdown of typical tech stacks found across different units:

In region 1:

- Monolithic architecture
- Backend: PHP with a popular enterprise framework (for example, Symfony/Laravel)
- Frontend: React + TypeScript
- UI: Material UI + Legacy Self-Developed UI Library

In region 2:

- Monolithic and distributed systems
- Backend: Java with a popular enterprise framework (for example, Spring)
- Frontend: React + TypeScript + Next.js
- UI: Headless UI components with custom integrations

In region 3:

A Distributed Application Stack

- NestJS
- React + TypeScript
- Material UI

A Legacy Application Stack

- PHP with an E-commerce Framework
- jQuery

This constellation of technologies, as well as their respective applications, can generally be visualized with the following diagram:

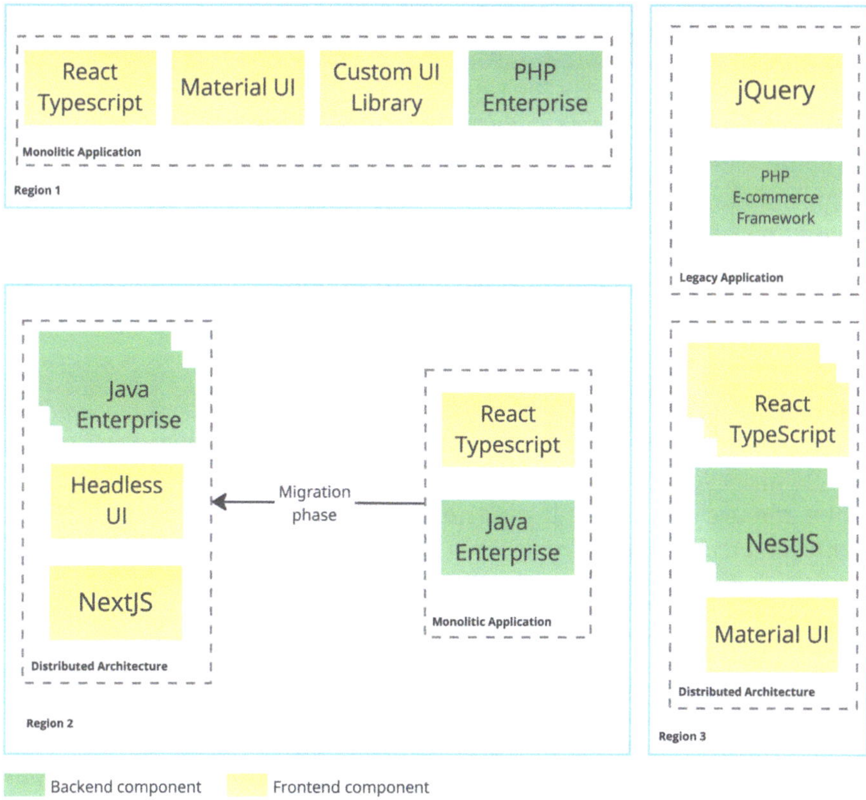

Figure 12.2: *Tech Stack*

In this scheme, the main system components are highlighted, distributed across regions, and categorized as either architecture application (distributed architecture or monolithic application).

The major challenge was to implement architectural strategies and principles to ensure effective integration between the various components.

This scheme also reflects the key components related to frontend implementation efforts, highlighting the vast diversity of initiatives, ranging from jQuery to the Next. js full-stack framework.

Architectural Considerations

Considering the aspects covered in *Chapter 2, Valuable Architecture*, the first exercise of the Architecture Review Board was to define the elements of importance for the project–in other words, the elements that, if done wrong, would require the most effort to correct. Based on this principle, and after many rounds of "relaxed" discussions, the following elements were defined:

Evolutionary Architecture

We embrace change as the principal and most important element. This paradigm brought greater peace of mind and acceptance of decisions for all involved while also mitigating some "decision fatigue." It helped everyone understand that every decision made at a given moment reflects the needs and concerns of that moment, rather than an imagined hypothetical future.

Secondly, changes were implemented gradually–we did not aim to revolutionize how the system and people worked but rather to evolve through small and manageable modifications.

Note: *Evolutionary Architecture is an approach to software development that acknowledges and plans for the inevitable changes that a software system will undergo throughout its lifecycle. Instead of aiming for a fixed, perfect initial design, it embraces the idea that the architecture will need to adapt and evolve as business needs, user requirements, and technological landscapes shift.*

From this fundamental principle, we derive the necessity for an architecture and design that is friendly to change, leading to the following key elements:

Business and Technology Alignment

It may sound cliché, but considering a scenario where three distinct companies (geographically and culturally) came together to work, discussions often felt like different languages being spoken, leaving people embarrassed about not understanding each other. Thus, the cliché was indeed applicable in this context, and a considerable effort was, and still is, dedicated to aligning the vocabulary of business and technology personnel through a ubiquitous language. The second step was mapping the primary domains of the new system, considering the three platforms.

Note: *The term "ubiquitous language" still sounds too "tech" for many business people–at least in this use case. However, despite the lack of alignment on the term itself, the shared understanding of the need for a unified vocabulary was achieved. This is one of those things that many books do not tell you but often happen in real life.*

With this effort producing its first results, the system's primary domains could be mapped, laying the foundation for implementing domain-driven design.

Distributed Technology

The decision to adopt a distributed architecture was both a necessity and a reflection of the structural organization of the group, which was already regionally distributed.

The main challenge was establishing workflows to manage the transition phase, in which monolithic applications would be updated by distributed teams.

It is important to highlight that the term "transition" in this context reflects the goal rather than the reality. Since architectural evolution is gradual, there will be a long and considerable period of transition–essentially, a prolonged phase where the system operates with a mix of monolithic and distributed applications. This is a fundamental characteristic of the system that architectural considerations must not overlook.

Micro Frontends

Driven by the need for distributed technological standards, adopting a micro frontend architectural pattern enabled the team to meet the often conflicting demands of different development teams. The Architecture Review Board's primary effort was to establish the minimal necessary contracts–that is, the implementation strategies–to allow various frontend development initiatives to work independently.

Event Carried State Transfer (ECST)

As a corollary to the distributed architecture, adopting ECST became necessary to ensure decoupling between each microservice implementation.

Note: *Event-Carried State Transfer* (ECST) *is an event-driven pattern where events not only announce that a change has occurred but also include all the necessary data related to that change within their payload, enabling consuming services to update their local copies of data and operate independently without needing to query the original source, thereby promoting loose coupling and eventual consistency in distributed systems.*

It is important to emphasize that this initiative is not a one-time action but rather a continuous effort throughout the system's life cycle. Therefore, this list should not be seen as a "definitive guide" but rather as a reflection of the system's architectural concerns at a given moment.

Challenges Faced

This session, together with the following: *main outcomes*, are the ones we could highlight as the most insightful for everyone involved in the project and, hopefully, for all the readers, who, with this understanding, will be able to actively work on these aspects.

It is important to emphasize that the following items do not aim to establish an order of importance or be an exhaustive list of items. Instead, it highlights the main points, especially those where adopting a micro frontend architecture has brought significant benefits.

Scale Frontend Development

This is the million-dollar question when it comes to scalable systems. A system that initially started with a small group of developers working harmoniously in a single repository (code base), with a well-defined set of features understood by all, begins to gain significant adoption. Along with this growth, the number of requests increases exponentially, leading to higher user expectations. This, in turn, results in the expansion of the team, the codebase, and all the challenges extensively discussed throughout the book.

In this use case, the existence of three relatively large applications operating in their respective regions–facing the demand to scale from a regional level to a global scale–makes the challenges even more interesting.

To mainly address the business question: How to maintain a consistent UI while allowing team autonomy? The Architecture Review Board's team initially mapped out the key frontend components. The following is a diagram derived from *Figure 12.2: Tech Stack*, focusing on frontend components:

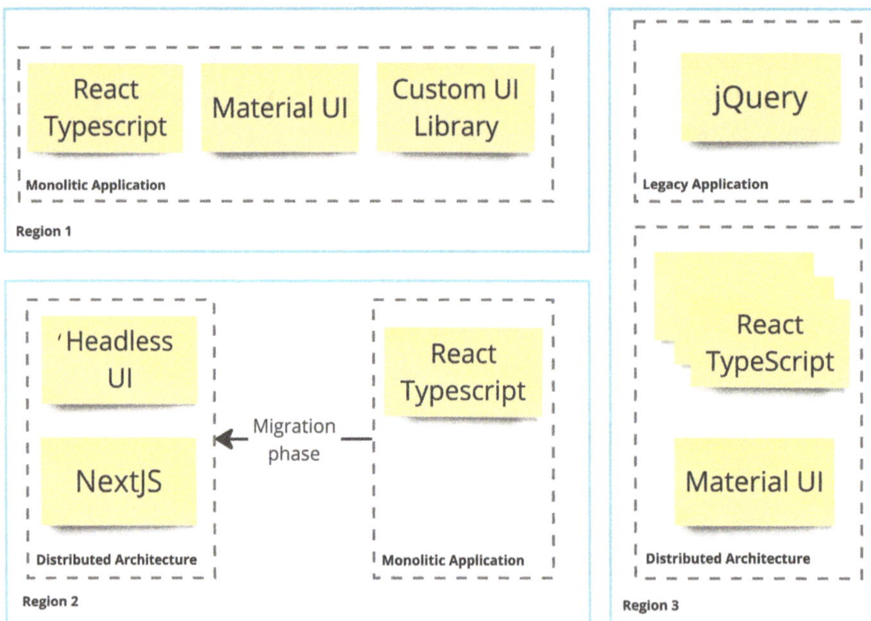

Figure 12.3: *Frontend Tech Stack*

Based on this mapping, some considerations were made:

First, regarding scope, the system based on jQuery was classified as legacy and was therefore excluded from considerations for the new project, some effort would still be required for it, but would strictly be focused on maintenance.

Second, given the complexity and diversity of existing frontend implementations, the most viable approach for effectively integrating applications into the system–while adhering to the principles of evolutionary architecture–was the adoption of a micro frontend architecture. With this decision, it was defined that shell applications would coexist, one in Region 1 and another in Region 2, each integrating distinct micro frontends. This structure is illustrated in the figure as follows:

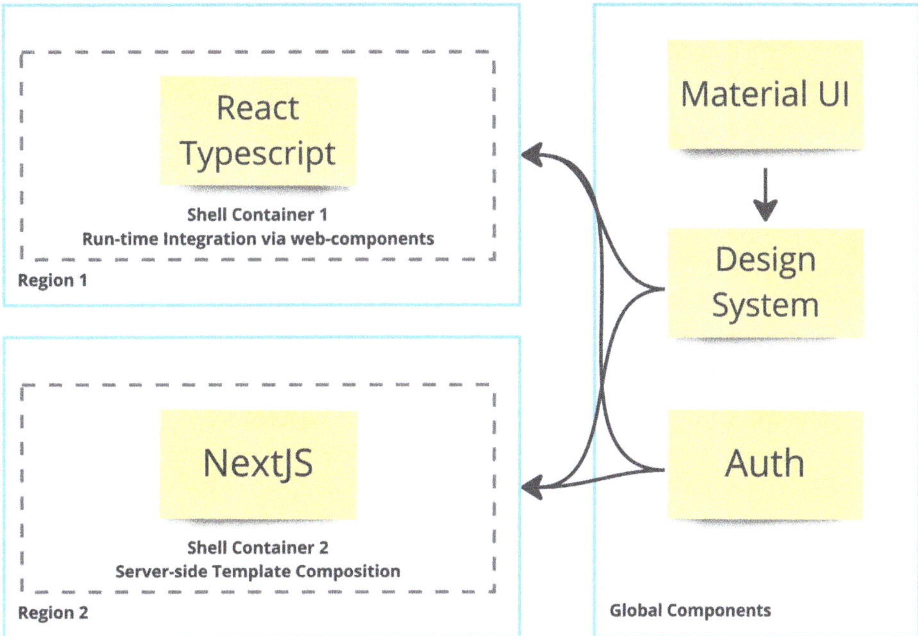

Figure 12.4: *Use-case containers diagram*

In the container diagram, each region has two monolithic applications acting as shell containers, where new micro frontends are gradually added as the system evolves. Additionally, global components–many of which were already part of the distributed architecture previously present in Region 3–now function as global components that can be instantiated by any of the different shell applications.

Regarding the shell applications, while this setup slightly increases complexity, it leverages existing implementations. To support this, two micro frontend integration patterns were adopted:

Run-time Integration via Web Components

This integration method was defined considering the desired low coupling with the shell application, which is based on PHP. Server-side component rendering would not be possible without significant structural modifications to the shell application. Additionally, since the application is for internal use only, accessed exclusively by authorized users, there was no need for major efforts regarding search engine optimization. The scope was also more limited in terms of the diversity of clients (browsers, native applications, and so on) accessing the application.

Server-side Template Composition

In this Next.js-based shell application, server-side integrations were more realistic and aligned with the framework's philosophy (so to say composability and modular architecture), as well as the preferences of the involved teams. Therefore, Server-Side Template Composition was chosen as the integration method.

As a result, global micro frontends need to support rendering both on the client (browser) and the server.

Note: *Ideally, a single integration method would be used in a micro frontend architecture. However, this real-world case demonstrates how adaptations can–and should–be made to address specific requirements. This highlights the importance of viewing micro frontend architecture not as a rigid, unchangeable set of principles but rather as a collection of best practices for implementation.*

React was chosen as the primary library/framework for implementation, and Material-UI was selected as the base component library upon which the design system would be built. These decisions were primarily influenced by previous choices, as React and Material-UI were already the preferred technologies in most individual application implementations.

Finally, a backend-only authentication and authorization npm package library for Node.js server environments (supporting Role-Based Access Control (RBAC) and Access Control Lists (ACL)-based permission checks, and including utilities for NestJS applications to enforce access control at the endpoint level) was implemented to ensure compliance with authentication and authorization requirements.

Design System and UI Unification

One of the most complex aspects of evolving a large-scale system toward a micro frontend architecture is achieving visual and interaction consistency without halting development. In this particular case, three distinct frontend codebases were already in active use across different regions, each with varying degrees of adherence to UX guidelines and implementation standards.

A transitional phase with inconsistent UI was accepted. During this period, new features built with the emerging design system would coexist alongside legacy screens with older, divergent styles. Rather than attempting a top-down rewrite–which would have stalled progress and strained delivery timelines–teams agreed to prioritize forward momentum while gradually introducing alignment through the design system.

With this basic setup, a smooth and gradual transition from the legacy architectural pattern to the new micro frontend-based approach was ensured. Moreover, while maintaining a consistent UX remains an ongoing collaborative effort between development and design teams, the setup provides the technical foundation for teams to evolve the system as new demands arise.

Aligning Different Development Cultures

Each acquired company had its own development culture, shaped by years of independent decision-making, tools, and processes. The perception of quality, testing practices, and deployment strategies varied significantly.

Communication Across Distributed Teams and Time Zones

When teams are spread across multiple locations and time zones (North America, Europe, Asia), several communication barriers arise:

- **Time Zone Misalignment**: Teams working in different time zones may have very limited overlapping hours.
- **Language and Communication Styles**: Some teams prefer written documentation, while others rely on verbal discussions.
- **Decision-Making Delays**: When discussions happen asynchronously, it may take days to finalize a decision.
- **Too Many Meetings or Not Enough**: Some teams may feel overwhelmed by too many sync calls, while others feel disconnected due to a lack of real-time discussions.

Main Outcomes

The journey towards a unified booking platform was a complex undertaking, fraught with challenges but ultimately yielding significant and insightful outcomes. This endeavor, spanning three continents and merging disparate legacy systems, offers valuable lessons for any organization facing similar large-scale transformations. Here is a breakdown of the main outcomes:

Evolutionary Architecture as a Guiding Principle:

The most fundamental outcome was the adoption and successful implementation of an evolutionary architecture. Recognizing the inherent complexity and the need for flexibility, the team embraced change as a constant, rather than a disruption. This mindset fostered a culture of continuous improvement and mitigated the paralysis often caused by "decision fatigue." Incremental changes, rather than a "big bang" approach, allowed for smoother transitions and minimized risks.

Bridging the Business-Technology Divide through Ubiquitous Language (with Real-World Nuances):

The effort to align business and technology teams through a ubiquitous language proved crucial, albeit with practical adjustments. While the theoretical concept resonated, the term itself proved too "techy" for some business stakeholders. However, the underlying principle of establishing a shared vocabulary was successfully implemented. This outcome highlights the importance of adapting theoretical frameworks to real-world contexts and focusing on achieving the desired result, even if the terminology needs to be modified.

Successful Implementation of a Distributed Architecture (Despite Transition Challenges):

The move to a distributed architecture was both a strategic necessity and a reflection of the geographically dispersed teams. While the transition from monolithic systems posed significant challenges, the team managed to establish workflows for managing this hybrid environment. The acknowledgment that the "transition" would be a prolonged phase allowed for realistic planning and resource allocation.

Strategic Adoption of Micro Frontends for Scalable Frontend Development:

The adoption of a micro frontend architecture proved instrumental in scaling frontend development and enabling team autonomy while maintaining a consistent user experience. The strategic decision to utilize two shell applications (one in Region 1 and one in Region 2) and implement both runtime integration via Web Components and server-side template composition addressed the specific needs of each region and technical stack.

Pragmatic Technology Choices and Framework Adaptations:

The selection of React and Material-UI as the primary frontend technologies, while influenced by existing preferences, provided a solid foundation for the design system. The team's willingness to adapt integration methods based on specific requirements, rather than adhering rigidly to theoretical principles, demonstrates a pragmatic approach to problem-solving.

Navigating Cultural and Communication Challenges in a Global Team:

The project shed light on the challenges of aligning diverse development cultures and facilitating communication across distributed teams and time zones. The emphasis on asynchronous communication, documentation, RFCs, and decision logs proved effective in mitigating the impact of time zone differences. The establishment of shared governance structures, such as the Architecture Review Board and Tech Leads Sync meetings, fostered collaboration and alignment.

Real-World Lessons in Balancing Consistency and Autonomy:

The project provided valuable lessons in balancing the need for consistency (in UI/UX and architectural patterns) with the desire for team autonomy. The delegation of UI/UX representatives to each team and the establishment of shared engineering principles helped maintain consistency while allowing regional teams to work independently.

ECST as a Cornerstone for Decoupling:

The adoption of ECST as a result of the distributed architecture provided a means to decouple microservices and ensure data consistency. Emphasizing that this was not a one-time endeavor but a continuous effort throughout the system's lifecycle proved crucial.

Design System and UI Unification

A design system was built to support gradual adoption across multiple levels of abstraction. At its core, the system defined design tokens—shared variables for color, spacing, typography, and other foundational styles—allowing even the most basic or legacy components to integrate visual consistency without complete rewrites.

On top of this foundation, reusable UI elements were built following an atomic design model:

- Molecules: composed components such as form groups or search bars.
- Organisms: larger modules such as navigation bars, and generic page statuses such as not found, no items found, and so on.

This layering enabled teams to adopt only what was necessary, depending on their use-case, and supported both server-rendered and client-rendered environments.

Critically, the design system was developed with backwards compatibility in mind. New components were introduced in a way that could coexist with legacy implementations, and no immediate migration was mandated. Instead, a gradual implementation strategy was followed: shared components were integrated as part of feature development or during planned refactoring, minimizing disruption while ensuring steady progress toward a unified experience.

This evolutionary path struck a balance between system-wide consistency and development velocity. Over time, it has reduced design fragmentation, improved accessibility and maintainability, and laid a scalable foundation for future growth.

A Continuing Evolution

It is vital to recognize that this transformation is not a completed project, but rather an ongoing process. The team's commitment to evolutionary architecture underscores the understanding that the platform will continue to adapt and evolve as business needs and technology landscapes change. The outcomes outlined above represent significant milestones, but they also serve as a foundation for future iterations.

The phrase "transition" was highlighted earlier, and it is essential to reiterate that it is a long-term state. The coexistence of monolithic and distributed architectures, the continuous refinement of the micro frontend strategy, and the ongoing effort to align business and technology through a ubiquitous language are all indicative of a living, breathing system.

Defining Success: Measuring the Impact of Micro Frontends

The successful implementation of micro frontends should not be defined merely by technical operability. Especially in migrations from monolithic frontends, success must be assessed through clear, outcome-driven criteria. A set of tangible indicators was used to evaluate whether the micro frontend architecture delivered on its architectural and organizational promises–particularly in terms of autonomy, scalability, resilience, and consistency.

Note: *These indicators were monitored (formally or informally), and we suggest future teams adopt similar Key Performance Indicators (KPIs) when evaluating micro frontend success.*

Team autonomy and development velocity emerged as primary indicators. It was assessed through the average time from feature definition to production deployment per team. A reduction in cycle time, particularly when multiple teams worked in parallel without blocking one another, demonstrated the ability of the architecture to eliminate cross-team dependencies and streamline delivery.

Deployment independence served as another key metric. By tracking the proportion of frontend deployments that were region- or team-specific and did not require global coordination, it became possible to evaluate how well the architecture enabled decoupled releases. A higher frequency of independent deployments indicated increased scalability and localized control.

The user experience consistency, to guard against fragmentation, was monitored across micro frontends and regions. Usability audits and UX deviation reports provided a view into perceptible differences in the interface. Minimal variation, as rated by end users or QA teams, confirmed that the distributed frontend still delivered a cohesive and seamless experience.

Resilience and fault isolation were evaluated by tracking incidents where failures in one micro frontend impacted others or the host shell. A noticeable reduction in the blast radius of failures, compared to the monolithic baseline, signaled improved containment and architectural robustness.

The developer experience, particularly in onboarding new engineers, served as a proxy for maintainability. Time-to-productivity for newcomers within specific micro frontend modules was compared to onboarding timelines in the legacy system. Shorter onboarding periods pointed to a reduction in cognitive load and clearer module boundaries.

Cross-region scalability was measured by the time required to roll out region-specific features through region-specific shell applications. Faster rollouts, coupled with fewer regression and backporting issues, validated the system's ability to support localized business needs efficiently.

Finally, **integration overhead**—the engineering effort needed to onboard a new MFE—was tracked through metrics such as developer hours and number of pull requests. Over time, successful adoption was reflected in predictable, minimal integration effort. A growing or unpredictable overhead would have suggested architectural misalignment or scalability concerns.

These dimensions offered a structured way to move beyond subjective or perceived success. Micro frontends, while a powerful architectural pattern, must be evaluated based on the value they deliver in context. In this case, their success was measured by their ability to enhance autonomy, resilience, and scalability—without compromising user experience or development flow.

Other Relevant Use Case

To scale the development of their shop web app across multiple teams—sometimes up to six—a large e-commerce company shop in Europe opted for a micro frontend architecture.

Their micro frontends are structured with a high level of granularity. Instead of simply assigning distinct applications to different routes, each page (or view) is assembled from multiple micro frontends, using therefore a per feature slicing for its micro frontend application.

Given the e-commerce nature of the application, optimizing for search engines and fast first paints were a priority. To achieve this, they implemented a *Server-side Template Composition* approach with server-side rendering capabilities, drawing inspiration from Zalando's Mosaic system.

Note: *Zalando's Mosaic system is Zalando's approach to frontend integration and composition for micro frontends. It allows teams to build and deploy independent* *frontend components that can be dynamically assembled into a cohesive user interface.*

The following sequence diagram shows how a given web page is assembled from multiple independent frontend fragments on the server side before being delivered to the browser.

Key Components

- **Browser**: The client requesting the web page
- **Nginx Reverse Proxy**: Routes requests and serves as the entry point
- **Composer**: The server-side composition service (also called in this context "orchestrator" or "aggregator", referred to in our book as shell container)
- **Fragments**: Independent micro frontends
    - Header fragment
    - Navigation fragment
    - Product-listing fragment
    - [name] fragment (any other dynamic/configurable fragment)

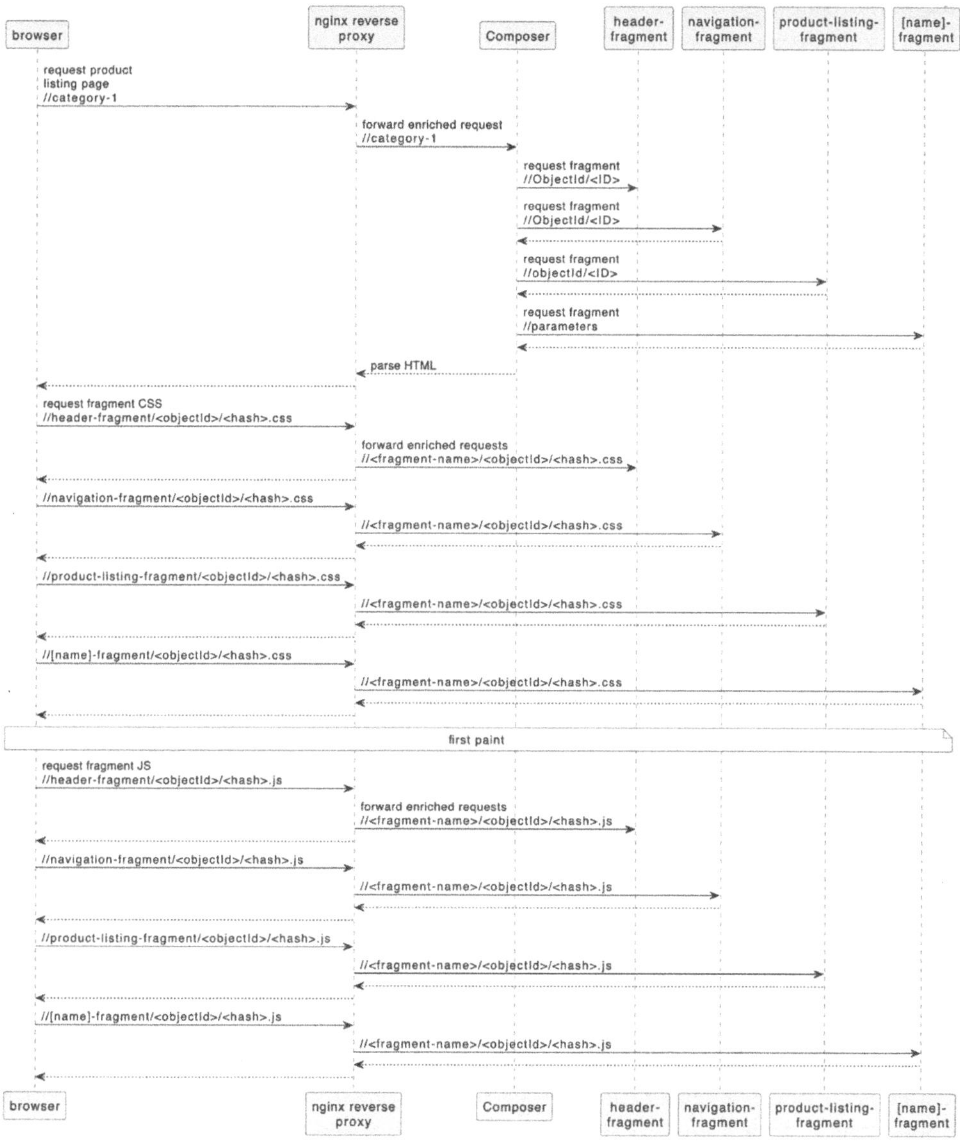

Figure 12.5: *Use-case Sequence Diagram*

The Flow

Initial Page Request

1. The browser requests a product listing page for a "category-1"
2. Nginx forwards this request with additional context to the Composer

3. The Composer then:
   a. Requests the necessary fragments from their respective services
   b. Each fragment returns its HTML content
   c. Assembles/composes these fragments into a complete HTML page
   d. Returns the composed HTML to Nginx, which forwards it to the browser

CSS Loading

After receiving the initial HTML, the browser requests CSS resources for each fragment:

1. The browser requests CSS files for each fragment
2. Nginx forwards these requests to the appropriate fragment services
3. Each fragment service returns its CSS
4. The browser receives and applies the styles
5. After all CSS is loaded, "first paint" occurs (as noted in the diagram)

JavaScript Loading

Finally, the browser loads JavaScript for each fragment:

1. The browser requests JS files for each fragment
2. Nginx forwards these requests to the appropriate fragment services
3. Each fragment service returns its JavaScript
4. The browser executes the JavaScript to enable interactive functionality (hydration process)

The Composer's Contract: Standardized Fragment Communication

The success of the architecture relies on a well-defined contract between the Composer and fragments. The contract established a consistent, predictable communication pattern:

```
GET http://<name>-fragment/?<input parameters>
```

The Composer enriches each fragment request using HTTP headers that provide contextual information—such as the current session, tenant identity, preferred language, and client capabilities, among others.

This standardized contract enables fragments to be truly independent while still receiving the context they need. It also facilitated:

- Consistent caching strategies

- Predictable authentication handling
- Uniform feature flag implementation
- Standardized internationalization approach

Note: *Differential serving is a frontend optimization technique where different versions of JavaScript and other assets are served based on the capabilities of the client (typically the browser). The primary goal is to improve performance by delivering modern, optimized code to newer browsers while maintaining compatibility with older ones.*

Migration Strategy: The Two-System Transition

One of the major challenges was migrating from the monolithic legacy application into the new micro frontend architecture without disrupting the user experience.

The organization needed to maintain full functionality while gradually moving features to the new architecture, with minimal user disruption and without duplicating all development efforts.

Solution: Per Page Slicing with Intelligent Routing

A strategic migration approach was implemented:

- Feature-Based Routing: The routing layer (API gateway) was configured to direct traffic based on feature paths:
- Requests to "*/new-available-feature*" (any feature already available in the new system) were routed to the new micro frontend system
- Legacy paths continued to be served by the monolithic application
- Data Synchronization: Where necessary, data synchronization mechanisms were implemented to ensure consistency between the legacy and new systems during the transition period.

With this approach incremental feature migrations were possible and rollbacks easily performed, they were just a matter of a rerouting update.

Challenges Faced

One of the most significant challenges emerged when certain fragments consistently underperformed, creating bottlenecks in page rendering.

As an example, the product recommendations fragment frequently took 800-1200ms to respond due to complex personalization algorithms, while most other fragments responded in under 200ms.

Some of the solutions implemented are listed below:

- **Timeout Policies**: The team implemented configurable timeout thresholds for each fragment. If a fragment does not respond within its allocated time, the Composer proceeds without it, inserting a lightweight placeholder instead.
- **Progressive Loading Strategy**: Critical fragments (header, navigation, main content) are loaded first, with non-critical fragments loaded asynchronously after initial page render.
- **Fragment-Specific Caching**: Different caching strategies were implemented for different fragments based on their update frequency and performance characteristics:
  - Static fragments: Long TTL with CDN caching
  - Semi-dynamic fragments: Short TTL with edge caching
  - Highly personalized fragments: Session-based caching
- **Skeleton Screens**: For slower fragments, skeleton UI placeholders were implemented that maintain the page layout while content loads.
- **Circuit Breakers**: Circuit breaker patterns were added to prevent cascading failures when a fragment service experiences issues.

Other challenges faced, especially during the transition phase between the legacy system and the new implementation, involved aspects related to visual identity, which differed considerably between the applications. To address this issue, minimal adjustments were made to the legacy application, and an "acceptable" level of divergence related to UI/UX was agreed upon among key stakeholders, considering the temporary nature of both applications running in parallel. A shared authentication mechanism also had to be implemented for both apps. Here again, understanding the transitional nature of the implementation, a more pragmatic approach was adopted.

Main Outcomes

The architecture has proven particularly valuable during expansion into new markets, where the organization was able to rapidly adapt the user experience for different regions by modifying only the relevant fragments, while maintaining core business logic.

By clearly separating infrastructure concerns (reverse proxy), composition logic (composer), and business functionality (fragments), with well-defined contracts, the organization created a system that can evolve incrementally, scale efficiently, and deliver exceptional user experiences even as business requirements continue to evolve.

Future of Micro Frontends

To begin exploring future trends in frontend development–particularly in the context of micro frontend architecture–it is helpful to consider the cyclical nature of technology. As a starting point, let us compare two technologies from different points in time: jQuery (representing the past) and React (representing the present). The specific technologies are not important; they serve only as temporal markers–Technology X and Technology Y.

We will focus our analysis on two key dimensions:

- **Developer Experience**: The overall quality of the experience developers have while building, maintaining, and deploying software
- **Codebase Size:** How the architecture and tools impact the scale and complexity of the resulting code

This historical perspective can help us identify repeating patterns and anticipate the direction frontend and micro frontend architectures might take in the future.

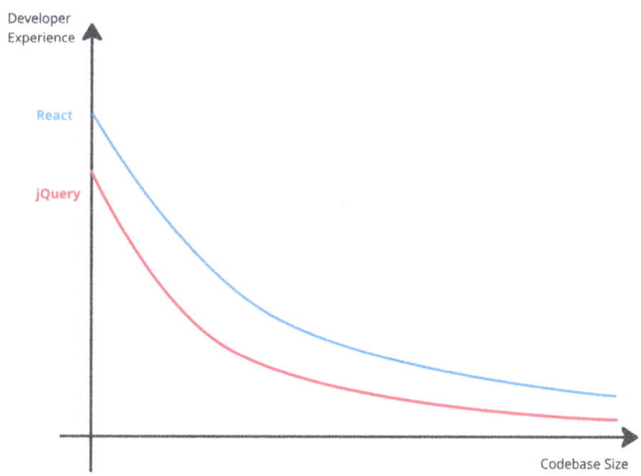

Figure 12.6: *DX/Code Base Size*

The chart reflects empirical evidence which supports that regardless of the technology choice, as codebases grow in size, developer productivity and experience often decline.

Supporting data includes:

Increased Code Volume: A survey by Sourcegraph revealed that 51% of respondents have over 100 times more code than they did a decade ago, leading to challenges in code management and understanding.

https://sourcegraph.com/blog/big-code-survey-2020

Developer Time Allocation: Amazon Web Services reported that developers spend only about one hour per day coding, with the remaining time consumed by tasks such as learning codebases, drafting documents, and fixing issues.

https://www.businessinsider.com/amazon-developers-spend-only-one-hour-coding-daily-aws-ai-2024-12

Complexity and Productivity: The growing complexity of codebases necessitates new tools and approaches to maintain productivity.

https://www.multitudes.com/blog/code-complexity

One may argue that using React since day one, will offer a better developer user experience than jQuery (a fact intentionally reflected in the chart), which can still be debatable; nevertheless, we can assume that for now.

And in the question of codebase size, jQuery, React, Angular, and technologies with widespread adoption have a special "disadvantage" when compared to the new, shiny, bright, revolutionary *yet-new-JavaScript-framework*. The scale of comparison is different: most likely, the *yet-new-JavaScript-framework* in a 100,000+ lines of code project will have similar difficulties; however, due to its initial lifecycle stage, 100,000+ lines of code project will be non-existing making real comparisons unviable.

Yet, what really differs the "past" *jQuery* from the "present" *react* is depicted in the following chart:

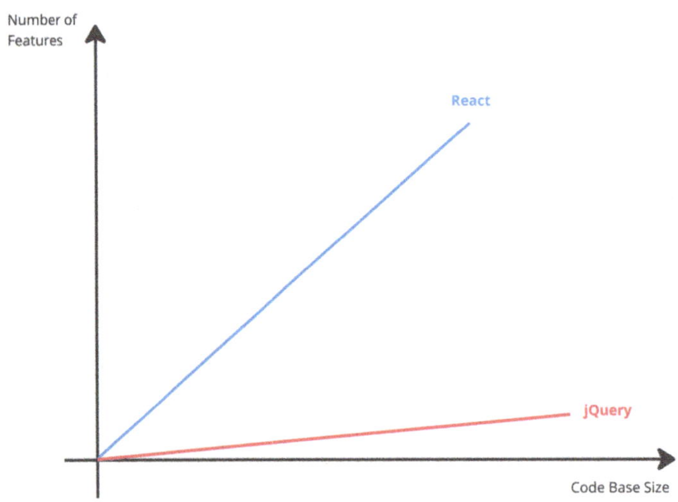

Figure 12.7: Number of Features/Codebase Size

Note: *The chart above is intended as an illustrative reflection, not a formal measurement. It visualizes a commonly held perspective among developers who have worked with both* *jQuery and modern frameworks such as React: as the number of application features increases, the codebase size and complexity tend to grow much more rapidly in jQuery than in React. While this is not based on empirical data, it reflects general development experience – particularly how modern abstractions, component models, and state management in modern frameworks, such as React, help manage complexity more effectively than imperative approaches such as jQuery.*

Advancements in programming languages and software development frameworks have significantly enhanced developer productivity by enabling the implementation of more features with less code.

Applications in *React* today have many more features, and if we were to hypothetically rewrite them using *jQuery*, the codebase size would likely be much larger and more tangled due to the lack of abstractions and tooling and consequently the developer experience would be way worse.

Therefore, what is the future of frontend development and micro frontend architecture?

In simple words, it is to continue implementing software with more features and fewer lines of code.

The technologies (React, Angular, Vue, and so on) offer the technical evolutions (High-Level Abstractions, Enhanced Tooling and Ecosystems, more efficient ways to organize code: Functional Programming, component-based frameworks, and so on), and the architectures, in our context the micro frontend architecture, the organizational means to keep the codebase "manageable," that is, within a manageable limit, thus achieving a scalable system, capable of growing indefinitely.

Artificial Intelligence and Micro Frontends

Nowadays one cannot completely cover any topic without drawing attention to the effects of Artificial Intelligence (AI) on it.

The relentless march of technological evolution continues to reshape the landscape of technology, and frontend development would not be different. As we navigate the cyclical nature of technology, the pairing of Artificial Intelligence (AI) with micro frontend architectures presents a compelling, yet complex, vision of the future. Just as React offered a leap forward from jQuery, AI promises to further enhance Developer Experience (DX) and streamline codebase management.

The Promise: AI as a Force Multiplier for Micro Frontends

AI is rapidly transforming micro frontend architectures, acting as a powerful and continuously improving force multiplier. It accelerates development through increasingly intelligent code generation and completion, minimizing errors and freeing developers for complex logic. Automated testing and debugging, driven by AI's evolving ability to analyze code and generate comprehensive test cases, ensures ever more robust integration between independent components.

Dynamic UI composition, tailored to user behavior and real-time data, delivers increasingly personalized experiences. Performance optimization, achieved through AI-driven analysis of metrics and constantly refined identification of bottlenecks, maintains and enhances application speed despite increasing complexity.

Ultimately, AI elevates the developer experience with real-time feedback, insightful analytics, and automated orchestration, simplifying management and boosting overall productivity, with each iteration of these AI tools bringing further enhancements.

The Pitfalls of AI Assistants

While the potential of AI in micro frontends is undeniable, several challenges need to be addressed:

AI Bias and Reliability: AI models can inherit biases from the data they are trained on, leading to unintended consequences. Ensuring the reliability and fairness of AI-powered micro frontend systems is essential.

Increased Abstraction and Reduced Understanding: Over-reliance on AI-generated code could lead to a decline in developers' understanding of the underlying architecture. This could make it more difficult to debug and maintain complex micro frontend systems.

Limited Context in Distributed Systems: Micro frontend architectures (just like its counterpart micro services), by their nature, are distributed. AI tools, even sophisticated ones, often lack a holistic understanding of the entire system's state and interactions. This can lead to generated code that introduces integration issues, performance bottlenecks, or conflicts with other micro frontends. The AI may not grasp the subtle dependencies and communication patterns that are critical for the system's overall functionality.

The Illusion of Productivity: The ease with which AI can generate code creates the illusion of increased productivity. While the sheer volume of code produced may rise, its relevance and quality are critical questions. Are we generating genuinely valuable, maintainable code, or simply more of the same, adding to the complexity without solving core problems? The ease of creating code can lead to a massive increase in code, that ultimately can be irrelevant, and create a larger burden on the overall system.

Lack of Holistic Design Capabilities: While AI assistants excel at generating code snippets or completing well-scoped tasks, they currently fall short in system-level design decisions. For example, choosing how to slice an application into micro frontends, deciding on the right communication model, or reasoning about cross-cutting concerns such as security, performance, or observability still requires human judgment. AI may confidently propose a solution, but often that confidence is superficial–its suggestions can seem well-thought-out but lack a true understanding of trade-offs, organizational context, or evolving constraints.

The Future of Micro Frontend Development with AI

Looking ahead, we can hypothesize several trends that will shape the future of micro frontend development with AI:

- **AI-Powered Micro Frontend Platforms**: We may see the emergence of specialized platforms that provide integrated AI tools for micro frontend development, deployment, and management. These platforms will simplify the process of building and maintaining complex micro frontend architectures.
- **Semantic Micro Frontends**: AI may enable the development of semantic micro frontends that understand the meaning and context of the data they display. This will lead to more intelligent and personalized user experiences.
- **Autonomous Micro Frontends**: In the future, micro frontends may become increasingly autonomous, capable of self-adapting and self-optimizing based on real-time data and user feedback. AI will play a crucial role in enabling this level of autonomy.
- **Low-Code/No-Code Micro Frontends with AI Assistance**: AI may help democratize micro frontend development by enabling low-code and no-code platforms. These platforms will allow non-technical users to create and customize micro frontends with the assistance of AI-powered tools.
- **AI as a Codebase Historian and Predictor**: AI will be used to analyze codebases and predict future changes. This will allow teams to anticipate potential issues and plan for future development efforts.

The integration of AI into micro frontend architectures is not just a trend, but a fundamental shift in how we build and maintain web applications. While challenges remain, the potential benefits are undeniable. As AI technology continues to evolve, we can expect to see a new era of intelligent, scalable, and personalized web experiences.

Conversational Interfaces: Reshaping User Experience

The convergence of AI and micro frontends is not limited to enhancing developer workflows or streamlining architecture. A more profound shift is unfolding at the user experience level–one that challenges the very foundations of how interfaces are designed and navigated. As large language models continue to advance, we are entering the era of conversational interfaces, where users interact with systems through natural language rather than through predefined routes, menus, or component trees.

In this new paradigm, users will not be restricted to clicking through hierarchical menus or discovering features through navigation. Instead, they will simply ask the system: "*Show me a chart of the most purchased experiences for families last summer,*" followed by "*Book that experience for this weekend.*" Interfaces must be ready to parse intent, extract meaning, fetch relevant data, and act–all through conversational input.

This shift introduces a new type of frontend responsibility: not just rendering views or encapsulating features, but participating in a larger, dynamic, language-driven orchestration layer. Traditional UI patterns will coexist with new components that can be programmatically assembled or queried through AI-powered agents. Developers will need to architect their systems for flexibility, enabling components to be surfaced, composed, or hidden based on user intent rather than predefined flows.

To support this, we will likely see the emergence of new API standards such as the Model Context Protocol (MCP)–designed specifically to support Retrieval-Augmented Generation (RAG) use cases in large-scale language models. These standards will define not only how data is retrieved, but also how context is structured, shared, and consumed across conversational and visual boundaries.

Note: *Retrieval-Augmented Generation (RAG) is an AI architecture that combines information retrieval with natural language generation. Instead of relying solely on what a Large Language Model (LLM) has memorized during training, RAG dynamically pulls relevant external knowledge at runtime and feeds it into the model to improve the accuracy, specificity, and freshness of its responses.*

The Model Context Protocol (MCP) is a proposed or emerging concept (not yet a formal standard as of now) that aims to standardize how context is structured, shared, and exchanged between applications and Large Language Models (LLMs) to support Retrieval-Augmented Generation (RAG) and other advanced AI behaviors.

From a tooling and architectural perspective, development stacks must evolve. Existing design-time assumptions about user flows, routing logic, and component trees will give way to runtime composition, intent-driven orchestration, and context-aware rendering. Micro frontend architectures will need to interoperate with semantic models, expose meaningful metadata, and maintain a consistent state accessible to conversational agents.

In short, the future of micro frontend development may not be entirely visible on the screen–it will increasingly reside in the invisible layers of understanding, context modeling, and real-time decision-making that bridge user intent and system action.

Conclusion

As we have journeyed through the intricacies of micro frontend architecture, from foundational principles to practical implementation, we have ultimately arrived at a crucial juncture: the real-world application of these concepts. This chapter served as a testament to the transformative power of this approach, illustrating how theoretical frameworks translate into tangible business outcomes.

The study case presented a comprehensive overview, starting with the contextual landscape, encompassing business requirements, organizational structures, and the existing tech stack. This foundation allowed us to delve into the core of architectural considerations and the strategic implementation of micro frontends. We witnessed firsthand the challenges that inevitably arise during such transitions, from technical hurdles to organizational adjustments, and the innovative solutions employed to overcome them.

The 'Main Outcomes' section highlighted the significant benefits reaped from adopting a micro frontend architecture, reinforcing the value proposition discussed throughout the book. We saw how this paradigm shift fostered increased agility, scalability, and maintainability, aligning technology with evolving business needs. Furthermore, the inclusion of 'Other Relevant Use Cases' broadened our perspective, demonstrating the versatility and adaptability of micro frontends across diverse scenarios.

Looking ahead, the discussion on the "Future of Micro Frontends" and their intersection with "Artificial Intelligence" provides a glimpse into the exciting possibilities that lie ahead. As technology continues to evolve, the principles and practices explored in this book will remain relevant, serving as a guide for building robust, scalable, and future-proof frontend systems.

The journey does not end here. The landscape of frontend development is dynamic and ever-changing. Embrace the principles, adapt the strategies, and continue to explore the potential of micro frontends to build exceptional user experiences. As technology advances, the ability to decompose complex frontends into manageable, independent units will become increasingly vital. We hope this book has provided you with a solid foundation and inspired you to innovate and excel in the world of frontend architecture.

References

1. https://react.dev/
2. https://mui.com/
3. https://engineering.zalando.com/posts/2021/03/micro-frontends-part1.html
4. https://engineering.zalando.com/posts/2021/09/micro-frontends-part2.html
5. https://sourcegraph.com/blog/big-code-survey-2020
6. https://www.businessinsider.com/amazon-developers-spend-only-one-hour-coding-daily-aws-ai-2024-12
7. https://www.multitudes.com/blog/code-complexity
8. https://github.com/features/copilot
9. https://www.cursor.com/
10. https://codeium.com/windsurf

Index

J

L

M

O

P

T

V

W